schooling
and
social change

Educational Policy, Planning and Theory
SERIES EDITOR: Don Adams, *University of Pittsburgh*

Adams *Education in National Development*
Adams and **Bjork** *Education in Developing Areas*
Adams (with **Reagan**) *Schooling and Social Change
in Modern America*
Carnoy *Schooling in a Corporate Society*
Mason *Contemporary Educational Theory*
Myers *Education and Emigration*
Perkinson *The Possibilities of Error*

schooling
and
social change
in
modern America

Don Adams
University of Pittsburgh

with Gerald M. Reagan
Ohio State University

DAVID McKAY COMPANY, INC.
NEW YORK

SCHOOLING AND SOCIAL CHANGE IN MODERN AMERICA

COPYRIGHT © 1972 BY DAVID MC KAY COMPANY, INC.

*Library of Congress Catalog Card Number: 72-75453
Manufactured in the United States of America*

For Janet

Contents

INTRODUCTION   *1*

Part 1/Education, Modernization, and the
     Industrial Social Order   *9*
     One: Perspectives on Social Change and
         Educational Change   11
     Two: Social and Educational Crises
         in Industrialized and
         Postindustrialized Society   37

Part 2/The Education Process and its Social
     Environment   *81*
     Three: Socialization, Schooling, and
         Education   83
     Four: Students and Schools   108

Part 3/Education, Occupation, and the Social
     Structure   *127*
     Five: Schooling, Manpower, and
         Occupation   129
     Six: Schooling and the Concern for
         Equity   172

Part 4/Choices in Control and Planning in
     Education   *217*
     Seven: The Struggle for Educational
         Authority: The Public and
         the Professionals   219
     Eight: Planning and Policy in
         Education   242

Part 5/Options in Designing Educational
     Change   *271*
     Nine: Alternatives in Education   273

INDEX   *301*

List of Tables

1 Index of Societies According to Degree of Differentiation *23*

2 Forecasts of Skilled Population and Scientific Personnel *44*

3 Educational and Instructional Technology *55–57*

4 Median Years of School Completed for Persons 25–29 Years of Age, by Color, 1940–67 *59*

5 School Enrollments in the United States, 1945–70 *64*

6 Major Occupational Groups of Employed Civilian Workers, United States, 1910, 1950, and 1959 *138*

7 Major Industry Groups of Employed Civilian Workers, United States, 1910 and 1950 *139*

8 Occupational Structure of the Total Labor Force and Output per Worker, by Country *140*

9 Work Life and Job-Changing Expectancies for Males, 1960–61 (at Beginning of Age Interval) *141*

10 Percentage of Male Workers not Continuing on One Job into the Second Year, by Age, January 1963 *141*

11 Median Years of School Completed by the Employed Civilian Labor Force 18 Years and Over, by Sex, Occupation Group, and Color, Selected Dates, 1948–70. Total Population *148–51*

12 Median Years of School Completed by the

Employed Civilian Labor Force 18 Years and Over, by Sex, Occupation Group, and Color, Selected Dates, 1959–70. Negro and Other Races   *152–54*

13 Projected Demand for New Elementary and Secondary Teachers, 1959–80   *167*

14 Some Scales of Reward or Status   *177*

15 Comparative Indices of Equality of Opportunity for Entry into Elite, Middle-Class, Skilled, Semiskilled, and Unskilled Strata (Base, Great Britain)   *183*

16 Mobility from Father's Occupation to 1962 Occupation for Males Aged 25–64: Outflow Percentages   *184–85*

17 College Attendance in 1967 Among High School Graduates, by Family Income   *188*

18 Selected Measures of Educational Attainment for Persons 25 Years Old and Over, and 25 to 29 Years Old, by Color and Sex, 1960 and 1940: USA   *190*

19 Some Characteristics of Nonformal and Formal Educational Programs   *281–83*

List of Figures

1 Speed Trend Curve   *39*
2 Structure of the Labor Force   *51*
3 Education, Manpower, and Industry Systems   *136*
4 A Systems Model of Education   *259*
5 The Educational Planning Process   *262*

schooling
and
social change
in
modern America

Introduction

No textbook today can provide enough information about educational problems for the educational decisions you will confront in the future. Whether you participate in educational decision making as a teacher, administrator, parent, or concerned citizen, the issues to be resolved and the decisions to be made will be difficult, complex, and extremely important. Problems of education and schooling will change as the wider society changes, and today's much-needed educational reforms may well harden into tomorrow's orthodoxy.

As social conditions change, some educational practices and policies will be viewed as problems in the society until they are modified to reflect the new conditions. Educational practices and policies geared to educating a small percentage of the total population become outmoded when social changes demand that most or all be educated. An educational system geared to train the majority as industrial workers becomes unsatisfactory as society moves toward automation and cybernation. Educational programs that encourage females to view themselves as less capable than males in certain fields are unrealistic when society commits itself to the liberation of women. The list could go on and on, but perhaps the point is made. Since it is highly likely that rapid social change will continue, new educational problems will continue to appear. The concern with educational reform should be a continuing concern: nothing in our schools, no set of educational policies or practices, ought be considered sacred simply because it has functioned satisfactorily in some previous era.

If new educational problems are likely to arise almost as soon as current problems are solved, what can possibly be accomplished by a textbook that deals with the interaction between education and its social and economic environment and with educational problems? Clearly one thing that *cannot* be accomplished is providing ready-made answers for future problems, since we do not even know what these problems will be. Nevertheless, a better understanding of education and schooling in our society provides the best vantage point we have for anticipating the nature of the future. We have further attempted to strengthen this vantage point (1) by using a conceptual frame within which certain generalizations may be possible regarding schooling and society and (2) by making a modest attempt at comparison of conditions in the American context with those of other societies. The implicit assumption in this organization is that the ability to conceptualize educational change and the perspective of occasional comparative references assist in the selection of meaningful questions concerning the future, and may provide a sense of the direction of current trends.

What Teachers Need to Know

Why should teachers learn to analyze broad educational conditions and problems? Why should they not limit themselves to the day-to-day problems of classroom teaching? Do teachers really *need* to understand general problems of schools and schooling? Isn't it enough that they be expected to become experts at the technical task of getting students to learn? Policy makers, and perhaps administrators, may need this broad understanding and knowledge of schools, but not classroom teachers. Teachers need to understand problems of *teaching,* and this is as much as can be reasonably expected. Whenever in the training of teachers valuable time is given over to nonessential subject matter such as analysis of educational problems, a mistake has been made. Those engaged in the training of teachers should direct their attention and time to developing the technical competence of teachers, not to general educational problems.

This argument raises the question of what constitutes teacher competence. There is considerable disagreement not so much with regard to what teachers know and do as from judgments about what they ought to know and ought to do.

These disagreements cannot be resolved here. But we can attempt to clarify our own attitude and to point out some other common views of the matter. Let us look at some of the possible criteria for defining a competent teacher.

First, almost everyone would agree that adequate knowledge of subject matter is essential for a teacher, although there may be disagreement as to what counts as adequacy. Clearly if we claim to teach someone, there must be something we claim to teach him, and it would be more than a little curious to assert that we are teaching something we ourselves do not know. But is competence in subject matter *all* that is necessary in teaching, or all that can be taught to prospective teachers? Certainly it has been frequently argued that knowledge coupled with certain natural endowments, e.g., pleasing personality and patience, constitute all the requisites for teaching.

The subject-matter-plus-natural-endowments view of teaching competence is, however, regarded as inadequate by most persons engaging in teacher education. In addition, they claim, it is crucial that those who teach are knowledgeable about those whom they teach. In teacher education programs this view is commonly reflected by study in developmental psychology, learning theory, individual child study, and some applied educational sociology. Thus, knowledge of students, plus knowledge of subject matter and natural endowments, are viewed by many as necessary conditions for teacher competence. Some would hold that these conditions are also sufficient, while others would argue for additional knowledge and skill.

In most teacher education programs one finds at least one additional assumption about teacher competence, namely, that teachers need to acquire knowledge of and skill in teaching methods and techniques. To teachers-in-training this aspect of teacher education is likely to be seen as the major purpose of professional education, as the core of teacher education. Prospective teachers would like, as would we all, some fail-safe recipe for successful teaching. Unfortunately, there is no such recipe, no bag of tricks, no set of rules that can guarantee success in teaching. Nonetheless, many would argue that there are techniques and methods which *can* be mastered and which are helpful in bringing the subject matter to the student in a way that will increase the likelihood that the student will learn. In short, mastery of techniques and methods is often viewed as a third aspect of teacher competence.

Learning About Schooling

Given mastery of these three aspects of teacher competence, we would have highly skilled teachers who could carry out many of the dictates of the educational managers, whoever those managers might be. There is much to be said for such skill. But this skill alone would not make teachers competent to deal with some of the problems they face at present and with many problems they will face in the future. The assumption upon which this book is based, and one which is explained and defended in various ways throughout our discussions, is that teachers, individually and collectively, make decisions that have sweeping implications for themselves, their students, and the society as a whole. The teacher may or may not recognize that he is participating in the making of such decisions. In either case, if our assumption is accurate, then the education of teachers should include attention to making these decisions more conscious, more informed, and hopefully, more humane. First we assume that the growing need for people to learn *within* schools is more than matched by a need to learn more *about* schools, that decisions about education and schooling are among the most important decisions to be made in our society. All citizens need to learn more about schools, but it is especially important that teachers do so.

Many may argue that it is unnecessary to teach about schools, that students, including those who plan to become teachers, automatically learn *about* schools while they learn *within* them. Of course students learn a great deal about schools without any intentional teaching. But there is much about schools that students do not learn, and some things about schools that they do learn are erroneous. To assume that anyone learns all he will need to know about schooling by being a student makes no more sense than to assume that a long-time prisoner in a jail learns all he needs to know about the legal system.

It is important that we back away and review problems of education and our schools and the way we go about making educational decisions. Not only may our information, our perceptions, and our convictions need updating but there has also been a growth in the *importance attached to schooling* by the wider society. One result of this is that teacher judgments about students are used in such a way that they go far in determining the "life chances" of the students, i.e., the student's chances of acquiring those things generally considered in the society as evidence of success. Teachers need a better understanding of the judgments they make, both in terms of the warrant of those judgments and in terms of the consequences of the judgments for students and for the society. To achieve such understanding, a teacher must go far beyond simply understanding classroom dynamics, child psychology, and his subject matter.

There is yet another reason today to broaden our notion of teacher competence, and this has to do with the growing political and economic power of teachers as they engage in various kinds of collective action. Often in the past teachers exercised little influence in making educational policy decisions. Times have changed. To regard today's teacher as a semi-interested observer in educational policy making is akin to regarding Attila the Hun as just another tourist. Teachers strike, lobby, negotiate, and demand with great effectiveness. And, increasingly, the focus of this new power will be on questions of educational policy. Unless we broaden our notions of teacher competence, we are likely to find teachers making more and more policy decisions, but doing so with a wages-and-hours mentality. This is not to argue against the legitimacy of salary concerns, but simply to point out that they are not, even when coupled with technical proficiency, sufficient to the task of policy making. In short, teachers have gained and are continuing to gain power. The fact should be reflected in the education of new teachers, and this book is an attempt at such reflection.

The Conceptual Framework

Many facile terms are used in describing the American society: "achieving society," "active society," "learning society," "education-centered society." But for any depth of understanding it is not enough to highlight a single apparent characteristic nor even, for that matter, to focus exclusively on the contemporary American scene. Moreover, one more book offering ad hoc structural descriptions of pieces of the school systems in the United States would be difficult to justify. A certain conceptualization and a rhetoric are necessary to give wider meaning to the "facts" of educational change and to allow interpretation of the relationships between educational institutions and other social institutions. To be more precise, the following assumptions may be said to underlie the approach taken in this book:

1. American educational problems and conditions are best viewed within their social and economic environments;

2. The perspectives of modernization and its implied institutional and value commitments offer a useful context in which to examine social changes and their concomitant educational changes;

3. Utilization of such concepts as modernization, industrialization, and postindustrialization leads naturally to reference to social and educational changes taking place in other societies. Such informal comparisons sharpen our understanding of American education.

The reliance on an underlying conceptual theme emphasizing certain aspects of social change may cause some readers initial difficulty. The ideas as well as the language may initially appear strange and unduly abstract. As both teachers and students are well aware, rhetoric frequently has been used to mask a high level of ignorance about social institutions and processes. We are convinced, however, that the concepts employed will help many readers gain deeper insights into the functioning of educational systems.

education,
modernization,
and the
industrial social order

1

Acquiring even a superficial understanding of the changes taking place in contemporary society is a major undertaking. The decade of the 1960s was a turbulent one, with more than its share of wars, rebellions, and social unrest. In 1960 the United Nations, in a moment of optimism, labeled the coming ten years the "development decade," a period in which poorer nations could expect to proceed rapidly up the rungs of development. In the industrially more advanced nations expectations in terms of higher patterns of consumption and in terms of a more equitable distribution of income also ran high. In both groups a nation's formal education was expected to be a major means for increasing the availability of the desired goods and services.

In retrospect, the hopes for the 1960s appear to have been unrealistic. For the poorer nations the struggle for a minimum standard of living seemed frustratingly slow. In the more wealthy nations desire for more and more consumption continued unabated, and the disparity of wealth remained dangerously broad. Educational systems in both poor and rich nations felt the effects of the disillusionment.

But underneath such social and educational struggles lie more fundamental societal changes imbedded in such concepts as modernization, economic growth, and industrialization. These changes and the social problems they have engendered provide the environment for the growth and functioning of educational systems. Chapter 1, drawing heavily on the social sciences, provides perspectives on contemporary American society by examining the nature of institutional and individual changes in the processes of modernization and industrialization. While the terminology at times may be new, the basic ideas are simple. Chapter 2 emphasizes the social and technological characteristics of advanced industrialized societies and the functioning of education in such environments.

CHAPTER ONE

Perspectives on Social Change and Educational Change

We are all familiar with the catch phrases used to describe the contemporary social scene. The media bombard us with these phrases, which are designed to evoke images of the people and institutions about us. Because of advances in air travel and communication, the world is "smaller"; because sheer volume of production is no longer the all consuming industrial goal, we in the United States now have a "postindustrial society"; because efficiency appears to demand bigness, a few "giant" impersonal enterprises control our production, recreation, and information fields. We live in a "technocracy" that is wondrous in its material conveniences, but is showing strains and occasional breakdowns in some "subsystems," such as transportation, and is generating crises in others, such as environmental pollution. Moreover, we are told that, in a technocracy, institutions are run not by leaders but by "faceless managers," further reducing the individual's sense of "control," "belongingness," and "involvement." Reactions by individuals and social groups to these developments have included: (1) "dropping out," that is, reducing involvement in such basic social institutions as family, school, and work; (2) seeking ways to "turn on" through sex, drugs, and psychedelic happenings; (3) striving for social improvement and for individual meaning through civic action and work with disadvantaged peoples; (4) commitment to overt revolution; or (5) apathy.

Educational systems both reflect and generate the nature of the social environment. Contemporary societies and individuals place great demands on their educational institutions. Schooling is expected to produce, for example, a more equitable distribution of wealth and status, the necessary skills for the economy, and attitudes and values acceptable to the family and the community. However, schools throughout the world are being subjected to a level of criticism unparalleled in modern history. Schools appear to have lost their legitimacy as the sole purveyors of education. Even the milder critics are calling for radical reform in curriculum and teaching methods. A minority of critics are demanding nothing less than the abolition of schools, indeed a de-schooling of society. This latter group argues that schooling is an initiation ritual into society which has always functioned to perpetuate inequality. Therefore, control over learning must be taken from schools and teachers and returned to individuals. In the words of Illich, "Deschooling must be the secularization of teaching and learning . . . the learner must be guaranteed his freedom without guaranteeing to society what learning he will acquire and hold as his own." [1]

How does a student or educator gain perspective and deeper understanding of these varied events and crosscurrents of thought? Which changes are lasting and which ephemeral? Which social forces reflect major new orientations for institutions and individuals and which are merely minor and infrequent aberrations? What specific issues and problems for teachers and administrators are being generated? What trends are apparent in the emergence of new demands on the education profession? In this and the following chapter an attempt is made to respond to these questions by examining educa-

---

[1] Ivan Illich, "The Breakdown of Schools: A Problem or a SYMPTOM?" (Cuernavaca, Mexico: Working draft of a paper for discussion, CIDOC, 1971).

tional change within the context of its socioeconomic environment.

Our discussion and analysis of educational and social changes employs the concept of modernization to gain a certain perspective on contemporary American society. Modernization refers to particular changes in institutions and individuals and therefore facilitates comparisons between and within societies. This concept, then, can make more apparent the degree of uniqueness or pervasiveness of social and educational conditions, problems, and issues. Basically, we want to provide a conceptual framework to assist in interpretation so that a static examination of schooling in the United States can be avoided; without the possibilities of implicit or explicit comparisons we would learn little. Moreover, our interest lies in understanding *what is* in a dynamic context of change so that hypotheses may be generated as to *what might be*.

By many commonly used measures the United States stands as the most modernized and industrialized nation. But, in terms of social and economic characteristics, what precisely is assumed when such a conclusion is reached? And what educational achievements, problems, and crises appear to be accompaniments of advanced stages of modernization or postindustrialism? To a considerable degree chapters 1 and 2, in terminology, in concepts employed, and in topics and problems raised, set the stage for the more narrowly focused, problem-oriented later chapters.

The Process of Modernization

Man seemingly prefers to think in terms of dichotomies in viewing the broad sweep of social change and in describing patterns of social behavior. He has used such contrasting classifications or typologies as community-society, folk-urban, mechanical-organic, traditional-modern, underdeveloped-developed, and agrarian-industrial (and postindustrial). Such "ideal types" have proved useful in gaining a general perspective on changes within a given society and perhaps in making gross comparisons between societies. In this and subsequent chapters, we are largely concerned with contemporary America and contemporary American education. We prefer to examine our topic in terms of the social, cultural, and economic changes that are now taking place or are a part of the recent past. Further, when such treatment appears to contribute to a better understanding of the topic we prefer to view American society and American education in their comparative or international setting. And, as indicated above, in proceeding with these efforts, a core concept, namely, that type of social change depicted as modernization or development, provides one of the main contexts for examining the educational system.

Modernization has been given a variety of definitions by scholars who have used the term. As Weiner points out,

> Economists see modernization primarily in terms of man's application of technologies to the control of nature's resources in order to bring about a marked increase in the growth of output per head of population. Sociologists and social anthropologists have been primarily concerned with the process of differentiation that characterizes modern societies . . . political scientists have focused particularly on the problems of nation and government building as modernization occurs.[2]

The development and applications of technology hold a central place in most definitions of modernization. Debate continues as to which social and individual changes necessarily precede technological change. There is little controversy, however, that expanded knowledge and new tools which permit man to extend his control over his environ-

---

[2] Myron Weiner, ed., *Modernization* (New York: Basic Books, 1966), p. 3.

ment and increase his productivity have far-reaching implications.[3]

Other scholars suggest that, fundamentally, modernization must be viewed in psychological or individual terms. Attitudes, needs, and personality are sometimes seen as the starting place for vast institutional and societal changes. Lerner, for example, argues that persons move from traditional to modern styles of life as they increase their empathic capability, that is, their ability to project themselves psychologically across social and occupational class lines.[4] Using somewhat different academic lenses and a different rhetoric, McClelland describes the level of "achievement motivation" as the key to

---

[3] The centrality of knowledge expansion is posited by Black, a historian who views modernization as a general term referring to ". . . the process by which historically evolved institutions are adapted to the rapidly changing functions that reflect the unprecedented increase in man's knowledge, permitting control over his environment, that accompanied the scientific revolution." C. E. Black, *The Dynamics of Modernization* (New York: Harper and Row, 1967), p. 7.

Levy, a sociologist, sees the degree of modernization related to the use of inanimate sources of power and use of tools. A society will be considered more or less modernized to the extent that its members use inanimate sources of power and energy or use tools to multiply the effects of their efforts. Marion J. Levy, *Modernization and the Structure of Societies* (Princeton, N.J.: Princeton University Press, 1966), p. 11.

Levy is referring to sources of power that are not acquired from human or other animal energy; by "tool" is meant any physical device ordinarily separable from the body of an individual who applies it and used to accomplish that which he could not accomplish at all, or would not accomplish as well, without it. Many, but by no means all, of these tools and sources of power were first developed in Europe and North America and subsequently utilized by other societies about the world.

Using the core elements in his definition, Levy goes on to view contemporary societies as forming continua along these dimensions. Societies as they modernize through the use of new tools and new sources of power are transformed structurally with new institutions, new value systems, and new roles emerging.

[4] By way of illustration, Lerner offers contrasting examples of the responses of a shepherd and a shopkeeper in rural Turkey when asked the question: What would you do if you were president of your country? The shepherd, who was "shocked by the impropriety of the very question" responded: "My God! How can you ask such a thing? How can I . . . I cannot . . . president of Turkey . . . master of the whole world." The grocer, however, promptly responded: "I would make roads for the villagers to come to towns to see the world and would not let them stay in their holes all their life." Daniel Lerner, *The Passing of Traditional Society* (Glencoe, Ill.: Free Press, 1958), p. 24.

the level of modernization of individuals or groups.[5] McClelland concludes that "the higher the level of expressed concern over achievement, the more rapid the subsequent economic growth."

That the confines of one's academic discipline may be too restrictive has been demonstrated a number of times but perhaps most dramatically in an attempt to relate economic growth to the psychological attributes of individuals and social groups. Hagen, a practicing economist, bravely departs from the strictures of his discipline and speaks of the innovational personality, concluding that personality change is typically the first step in the modernization sequence, which involves urbanization, increased media participation, increased literacy, and further change in personality. In other words, urbanization, and so forth, are viewed as steps in the process of change, not its point of departure. The Hagen formula for social change that may lead to economic development is as follows: the withdrawal of status respect from some important societal group→retreatism→alienation from traditional values→possible increased productivity and technological progress.[6]

One of Hagen's illustrations is the samurai of nineteenth-century Japan. The virtual elimination of feudal warfare left the samurai without their traditional function as warriors. As a consequence of this withdrawal of status respect, samurai drifted from the feudal estates into a number of other pursuits. Many became *ronin*, i.e., wanderers, some in search of other heroic roles, some retiring to seclusion or meditation, and others succumbing to lives of dissipation. This with-

---

[5] David C. McClelland, "Changing Values for Progress," in *Education and the Development of Nations,* ed. Hobert Burns (Syracuse, N.Y.: Syracuse University, 1963), p. 3. See also David McClelland, *The Achieving Society* (Princeton, N.J.: Van Nostrand, 1961). McClelland defines need for achievement as "a spontaneous desire to do something well for its own sake rather than to gain power or love, recognition or profit." In his research he noted high levels of achievement concern preceding such cases of rapid economic growth as in Greece in the classical period, in Spain in the late Middle Ages, in England in Tudor times or just before the Industrial Revolution.

[6] Everett E. Hagen, *On The Theory of Social Change: How Economic Growth Begins* (Homewood, Ill.: Dorsey Press, 1962), pt. II.

drawal from their traditional societal role, Hagen argues, in time gave way to new commitments and new faith. Many of the merchants and early industrialists—the economic innovators—were samurai who devoted their energies in these directions with as much dedication as they had previously performed their military tasks. Samurai, particularly of the lower grades, filled the new "modern" roles in far greater proportions than their numbers would suggest.

Perhaps most controversy exists when an attempt is made to describe the political requisites for modernization. A modern polity is frequently characterized in terms of the involvement of citizens or the responsiveness of the government to citizens' needs. A number of scholars have also defined political development to include the capability of regulating conflict and tensions so that the direction of change can be influenced by the goals of the society.[7] Questions arise, however, over the form of the modern polity. Is democracy necessarily either a requisite or a goal? [8]

What political scientists call "participant political systems," i.e., nations with elected public officials, multiple political

---

[7] James Coleman, for example, gives the following definition of political development: the acquisition by a political system of a consciously sought and qualitatively new and enhanced political capacity as manifested in the successful institutionalization of (1) new patterns of integration regulating and containing the tensions and conflicts produced by increased differentiation and (2) new patterns of participation and resource distribution adequately responsive to the demands generated by the imperatives of equality. James Coleman, ed., *Education and Political Development* (Princeton, N.J.: Princeton University Press, 1965), p. 15.

[8] Coleman, in describing the "modern participatory state," identifies two possible models—the totalitarian and the democratic. His preference for the latter is obvious, and he finds the democratic model more viable for a modern society; that is, he believes that a democratic polity is a better vehicle for bringing about and sustaining development and social change. See Ibid.

Some scholars such as Ward and Rustow are more cautious. Whereas they emphasize that developed polities are characterized by interest and involvement, they do not argue that political development necessarily implies democratic decision making. Indeed, in commenting on the Communist belief that all societies move along a single path toward one preordained goal, these authors conclude that "this artless and simplistic notion does not gain in validity as we change the sign on the finish line from 'Communism' to 'Democracy.'" Robert E. Ward and D. A. Rustow, eds., *Political Modernization in Japan and Turkey* (Princton, N.J.: Princeton University Press, 1964), p. 5.

parties, and the like, are often associated with higher incomes. Nevertheless, successful economic performance has been associated with authoritarian governments as well as democratic ones. There appears, then, to be little direct evidence to suggest that the more participant forms of democarcy *ensure* rapid economic growth. More likely there are common social and individual indicators underlying transformation of political and economic institutions.

While democracy may be neither a prerequisite to, nor a necessary outcome of, modernization, several scholars note that the components of modernization may be prerequisites to democracy. As the result of empirical inquiry, Adelman and Morris conclude:

> It is reasonable to assume that before fully participant nationwide democratic institutions can evolve, certain levels of mass communication, urbanization, and literacy, for example, must be achieved and rationalist, positivist attitudes must be sufficiently diffused throughout the society.[9]

The variety of interpretations of the most fundamental ingredients of modernization hides the considerable agreement in the behavioral sciences about the direction of structural and value change in this process. As we have seen, there are a number of interpretations of the character of modernization.[10] In this complex and still somewhat mysterious process

---

[9] Irma Adelman and Cynthia Taft Morris, *Society, Politics, and Economic Development: A Quantitative Approach* (Baltimore, Md.: Johns Hopkins, 1967).

[10] In fact, some scholars attempt to distinguish between the notions of modernization and development. Modernization, one argument goes, refers more to the values, attitudes, and life styles of people, while development is fundamentally an application of technology to processes of production and distribution. From this interpretation, it follows that modernization may thwart development. That is, the effort expended in producing and acquiring modern clothing, entertainment, and services detracts from the accumulation of capital through savings and thereby limits investment in agriculture, industry, or infrastructure. While this distinction has merit, we will rely primarily on the term modernization to describe all the processes we are discussing. When it is necessary, for the sake of clarity, we will make explicit in the context distinctions between such concepts as economic development, industrialization, social development, and modernization.

there is perhaps a fairly general consensus that the following changes will take place:

Technology will change toward the increased application of scientific knowledge; agriculture will move from subsistence farming to cash crops to commercial production; in industry the trend will be away from muscle power to the use of machines that derive power from other forms of energy; in religion the belief patterns will become secularized; in ecological arrangements a movement toward urban concentration will be evident; in familial patterns there will be a reduction in the size and number of functions; in education growth will occur in the quantity available and the variety of curricula offered.[11]

In terms of individual propensities and commitments, the profile of modern man drawn by Inkeles may be considered a synthesis of widely expressed views. Modern man may be characterized by (1) receptivity to new experiences and openness to innovation and change; (2) a disposition to form or hold opinions over a large number of the problems and issues that arise not only in his immediate environment but also outside it; (3) orientation to the present or future, rather than to the past; (4) planning and organizing beliefs as a way of handling life; (5) mastery of the environment in order to advance individual purposes and goals, rather than being dominated entirely by environmental needs; (6) confidence that the world is calculable and that other people and institutions can be relied upon to fulfill or meet obligations and responsibilities; (7) awareness of the dignity of others and a disposition to show respect for them; (8) faith in science and technology; (9) belief in distributive justice, in rewards based upon social contribution and not according to either whim or special properties of the person not related to such a contribution.[12]

Modern society, then, is a form of human community

---

[11] See Neil S. Smelser, "The Modernization of Social Relations," in Weiner, *Modernization,* pp. 110–11.

[12] Alex Inkeles, "The Modernization of Man," in Weiner, *Modernization,* pp. 138–52.

characterized by an industrial life style and a complex occupational and social structure. Industrial life style implies a particular set of relations between the economy and the individual. Labor relations tend to be contractual and impersonal, the occupational structure differentiated and specialized, and access to consumer goods so widespread as to permit all sectors of the population to share in the fruits of the industrial infrastructure—power, communication, transportation, and the like.

Many social scientists would also suggest that in modern society the standards for morality, legality, and so on presumably are more "universal," that is, based on regulations and values that apply alike to all the various social, ethnic, or age groupings. Furthermore, in the modern society, individual success and social mobility are less likely to be the accidents of family, sex, or race, but rather depend more on individual qualifications and achievement. Gross generalities such as these are dangerous, and there are obvious exceptions in individual cases. It is easy, for example, to note the persistence of privileged groups in Western Europe and the United States. Nevertheless, these generalizations relate to certain fundamental characteristics of social change and at least offer a useful perspective in examining the process of modernization.

Measurements of Modernization

A number of attempts have been made to identify and quantify indicators of the level of modernization. Most of these attempts have resulted from an examination of available cross-national data on contemporary societies. The following list includes most of the indicators frequently used in the ranking of nations:

> Size of the traditional agricultural sector (inversely related to modernization)
> Extent of urbanization
> Extent of social mobility

Extent of literacy
Extent of mass communication
Degree of national integration and sense of national
    unity
Strength of democratic institutions
Degree of administrative efficiency
Extent of leadership commitment to economic development
Per capita GNP
Abundance of natural resources
Level of technology in industry
Level of technology in agriculture
Rate of improvement in human resources [13]

In addition to such attempts at describing variations in national wealth, production, consumption, and so on, efforts have also been made to describe the modernization level of societies in more basic structural terms. For example, many scholars focus on the concepts of differentiation and specialization in examining the structural attributes of social change. A variety of theorists including Parsons, Eisenstadt, Easton, Smelser, Buckley, Young, and Marsh have suggested that social differentiation is crucial to the understanding of modernization for at least two reasons: (1) it is *a,* if not *the,* principal process through which social systems adapt to changes in their environments; and (2) the level of differentiation at any point in time is a good index of the ability of a system to adapt further.[14]

The process of societal differentiation has been defined by MacIver and Page to include:

---

[13] Adelman and Morris, *Society, Politics, and Economic Development,* pp. 16–17.

[14] See, for example, Talcott Parsons, *The Social System* (New York: Free Press, 1951); S. N. Eisenstadt, *Modernization, Protest, and Change* (Englewood Cliffs, N.J.: Prentice-Hall, 1966); David Easton, *A Systems Analysis of Political Life* (New York: John Wiley, 1965); Walter F. Buckley, *Sociology and Modern Systems Theory* (Englewood Cliffs, N.J.: Prentice-Hall, 1967); Frank N. Young and Ruth C. Young, "Social Integration and Change in Twenty-Four Mexican Villages," in *Economic Development and Cultural Change* 8, no. 4 (July 1960): 366–77; Robert M. Marsh, *Comparative Sociology* (New York: Harcourt, Brace and World, 1967). See also, Smelser, "Modernization of Social Relations."

1. a greater division of labor, so that the energy of more individuals is concentrated on more specific tasks and so that thereby a more elaborate system of cooperation, a more intricate nexus of functional relationships is sustained within the group;

2. an increase in the number and variety of functional associations and institutions so that each is more defined or more limited in the range or character of its service;

3. a greater diversity and refinement in the instruments of social communication, perhaps above all in the medium of language.[15]

Perhaps an illustration will keep this somewhat technical language from obscuring what is a relatively simple notion. In undifferentiated societies the family or kinship group perform most of the crucial social tasks: finding and distributing food and other goods, making decisions about crime and punishment, and educating the young. In modern industrialized societies special organizations and entities make and distribute goals, educate, govern, and perform other specialized functions. The process of modernization may be viewed, then, as the separating out from the family of the economic, political, and educational institutions and creating a distinct place for them in the social order.

Marsh has developed an index of differentiation by utilizing two indicators: (1) the percentage of males in nonagricultural occupations, and (2) gross energy consumption in megawatt hours per capita for one year. On the basis of this index, one hundred fourteen contemporary national societies were ranked. By way of example, table 1 presents the ranking of a selected number of countries on a scale of differentiation.

Educational Change and Modernization

In examining educational change in the process of modernization, we are most concerned with two general questions:

---

[15] R. M. MacIver and Charles H. Page, *Society: An Introductory Analysis* (New York: Holt, Rinehart and Winston, 1962), p. 527.

TABLE 1

Index of Societies According to Degree
of Differentiation

Index of Differentiation Score	Nation
109.4	United States
84.6	United Kingdom
57.5	France
41.4	USSR
40.6	Chile
39.0	Venezuela
31.2	Kenya
29.3	Mexico
26.3	Brazil
25.7	Tunisia
23.5	Dominican Republic
23.0	Peru
22.6	Paraguay
21.4	Bolivia
21.1	Ghana
20.9	Philippines
20.3	India
19.2	Burma
13.8	Honduras
11.0	Haiti

SOURCE: Robert M. Marsh, *Comparative Sociology* (New York: Harcourt, Brace and World, 1967), pp. 338–47.

(1) What is the changing nature and direction of linkages between education and other systems? (2) What is the changing nature and direction of intraeducational system changes? Although the second question has at times been viewed as a subquestion of the first, we believe that changes inside the system are not totally dependent on the larger society. Before

proceeding directly to attempt to respond to these questions, however, some further discussion is in order of what is implied in the term *formal education.* (For convenience we will tend to use *education* as a synonym for formal education.)

Much of the literature on education and social change would seem to assume implicitly that education has a homogeneity which allows easy generalization and analysis. To the contrary, education as an institution, process, or system has a number of features inhibiting analysis:

1. Formal education has evolved as a gradual consequence of economic, political-military, and religious needs. Thus, historically, education has been an institution operated for very limited and inherently conservative ends. By contrast, modern or modernizing educational systems frequently constitute attempts to promote vast social and cultural changes.

2. Education is a composite of skills, techniques, and value systems, many of which have long-range rather than immediate consequences on the individual and on society.

3. Education develops a "culture" of its own that may interfere with the objectives formulated by parents, school boards, or government. This culture reflects to a varying degree the emphasis that educational systems may place on transmission of skills, community service, moral behavior, personality development, scholarship, and research.

4. Education is marked by a complexity of levels and programs that obstruct analysis. Three distinct stages of formal education, e.g., primary, secondary, and higher, may be found in most nations; nevertheless, great variation persists in the function and organization of institutions at each stage.

5. Formal education is multifunctional; for example, it plays some part in a number of aspects of socialization, occupational preparation, and in the development of self-concepts.

One way to describe and explain educational change within the general process of modernization is through use of the concept differentiation introduced earlier. As social differentiation proceeds, the educational system evolves with its own functional place in the society. Such evolution is characterized by a specialization of roles and organizations within the educational system and a growing differentiation between levels of education, creating new problems of articulation and coordination.

The clearest and most dramatic way to illustrate differentiation of the educational system is to compare "primitive" or "traditional" societies with modern societies. In the traditional society (as represented in contemporary times by tribal groups found in the more remote areas of Africa, Latin America, or Asia), the family or kinship unit has, along with its other functions, the function of education. The primary educational goal in traditional societies is the fostering of commitment to a number of adult obligations. Structurally, then, the educational system is undifferentiated from the family, and functionally it prepares for diffuse roles. In the more formal language of social scientists, the patterns of value orientations influencing relations within the educational system are said to be particularistic, ascriptive, diffuse, and affective.[16] Participation in the educational process is governed by such ascriptive criteria as sex, age, size, and lineage. Since the outcomes of education are primarily of concern to the kinship group, we may say that the process is circumscribed by particularistic norms.

A contrast may be made with an ideal modern society. Here the educational system is a recognized autonomous system with a large variety of subsystems. In keeping with the specialized demands of modern society, the functions of the educational system are numerous. The educational system, in

---

[16] These value orientations can be viewed as forming four sets of continua along which the norms or standards governing societal interaction can be conceptualized: (1) the movement along the continua from particularism to universalism refers to the increase in the degree to which people are expected to act in accordance with general norms rather than on the basis of particular cases (e.g., increased reliance on impartial legal codes); (2) the change from ascription toward achievement refers to the extent to which people are evaluated on the basis of their performance rather than in terms of characteristics of lineage, sex, race, and so on; (3) the movement from diffuseness toward specificity refers to the extent to which the basis for the way people act is lodged in narrowly defined categories (i.e., specialization of roles); (4) the change from affectivity to affective neutrality refers to the extent to which people are willing to act in accordance with the interests of the group (or society) rather than for their immediate personal gratification.

its most general purpose, provides a source for the human resources and creativity necessary to continue modernization.
The educational system also assists in the preparation for
highly specific occupational tasks. The value orientations
structuring relations within the system tend to be universalistic, achievement-based, specific, and neutral. That is, the
manner of selection and of rewarding and evaluating students
transcends the norms of particular social groups. Further, the
system seeks to promote commitments and obligations that
need not be immediately fulfilled.

Highlighting the contrasts between the educational systems of modern and traditional societies plays down their
similarities. Still, similar functions do exist. Thus, both
modern and traditional educational systems seek to transmit
a body of culture valued by the superordinate system, e.g.,
family or society. Both, then, contribute to the process of
socialization and the certification of individuals for new
roles. Moreover, educational systems in the full range of
societies from traditional to modern frequently reflect ascriptive norms in their admission procedures and in certain other
internal arrangements. Phrased differently, considerable
structural differentiation may take place within an educational system, with little functional change. Yet, as the "body
of culture" becomes larger and more complex, specialized
entities for the transmission of portions of it are established.
And as the roles within the society become more specialized
and differentiated, specialized entities for their preparation
are established. The following section describes this process
in a more detailed, though still simplistic, fashion.

Stages of Educational Differentiation

Elaborating on the simple typology of traditional and modern, it is possible, in a crude way, to hypothesize levels of
educational differentiation.[17]

---

[17] Some efforts have been made to hypothesize stages of educational development that parallel levels of modernization. Thus Beeby described educational
systems in the (1) dame-school stage, (2) stage of formalism, (3) stage of transi-

1. Education at a preliterate level of society is marked by informal learning within the family and organized relations between the generations to provide economic skills and an introduction to appropriate social behavior. At this level the roles of the student and teacher are determined by purely ascriptive criteria. Children are "students" because of their age; any difference in what they learn is determined by their sex. "Teachers" are teachers because they are adult members of the family and whatever "specialization" is present is determined by sex; i.e., females may teach cooking; males, hunting and the like.

2. At a somewhat more advanced stage, part of the socialization process differentiates out of the family to be provided for all adolescent members of the society under the guidance of a specialized adult group. While a practical content constitutes a part of the "curriculum," strong emphasis is also placed on metaphysical and conduct areas. The bush school of West Africa provides an example of education at this stage.[18]

At the second stage, then, ascription in terms of age, and often sex, is the basis for determining who the students are. Some attention to talent is in evidence in determining teacher roles; training beyond that given to the average person may

tion, and (4) stage of meaning. (C. E. Beeby, *The Quality of Education in Developing Countries* [Cambridge, Mass.: Harvard University Press, 1966].) While rich in insight into the educational problems of developing societies, this study is not particularly helpful in its avowed aim of being a starting point for a theory of educational change. There is, moreover, at least a modicum of truth in one reviewer's complaint that Beeby views economists as ogres and educators as Florence Nightingales. In contrast to Beeby's "qualitative" model, Laska built a quantitative model of educational development suggesting that "there may be an evolutionary sequence for the optimum development of educational systems in the modern or modernizing societies." In the Laska model the first stage requires a limited amount of higher education, universal primary education is achieved at the second stage, and the third stage is characterized by a vertical expansion of school enrollments eventuating in universal secondary education. John A. Laska, "The Stages of Educational Development," *Comparative Education Review* 8, no. 3 (1964): 251–63.

[18] See David G. Scanlon: "The Bush School," *Phi Delta Kappan* 41, no. 4 (January 1960): 148–52. The bush school refers to ceremonial rites and practical training received by some boys and girls (separately) at the age of puberty. Instruction at the bush school would typically include the inculcation of traditional cultural values and spiritual beliefs and a certain amount of training in such skills as farming or cooking.

be required. A beginning of specialization is also evident as certain adult members of the society have more responsibility than others for training children. These teachers are not specialized to any appreciable extent, however, for the teacher is regarded as the guide to the meaning of life, the source of all knowledge. Furthermore, some degree of universalism may be observed when standardized tests must be passed (i.e., bravery proved) according to procedures accepted by the society.

3. However, as the society itself becomes more differentiated and problems of social selection greater, certain families or groups gain increased power or economic advantage over others, and formalized education ceases to be the prerogative of all societal members. Education can lay claim to a long history as an institution tied to those relatively small groups who wielded political, economic, or religious power. This condition accords with the differentiation concept, for those groups at the center of the societal differentiation process in economic, political, and cultural spheres are the ones who would find it most necessary to build an educational institution to provide the skills, attitudes, and values through which they could maintain, adapt, and develop themselves and their institutions.

Standards based on ascription, particularly in terms of class lineage, are strong in determining who the students are in this context. Criteria for determining who the teachers are may be considered related to intelligence or talent only to the limited extent that teachers are required to have a greater degree of knowledge. The "curriculum" exhibits differentiation in that concern is focused on language, liberal arts, and philosophy, in addition to conduct, law, and theology. Particularism is a norm when individuals are educated according to their station.

The teacher continues to assume the role, at least at what is now termed primary and secondary levels, of the fount of knowledge about life rather than as a specialist in one branch of learning, and the educational institution may be described as Mark Hopkins sitting on one end of the log and the student sitting on the other. Some differentiation in terms of role specialization may be discernible at the level of higher education both in terms of administrative roles and specialized teaching roles.

4. At a yet more advanced stage the relation between education and society becomes decidedly complicated. Industrialization and ever-increasing societal differentiation as measured by division of labor and role specialization become outstanding characteristics of the society. Educators frequently claim that the many levels and problems in education supervised and taught by a wide range of specialists play a significant role in promoting industrialization and inculcating modern values. This stage places new burdens on schooling in terms of mass instruction, occupational recruitment, and social selection.

Accompanying differentiation and specialization during recent decades are two other visible educational changes: (1) the diffusion and expansion of schooling; and (2) the assumption of an increasingly significant role of formal education in further socioeconomic change. Mass education has become the goal of every contemporary nation. Although in many nations universal schooling is as yet an unfulfilled goal, even in the least developed nations rudimentary schooling is being offered to large numbers of young children who, in earlier periods, would have gone unschooled. In Western Europe, Australasia, Japan, Canada, and the United States nearly all children are provided with education through the primary grades, and increasingly through the lower secondary grades. Moreover, in these nations literacy approaches 100 percent.

The increased centrality of the educational system in planned and unplanned socioeconomic change is manifested in a number of ways. As progress is made toward modernization, educational attainment is increasingly associated with social prestige and occupational status. Moreover, in contemporary societies formal education frequently appears to be a major factor in intra- and intergenerational social mobility. Thus, both the path to success for the poor and the route to safeguarding status already acquired lead through the educational system. Further, the growing emphasis on human resources as the key to economic growth has given added justification for expansion of education. Thus, the powerful driving forces of greater development and of greater equity contribute to the increased stature of education.

Although the precise nature of education's contribution to modernization may for some time remain unspecified, and the exact course of educational change is as yet uncharted, there probably would be little controversy regarding the generalization that modern societies require the support of well-developed educational systems. A very good case indeed can be made for the view that the level of education in the more modern societies is an important element in the maintenance of a high level of development. First, in developed societies, production and trade are almost wholly monetized. This implies a vast system of abstract bookkeeping, information gathering and storing, and complex contractual arrangements. Nearly all social roles demand a more sophisticated or technical knowledge than is required in less complex societies. Whether or not such knowledge is best acquired through schooling may, of course, be debated.

Second, in the developed societies important communication is frequently in written rather than oral form. Written law has replaced customary law and simple mores. Further, that crucial social necessity, the allocation of labor, is built on employment records, written applications, letters of recommendation, and so on. Factory rules, instructions, regulations, wage-and-hour laws, and myriads of similar written notices make life for the illiterate in these societies virtually impossible.

Third, the dependence of the developed society on advanced technology is absolute. The large urban masses in developed societies are dependent for their food and other necessities on their ability to command these things, either from technically advanced agriculture in their own society or from abroad, by the trading power of goods produced by advanced techniques. The large number of people who must be able to manage and manipulate this technical apparatus tends to grow continually in developed societies. A large and constant stream of technically competent people must be trained in each generation, implying higher schooling for many.[19]

A Critique of the Foregoing

We have described modernization as a movement toward more universalistic and achievement bases for norms and behavior. An important focus has been the notion of differentiation—a process visible in all societal institutions. The development and applications of technology have been catalysts and consequences of differentiation. However, some criticisms of this interpretation can be made.[20]

First, some critics have argued that such terms as universalism and achievement orientation smack of ethnocentricity. Are these necessary values for modernization or are they merely found in those existing societies we term "modern"? Indeed, are these concepts, as well as the broader notion of modernization, examples of our value-ridden social sciences?

Others have questioned the level of commitment to such values and norms in the modern societies. For example, are rewards in the United States today given more on the basis of achievement than in the past? Certainly the educational level of a person in the United States has become an increasingly important criterion for employment. But, can this be equated to achievement orientation? More and more we have become a "credential society," allocating and rewarding persons on the basis of diplomas and degrees.[21] Yet, as many empirical studies have shown, a student's success in schooling is associ-

---

[19] See Don Adams and Robert Bjork, *Education in Developing Areas* (New York: David McKay, 1969), chap. 2.

[20] Much of the description of modernization presented thus far draws heavily from the loosely knit movement in the social sciences known as structural functionalism. The efforts of scholars associated with structural functionalism, such as Talcott Parsons, Robert Merton, and Marion Levy have been roundly criticized in the past few years from a number of points of view.

[21] See S. M. Miller and Frank Riessman, *Social Class and Social Policy* (New York: Basic Books, 1968).

ated closely with his socioeconomic background. What passes for achievement, then, when the schools are the selection instruments, may in part be ascriptive attributes. At a more conceptual level, the criticisms have concentrated on the inadequacy of the structural functionalists in describing social change.

For example, many contemporary social scientists believe that the differentiation concept used to describe social change relies too heavily on equilibrium, order, and orderly change, and that too little attention has been given to conflict as initiator and consequence of change. The idea of differentiation suggests an evolutionary process, if not necessarily without tensions, at least representing change along predictable lines and even perhaps under central control.

To some scholars who view conflict and revolution as the mechanisms of change, focusing on differentiation avoids important questions. Social change and modernization result from the interaction of social groups and the exercise of political and economic power. Moreover, it is argued, concentration on these processes makes more visible the social problems and tensions that arise.

Discussions of modernization in terms of evolutionary change toward utilization of universalistic and achievement criteria in the assessment of behavior particularly incur the wrath of the more radical—whether Marxist or non-Marxist—scholars and students. These observers argue that the optimism engendered by such interpretation is unfounded and that much of the assumed progress in modernizing societies is illusory. The good life, rather than being shared among increasing numbers in industrialized societies, remains restricted to a comparative few. Or, by way of slight modification, the fruits of technology and productivity are disseminated by the upper class (or power elite) only to the extent necessary to obstruct social upheaval. Evidence presented in support of this position includes:

1. In a number of developing nations (perhaps Pakistan serves as one of the better examples), economists have demon-

strated with aggregate data that rapid advances are being made. Yet a closer examination frequently indicates that a few families have greatly increased their wealth and power while the lives of the great masses of poor remain untouched.

2. In the United States an interlocking power elite functions through bureaucracy and through the military-industrial complex to keep the rich rich. The privilege and position of the elite are maintained through economic productivity, military power, and even ideological machinations, e.g., CIA activities. Domhoff comments: "All power elite foundations, institutes, and associations are propaganda fronts which are involved in maintaining the legitimacy and respectability of the present establishment. . . ." [22]

3. In Western Europe, after decades of struggle led by liberal intellectuals, trade unionists, and others, expansion of enrollments in the highly privileged secondary schools came about after World War II. Nevertheless, selection and promotion criteria being what they are, such expansion has benefited the poor comparatively little.

A balanced view of modernization would certainly conclude that progress toward a more equitable distribution of wealth, status, and power has been frustratingly slow. And, undoubtedly, at a conceptual level the notions of development and modernization have been strongly colored by Western history. Yet such core ideas as technological change, social differentiation, and achievement values have demonstrated their utility in describing social and educational change. These and other concepts presented earlier need not be viewed as constituting a theory that has explanatory power in all cases. They do, however, provide bases for departure in empirically observing social and educational change.

In the subsequent chapters we will take careful note of the questions implicit in these criticisms. What has been the relationship between modernization, postindustrialization,

---

[22] G. William Domhoff, *The Higher Circles* (New York: Vintage Books, 1971).

and equity? Between quality, ability, and equity? How do the educational system and the society define and reward ability? Has education, as some radicals argue, largely been a tool of cultural imperialism within nations and between nations, employed either to reinforce the privileged culture or to provide a minimum level of social stability?

Summary

The concept of modernization offers one way to view variations in the patterns of living and working. Modernization is not, however, easy to define, for it is filtered by the distinctive lenses of the observers. On one hand this may reflect only variations in academic training. If this is the case, then perhaps synthesis and agreement are possible. On the other hand, differing views of modernization may be the result of deep-seated ideological convictions. Training and convictions, of course, are not unrelated; indeed, some would argue that they are necessarily intertwined.

In our interpretations of modernization we have drawn heavily from the social sciences—some might say the traditional social sciences. We have given some attention to radical positions on social change and on education and will continue to do so, for it is important that the reader be aware of the many variations of opinion that exist. However, we make no promise of giving equal space to all interpretations of social and educational change. Our focus and conclusions tend to be most strongly influenced by our experience and our understanding of available research and data. We like to think that our analyses cannot in toto be labeled either conservative, liberal, or radical. Nevertheless, as will be made clear in the next chapter, the contemporary social and educational problems are so overwhelming and so demanding of immediate attention that a defense of a status quo posture in education is untenable.

References

Adams, Don, and Bjork, Robert. *Education in Developing Areas.* New York: David McKay, 1969.

Black, Cyril E. *The Dynamics of Modernization.* New York: Harper and Row, 1967.

Coombs, Philip A. *The World Educational Crisis.* New York: Oxford University Press, 1968.

Eisenstadt, S. N. *Modernization, Protest and Change.* Englewood Cliffs, N.J.: Prentice-Hall, 1966.

Levy, Marion J. *Modernization and the Structure of Societies.* 2 vols. Princeton, N.J.: Princeton University Press, 1966.

Thut, I. N., and Adams, Don. *Patterns of Education in Contemporary Societies.* New York: McGraw-Hill, 1964.

Weiner, Myron, ed. *Modernization.* New York: Basic Books, 1966.

Discussion Questions

1. How does the definition of modernization vary, depending on the academic training of the observer? Give examples.

2. What are the more common measures of national development? What can these measures tell you about the life of a people?

3. Do you find at least a hint of ethnocentricity about the concept and measures of modernization? What may be some of the pitfalls in using the more developed nations as models for the poorer nations to follow?

4. If modernization were defined to include absence of pollution of the environment, would your ranking of nations differ?

5. Can you cite support for the concept of social differentiation by drawing from American history?

6. Can you cite support for the concept of educational differentiation by drawing from American history?

CHAPTER TWO

Social and Educational Crises in Industrialized and Postindustrialized Society

The preceding chapter, which offered a brief outline of the nature of modernization and its accompanying educational changes, lends perspective to some of the historical developments in American society and to some of the variations existing among contemporary societies. It falls far short, however, of describing the complex stresses and strains of advanced industrialized societies. In this chapter the focus will be on such societies—although for the sake of contrast and comparison reference will be made to developing nations.

The Social Environment

As we have seen, by most indices, the United States is the most developed of nations. Its level of productivity, per capita income, consumption rates of food, recreation, etc. are rarely surpassed. Moreover, the United States is sometimes viewed as the most equitable of all contemporary societies. However, contemporary America has also been described by social critics as a "warfare state," engaging in "corporate imperialism," valuing and practicing racism, and generally dehumanizing and repressive to the individual.

The caliber of the critics, the growth internationally of disenchantment with U.S. military, political, and economic postures, and the extent of unrest and even revolution among young Americans suggest that these accusations should not be lightly dismissed. While it is impossible here to undertake an analysis of the nature of conflict, inequality, and dissatisfaction in American society, it may be possible to identify some of the more significant social conditions impinging most directly on the educational system.

Rapidity of Social Change

The rapidity of social change is reflected in all major American institutions. A major stimulant and reflector of change has been the process of urbanization. Between 1790 and 1970 the population of the United States grew from less than 4 million to more than 200 million. At the earlier date approximately 95 percent of the population lived in rural areas; by 1970 more than 70 percent of Americans lived in urban areas. The urban style of living facilitates the interaction of people and ideas and is associated with greater secularization, greater empathy (ability to perceive oneself in another role, see chapter 1), and greater propensity for innovation. Moreover, because of advances in transportation and communication (see fig. 1), even the dwindling rural population is aware of, and to some extent participates in, the urban style of life.[1]

A world perspective on expansion of population offers a picture of equally dramatic change. It was not until approxi-

---

[1] It is interesting to note, however, that throughout its rapid social and economic change America's political structure has remained remarkably stable. "This nation possesses the oldest operative written constitution, the oldest continuous two-party system, and the oldest recurrent set of peaceful elections in history." Eleanor Bernert Sheldon and Wilbert E. Moore, "Monitoring Social Change in American Society," in *Indicators of Social Change*, eds. Sheldon and Moore, (New York: Russell Sage Foundation, 1968), p. 14.

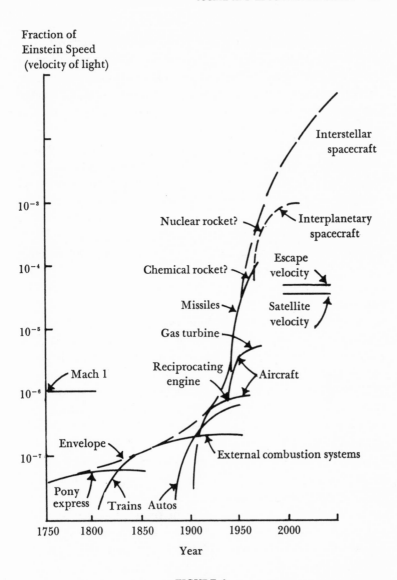

FIGURE 1

Speed Trend Curve

SOURCE: Daniel Bell, "The Measurement of Knowledge and Technology," in Sheldon and Moore, *Indicators of Social Change,* p. 188. Original source: Courtesy Robert U. Ayres, Hudson Institute.

mately 1860 that the world achieved a population of 1 billion persons. By 1925 the world's population had grown to 2 billion; by 1960, to 3 billion. By 1980 it is estimated that we will have passed the 4-billion mark. One dramatic perspective on this rate of growth is to note that it has been estimated that "of all the people who have ever lived, one-fifth are alive today." [2]

In the more industrialized societies even the core societal unit, the family, has undergone fundamental change although its basic stability has persisted beyond the expectations of many social analysts. The past several decades have seen (1) a reduction in the age of marriage, (2) smaller families, (3) a declining mortality, and (4) a rising life expectancy. These conditions in the context of other social and economic change have given rise to "an increase in the labor force participation by women, an increase in the span of years husband and wife have together after the last child has left home, and a change in demand for new forms of housing and recreation." [3] Rates of divorce and illegitimacy have increased, but the great preponderance of adults marry (over 95 percent of women 30–44 years old are married), and the family unit has not disintegrated into informal communalism. Liberalization of abortion laws is progressing steadily; however, it is too early to determine the effect of this change in the law on marriage and family life.

The rapidity of social change is nowhere more apparent than in the world of work. It has been suggested that craftsmen living before the time of Christ were not dissimilar from the craftsmen of Europe in 1800 in their work habits or in the range of skills demanded. Yet, who would suggest that vocational or technical skills of any occupational group in 1800 would be adequate to meet the needs of today's economy? Or even that in many areas those skills adequate in 1970 would suffice in 1975?

---

[2] Bell, "Measurement of Knowledge and Technology," p. 150.
[3] Sheldon and Moore, *Indicators of Social Change,* p. 16.

Nor should it be supposed that the effects of changing technology are limited to, or most dramatically represented in, occupational roles. Some scientists are now forecasting changes in biological technology during the twenty-first century, discussions of which currently are limited largely to books of science fiction. To list a few of the anticipated developments:

a. Laboratory demonstration of electronically amplified or augmented communication between brains (controlled ESP)

b. Maintenance of the human brain extracorporeally for several days

c. Feasibility of safe reduction of sleep required

d. Demonstration of long-duration coma or hibernation to permit a form of time travel

e. Widespread use of physical, chemical, or psychological manipulation to modify the minds of children to accomplish societal purposes.

For millennia children throughout the world retraced the steps of their parents. Today, except in a few isolated traditional societies, children face a severe rupture from the world their parents grew up in. As never before it is now true that children face an unknown future. And, although surely it will be a world in which our scientific understanding of man and his universe will be vastly superior to that which we hold today, less certain is our ability to apply this knowledge in creating a significantly safer, healthier, materially more abundant life.[4]

---

[4] A list of "continuous critical problems" to the world is offered by Ozbekhan.*   1. Generalized poverty within affluence   2. Discrimination of minorities   3. Obsolete welfare practices   4. Insufficient medical care   5. Hunger and malnutrition   6. Inadequate education   7. Inadequate shelter   8. Inadequate transportation   9. Urban and suburban sprawl   10. Decay of inner cities (slums)   11. Environmental pollution   12. Inadequate crime control   13. Inadequate law enforcement   14. Obsolete correctional practices   15. Spoilage of nature   16. Inadequate recreational facilities   17. Discrimination toward the aged   18. Wastage of natural resources   19. Uncontrolled population growth and size   20. Un-

Development of a Technostructure

American society has completed the transformation from an agricultural economy to an industrial economy and is currently emerging into a postindustrial society. In this movement the emphasis in economic activity has changed from farming to manufacturing to services. Great increases in productivity have accompanied economic change and growth, largely as the result of technological advances; these advances in turn have profoundly affected the nature of work and the nature of life.[5] Five dimensions of the postindustrial society have been suggested:

1. The creation of a service economy
2. The pre-eminence of the professional and technical class
3. The centrality of theoretical knowledge as the source of innovation and policy formulation in society
4. The possibility of self-sustaining technological growth
5. The creation of a new "intellectual technology" [6]

The first two of these dimensions are relatively self-explanatory; moreover, they are described in chapter 5. The latter three points are more subtle and may require elaboration. To illustrate the centrality of theoretical knowledge, Bell suggests the contrast between the inventions of the early twentieth century and those of today. Such inventions as the tele-

---

balanced population distribution   21. Obsolete system of world trade
22. Underemployment   23. Spreading social discontent   24. Polarization
of military power   25. Inadequate participation in public decisions
26. Inadequate understanding of international communism   27. Inadequate
conception of world order   28. Insufficient authority of international
agencies.

* Hasan Ozbekhan, "Toward a General Theory of Planning," in *Perspectives of Planning*, ed. Erich Jantsch (Bellagio: Organization for Economic Cooperation and Development, 1968), p. 85.

[5] One of the more precise definitions of the term postindustrial society is offered by Sheldon and Moore: "A post-industrial society is one in which more than half of the economic activity is devoted to services, whether measured by value of product or by distribution of the labor force." Sheldon and Moore, *Indicators of Social Change*, p. 13.

[6] Bell, "Measurement of Knowledge and Technology," pp. 152–53.

graph, telephone, and automobile resulted largely from the work of "talented tinkerers" who generally were unconcerned with the fundamental laws underlying their experimentations. By contrast today we have, for example, "chemically created synthetics—based on the theoretical properties of the macromolecules which are manipulated to achieve the planned creation of new materials." [7]

By "self-sustaining technological growth" is meant the avoidance of stagnation by opening up "new technological frontiers in order to maintain productivity and expansion." In effect this means we are entering a period when we can plan technological change and hence plan productivity.

The term "intellectual technology" as used by Bell includes such technologies as linear programming, systems analysis, information theory, games, simulation, and so forth. These techniques, assisted by the computer, allow the accumulation and manipulation of large amounts of data. Further, by simulating scientific, social, or political situations, "controlled experiments" may be undertaken of vastly greater magnitude than has been hitherto possible. [8]

Recent technological developments in our postindustrial society have required the introduction of new machines and new production methods. Efficient operation of the new machines has demanded new skills and the adoption of new managerial techniques. Technological advances have generally meant great increases in production and increased capability in the dissemination and distribution of goods. However, a number of social and educational problems have accompanied technological change. New machines and techniques have not always meant sizable increases in employment, and between 1950 and 1970 in the United States, for example, the rate of unemployment in the labor force fluctuated between 4 percent and 6 percent. (In addition to not solving, and at times heightening, the problem of unemployment,

---

[7] Ibid., p. 157.
[8] Ibid., pp. 157–58.

TABLE 2

Forecasts of Skilled Population and
Scientific Personnel

	1963	1970	1975
Population of the United States (in millions)	190	209	227
Work force (millions)	76	86	
Civil employment (millions)	70.3 (1964)		88.7
White-collar workers	31.12 (1964)		42.8
(as a percentage of civil employment)	(44.2%)		(48%)
Professional and technical	8.5 (1964)		13.2
(as a percentage of civil employment)	(12.2%)		(14.9%)
Scientific population (millions)	2.7	4	
(as a percentage of active population)	(3.6%)	(4.7%)	
Scientists in the strict sense	0.5 ⎱ 1.43	0.74 ⎱ 2.14	
Engineers	0.93 ⎰	1.4 ⎰	
Technicians	1	1.6	
Science teachers in secondary schools	0.25	0.3	
Doctorate degrees (in thousands)	106	170	
In science	96	153	
In engineering	10	17	

SOURCE: *Reviews of National Science Policy: United States* (Paris: Organization for Economic Cooperation and Development, 1968), p. 45.

technological change and automation have affected skill levels and the nature of the relationship between work and schooling. Chapter 5 further discusses these conditions.)

A second problem has been that of size. A society of highly developed and rapidly changing technology tends to rely on large-scale planning. In the United States, for example, the five hundred largest corporations produce nearly half of all the goods and services available annually.[9] Size may be the servant of technology, but is it inhibitive to the freedom of the individual? If the imperatives of technology and organization dictate the shape of society, then may not man be relegated to servitude to the machine? Does man relate to the world only through technique? Has man become a means, not an end? Can the continual creation of bigger and better material things remain for long a meaningful goal? [10] There is no easy agreement among observers on the answers to these questions, but they are being asked with increased frequency.

Loss of Community and Identity

During the decade roughly paralleling the 1960s, there was considerable sociological and psychological literature on the problems of the individual in coping with the implications of contemporary postindustrial society. The breakdown of intimate family ties, the loss of community, the development of anomie, or normlessness, and the alienation of the individual from society have all been topics for analysis and debate.

The condition of alienation, especially, requires further explanation and elaboration. It is popular to say that modern society, particularly in its technological developments, has promoted alienation. That is, man (in the generic sense) has created institutions, ideologies, and patterns of life that now confront him as alien and act to constrain his individual freedom. This argument tends to run as follows: the fewer the ways in which man can achieve independence of action, the fewer the possibilities for overcoming the constraints of

---

[9] As Galbraith points out, the period is long past when the operation of a lemonade stand under a tree by children bears any resemblance to business enterprises in the real world. See John Kenneth Galbraith, *The New Industrial State* (Boston: Houghton Mifflin, 1967), p. 2.

[10] The extreme in the U.S. commitment to things bigger is perhaps suggested in the story of the wreath placed by Khrushchev and Bulganin on the grave of Mahatma Gandhi. It is said that this wreath held the record for sheer size until, following a visit by John Foster Dulles, the journal of the U.S. Embassy informed its Indian readers with quiet pride that the diameter of the American wreath exceeded that of the Russians by a good six inches.

social, political, or economic institutions and the greater the possibility of alienation—that is, of conceiving oneself as alien.[11]

Clearly alienation may exist in varying degrees of intensity. Presumably it is the pervasiveness of alienation as experienced in a number of life activities in contemporary post-industrial society that can have a profound destructive effect. But alienation cannot be explained, as is frequently attempted, merely as a result of (1) poverty, (2) subjugation to political or economic despotism, (3) pressure to seek ever-higher material goals, or (4) the lack of brotherhood or lack of faith. Rather, it is the lack of expectation that one can ever cope with the given reality. Isolation appears to be implicit in this picture. Therefore, when individuals acquire the capacity to communicate and share experiences with one another, when a sense of community is formed, their alienation is mitigated.

But which groups in contemporary America are most alienated? What actions and policies might ameliorate this condition? What is the role, if any, of the educational system in such improvement?[12]

In answer to the first question, the most obvious possibility

---

[11] Perhaps, as Bell suggests, this condition is enhanced by the "end of linearity" in our culture. "In our culture today we see the end of . . . rational cosmology. In a very simplified sense, there is an end of linearity and the emergence of the problem of the creation of simultaneity. People no longer can have a sense of linearity, of beginning, middle, and end, foreground and background." Daniel Bell, "The Post-Industrial Society," in *Technology and Social Change,* ed. Eli Ginzberg (New York: Columbia University Press, 1964), p. 44.

[12] In a definition still relevant today Seeman suggests five variants of alienation: 1. *Powerlessness:* An individual's belief that he is incapable of influencing his social and political world under the present social and political ground rules. 2. *Meaninglessness:* The individual's lack of a clear belief system by which to interpret and judge behavior outcomes. 3. *Normlessness:* A breakdown in the regulatory power of social norms over individual behavior, and the expectation that certain goals can only be achieved through socially unapproved behavior. 4. *Isolation:* The individual's feeling of apartness from society, which he expresses by disputing the high values it attaches to its belief systems. 5. *Self-estrangement:* The heavy dependence of an individual's behavior on external rewards and expectations rather than on intrinsic meaningfulness.*

* Melvin Seeman, "On the Meaning of Alienation," *American Sociological Review* 24 (December 1959): 783–91.

for alienation lies in our minority groups. The following quotation of a Negro youth and its analysis by a social scientist suggest some of the reasons why such potential exists.

> "I'm not out to get Whitey—I'm just out to get out.
> . . . They talk about gettin out. . . . They carried
> signs about gettin out. . . . Now looks like you got to
> burn the place down and shoot your way out. . . ."

The comments are those of a seventeen-year-old black male who was actively involved in the Newark riots of 1967. He was not part of an organized movement. He does not believe that he has to confirm his masculinity through acts of violence. He does not explain his behavior by stressing the many years that blacks have been exploited and discriminated against. He is not seeking vengeance. Although he has heard of Carmichael, Brown, and King he knows little of their ideologies nor is he overly concerned with their intentions. He seeks neither intimate contact with whites nor continued existence within a racial ghetto.

His actions and his words make one thing clear—he wants a change of status and he wants it now. He wants out of the slums. He wants out of unemployment. He wants out of a physical setting which restricts mobility and maximizes feelings of personal defeat. He sees himself as standing on the outside and he wants in.[15]

Yet, controversy persists regarding what the poor actually want. Gottlieb argues above that they want "in," that is, they want many of the things associated with middle-class status. Others have argued that the behavior of lower-class youth is not so much a reaction against a society that does not allow them participation in the good life as it is a reflection of the unique culture of the lower class.[14] Curiously, in spite of a

---

[13] David Gottlieb, "Poor Youth: A Study in Forced Alienation," *Journal of Social Issues* 25, no. 2 (1969).
[14] See, for example, W. B. Miller, "Lower-Class Culture as a Generating Milieu of Gang Delinquency," *Journal of Social Issues* 14, no. 3 (1958): 5–19; and Edgar Z. Friedenberg, *An Ideology of School Withdrawal: The School Dropout* (Washington, D.C.: National Educational Association, 1964), pp. 25–29.

rather substantial amount of research, it is impossible to identify the goals of the poor. Perhaps the problem lies in trying to treat the poor as being all alike. Undoubtedly many poor "want in." But wishing to become a member of that heterogeneous, ill-defined body called the middle class offers a limited description of aspirations. Surely some poor first want status and respect while maintaining identity within minority groups, regardless of whether this entitles them to be defined as middle class. (In chapter 6—where attention is focused on problems of equalization of educational opportunity—this topic will be explored further.)

Yet alienation is not limited to the relatively disenfranchised minority groups. Some have argued, as Marx did in nineteenth-century Europe, that alienation can be applied universally to the working class.[15] However, the evidence in this regard appears to be less than conclusive. Many recent studies question whether most workers are alienated or estranged. The development of unions, the lessening of routinized work, and concomitant advances in required and recognized specialized knowledge have somewhat protected the worker from alienation. Indeed it has sometimes been argued that, in contrast, the middle-class college-bound or college-educated person finds himself in a much more frustrating, open-ended situation than the worker. This person is led to believe, for example, that academic success and hard work will inevitably carry him to the top.

> American education reflects the norms of "contest mobility," a system in which elite status is the prize in an open contest and is taken by the aspirant's own efforts. . . . Every individual is encouraged to think of himself as competing for an elite position, so that in preparation he cultivates loyalty to the system and conventional attitudes.[16]

---

[15] See, for example, Harvey Swados, "The Myth of the Happy Worker," in *Man Alone*, ed. Eric and Mary Josephson (New York: Dell Publishing, 1969).
[16] Melvin Seeman, "On the Personal Consequences of Alienation in Work," *American Sociological Review* 32, no. 2 (April 1967): 273–85.

But, as many observers have pointed out (C. Wright Mills perhaps most dramatically in *The Power Elite*), the very top positions in society are rarely available through the process of contest mobility. Rather, they are reserved for a small elite group and will be unobtainable to all but a very few middle-class aspirants. Herein lies a possible source for middle-class alienation.

Moreover, the demands of geographic mobility and the resultant rootlessness, the need to affect certain status symbols, the pressures for conformity in business and social situations are felt by the middle class at least as much as they are by the poor.

Alienation between the generations has been a topic for considerable attention in recent years. The question "What are young people looking for?" has been asked by a wide range of journalists, scholars, students, politicians, and parents. Clearly the young (frequently merely defined as those under thirty years of age) are not homogeneous with respect to values or beliefs. In spite of what appears to many older adults as a uniform youth culture and in spite of the fact that Pope Paul VI described modern youth as "reeds that bend before the winds of any new ideas or like sheep who flock along after anyone who sets the pace," [17] diversity among the young should not be discounted. For example, at least in the United States, many students reject the more ideologically radical students groups such as the Students for a Democratic Society. Many girls and young women watch the "Women's Lib" movement with only mild enthusiasm or even open disdain. The basic revolutionary notion that most essential social ills around the world are the result of a conscious capitalistic (and imperialistic) plot appears not to have overwhelming youth support.

Yet the level of dissatisfaction and frustration among the young is clearly high. As has been noted by Jon Van Dyke (who at the age of twenty-seven found it "presumptuous" to

---

[17] *Pittsburgh Post-Gazette,* 5 April 1971.

speak on behalf of the young), "The young are not burdened with a sense of history. Unlike the old, they are not concerned with whether we are better now *than we used to be*. Instead, they are only conscious of how bad our society is *compared with what it could be*." [18]

A few of the perceived gaps between where we are and where we might be as identified by Van Dyke are:

> The young also see that despite our rhetoric favoring progressive taxation, the rich in fact do not pay a significantly higher percentage tax than the middle class and the poor. Because of loopholes that still exist, some of the rich pay virtually no tax.
>
> They note that our government has spent some $200 billion on a war in Southeast Asia that has served no goal except to destroy the lives of millions of Vietnamese, and to create more turmoil and hate among Americans than we have known in the previous hundred years.
>
> The young are told that violence is evil, but they know that guns can be bought and sold in the United States more freely than in any other civilized nation.
>
> The young are lectured ad nauseam about the evils of marijuana, even though there has never been any proof whatsoever that there are any evils. Many of the young are sent to jail for using marijuana. And at the same time billions of dollars are spent, legally, to promote the use of two proven narcotics, alcohol and tobacco.
>
> The young notice that our cities are being choked by smog and that diseases directly related to smog are increasing rapidly. At the same time, they notice that we spend about a hundred times as much money on automobile transportation as on public, smog-free transportation and that this ratio is getting worse rather than better.
>
> The young see that Congress, the only legislative body in the world that selects committee chairmen

---

[18] Jon Van Dyke, "What Young People are Looking For," *Center Report* 4, no. 1, Center for the Study of Democratic Institutions: 21.

solely on the basis of seniority, is controlled by an oligarchy of old men who continually throttle progressive legislation. The average age of the chairmen of committees is seventy years, and each of these chairmen has spent an average of twenty-eight years in the House. This same Congress forces employees of the executive branch to retire at 65, yet they stay on themselves long after they have lost touch with the needs and interests of their countrymen.[19]

Challenges for Education

The changes described in the preceding pages impinge on education in at least five major ways:

1. *Technological change and its reverberations throughout society have made new demands on, and given new prestige to, education.* The traditional view of the labor force as triangular in shape, with the preponderance of unskilled and semiskilled workers at the bottom and room only for a few highly skilled at the top, has given way to a diamond-shaped structure. Some have predicted that soon an inverted triangle would be the most appropriate representation.

FIGURE 2

Structure of the Labor Force

Triangle 1 represents the view of the labor force widely held in the United States until World War II and perhaps until the last decade in Western Europe. It would still be an accurate characterization of the less-developed nations where

---

[19] Ibid., p. 21.

the demand by the economy for most high-level skills is relatively small. The development of industry, the technologizing of agriculture, the administrative, transportation, and service demands of urbanization all influence the shift in the average skill level of a population toward the diamond form (2). Continued technological advances coupled with new affluence and aspirations move the labor force toward the form of the inverted triangle (3) Ultimately, perhaps, the expression "no room at the bottom" will replace the phrase "no room at the top." [20]

It is generally assumed that the requisite knowledge as well as the necessary certification for advanced skills will be the task of the educational system. Thus, in quantitative terms, the trend is toward expansion of educational enrollments at the secondary and higher levels. To a large extent the trend is also toward growing specialization in a wide range of ever-increasing technical and professional areas. The extent of change varies with level and pattern of economic development. Educational expansion in the less developed nations has frequently outstripped the occupational opportunities for graduates. In Western Europe and the United States, however, the output of the educational systems has often not kept abreast of the technical and professional demands of the economies.

The swiftness of technological change requires not only new and increased amounts of technical knowledge but also flexibility regarding the time and place of acquiring such knowledge. In a relatively static society, learning is comparatively fixed and limited. The transmission of knowledge from one generation to the next is thus an easy task. Under conditions of technological and social change, schools must adapt

---

[20] Moreover, advances in technology have created a new kind of leader and thus have raised questions about the education appropriate for leadership. The scientist-technologist has begun to acquire power in both business corporations and in the councils of government, for it is assumed that he alone is capable of understanding the new technological processes. Indeed, a few observers envision a small esoteric group of intellectuals eventually taking over all the major decision-making posts in industry and government.

quickly to new demands.[21] Moreover, the rapid obsolescence of skills and knowledge means that learning and probably all formal instruction must take place during many points in a person's life. The old singular schedule of schooling, then work, must give way to repetition of this sequence many times in a person's life or in a paralleling of these activities throughout life.

Furthermore, a question is raised regarding what is to be taken as constituting educational activity. Traditionally, our view and analyses of education have focused on the core institutions of learning, that is, the educational system, and have taken little account of such peripheral activities as vocationally oriented programs in business, government, and the military; planned instruction through television; correspondence courses, antipoverty programs; religious education; and the like. Information on education in the periphery has not been systematically acquired—even though one estimate suggests that there are as many as 40 million participants in formal learning experiences outside the school system. Regardless, however, of the precise dimensions and form of educational activity in the periphery, its magnitude is such that those concerned with educational and public policy must give it careful study.

---

[21] One source summarizes the educational implications of technological change as follows: 1. Technological change will continue as a master of all or as a servant for all.   2. Education, although not the sole means, is the best means by which the individual and society can adjust to technological change.   3. The new technology has removed the margin for educational error.   4. Technological change has immediate impact, which is nationwide in scope.   5. Manpower needs in a technological society can be met only through education.   6. Occupational education must become a responsibility of society.   7. Occupational education must become an integral part of total education.   8. Occupational education is the responsibility of every segment of the educational system.   9. Continuing education has become necessary for everyone.   10. Higher education has a responsibility to raise the educational level of all American youth.   11. Sound occupational choice is made in direct proportion to information, guidance, and opportunity available to the individual.   12. The necessity of occupational education for all could, if present institutions fail in their responsibilities, lead to a separate [another] system of education in the nation.*

* Grant Vehn, *Man, Education and Work: Post-Secondary Vocational and Technical Education* (Washington, D.C.: American Council on Education, 1964), pp. 158–60.

More obvious than the effect of technological change on the structure of education are the continual revisions and alterations in curriculum it fosters. New applications of technology, for example, have affected the nature of the curriculum in mathematics and sciences even in the earliest grades. New variants of the traditional subject-matter divisions have appeared at all levels. In the social studies the tools of technology are providing new confidence in the examination of sensitive and subtle areas of human discourse—areas that may have been created by technological change. Moreover, technological change has stimulated a more open point of view toward curriculum—customary boundaries between subjects and disciplines have become less firm and specific content less sacrosanct. Subject matter has become viewed as a changing body of knowledge rather than as a rigidly fixed set of principles and facts.

These changes alter the role of the teacher:

> Up to now the formal attitude toward knowledge has been characteristic of the university scholar but only rarely of the primary and secondary school teacher. From the standpoint of the latter group of teachers, this represents a potentially revolutionary alteration in the requirements of their jobs. The elementary or secondary teacher has not been required to keep up with the literature in the same way that the university or college teacher is expected to keep abreast of new developments in his field. Consequently, it has not been the practice to make allowances for this requirement of the job when establishing teaching loads for such teachers. The impact of requiring increased scholarship of elementary and secondary school teachers on such things as school budgets, salary scales, the availability of library facilities and the recruitment and training of new teachers is not difficult to imagine.[22]

_____

[22] David Goslin, *The School in Contemporary Society* (Glenview, Ill.: Scott Foresman, 1965), p. 46.

One aspect of technological change has been the growth in the direct application of the concept and process of technology to a number of economic, social and educational processes. Thus, the very activities of education and teaching may be viewed as technologies, that is, applications of science. The following chart suggests some of the activities that might be involved in educational and instructional technology.

TABLE 3

Educational and Instructional Technology

Educational Technology	*Instructional Technology*
(Goals or Behavioral Objectives)	
1. Selection of the priorities of the curricula for the nation or community. Statement of the classes of skills and other behavioral competencies in terms of regional or national needs. (e.g., secretaries, machine operators, carpenters, mechanics, teachers, nurses, etc.)	1. Selection of curricular priorities in terms of availability of resources and needs of the learners. Specification of behaviors which the pupils are expected to perform at the end of the lesson, unit of study, or year's curriculum. (e.g., "On completion of the unit the pupil will be able to dissect a frog and name the bones in its skeletal structure.") Test and analysis of behaviors desired.
(Analyses of the Characteristics of the Learners)	
2. Specification of the present skills and competencies of the pupils within the age ranges for which the goals are possible. Determination of the special testing that may be needed.	2. Discovering the existing levels of the pupil's knowledge and skills in given subject areas (for example, in biology, "Can the pupil identify the bones of a frog?") Development and administration of appropriate pretest to determine the best entry point into learning the content and performance required by the terminal behavior. Consideration of the pupil's learning styles.

*(Organization of the Educational Content
or Subject Matter)*

Educational Technology	*Instructional Technology*
3. Curriculum review—analysis of relationships between similar courses of study to determine what revisions are necessary. Up-dating content where feasible, elimination of obsolescent information and unnecessary skills. Survey of persons presently performing the behaviors for which the pupils are to be taught.	3. Analysis of the content of the particular subject in order to select and organize the lesson or unit of study. Addition or elimination of inappropriate content. Providing amounts sufficient for fast, average, and slow pupils, or providing alternative content, if appropriate.

*(Mediating the Educational Content and Resources
for Presentation to and Utilization by the Learner)*

4. Selection of the educational media which will most efficiently and effectively permit simultaneous teaching and learning of the required skills and knowledge (behaviors).	4. Selection of instructional media (i.e., charts, books, films, television, etc.) which are most appropriate for the types and conditions of learning to take place. Utilizing different styles of presentation as required by the pupils for achievement of the objectives. Development of reinforcement experiences at appropriate points in the learning sequence.

*(Measurement and Evaluation of the
Learner's Performance)*

5. Constant monitoring of the achievement levels of pupils in all of the schools, national (regional or district) evaluation by testing. Surveying the output of personnel with the skills or other behavioral competencies specified by the goals (see point 3 preceding). Comparison with gains (or losses) for similar efforts and expenditures in other	5. Testing and evaluating the influence of specific parts of the content as presented by the media of instruction to find that which may have most (or least) influenced pupil learning. This step may lead to teacher's revision of content or change of media to produce more efficiency and effectiveness in future instruction.

Educational Technology	*Instructional Technology*
districts, regions, or nations. Evaluation should lead to continued revision to increase efficiency of future efforts.	

(Feedback Among the Other Components)

6. Feedback must occur throughout the process of educational or instructional technology in order to be certain that the established educational goals or specific behavioral objectives are still valid and, in fact, are being achieved.

SOURCE: Adapted from Robert Cox, "The Process of Educational Technology," in *Education in National Development,* ed. Don Adams (New York: David McKay, 1971), pp. 69–72.

Finally, as indicated earlier, technological change and increased technological complexity give rise to specialization of function and differentiation of roles. Bureaucratization and increase in size of organization have been accompaniments of this change and have had their effect on schooling. Among the more significant of these influences are:

1. The demand for an increasing number of specialized courses with the concomitant pressure for earlier decisions regarding courses of study.

2. The development of a more highly organized process of teaching and "managing" learning (see table 3). Children have been grouped in a variety of ways relating to their abilities and interests. Likewise, teachers have been utilized not only in the usual classroom arrangement but in teams, as television lecturer, etc.

3. An increasingly complex administrative hierarchy, which in the larger educational systems functions similarly to the administrative structure of a large business.

As Goslin notes:

These innovations have been made both possible and necessary by the increasing size of schools and the changing public conception of the school from an in-

formal gathering place for children of all ages and
abilities presided over by the stern but kindly spinster
lady to an efficiently functioning organization staffed
by well-trained professionals.[23]

2. *A second major influence on contemporary education is
the nature of demographic change.* A study of demography
and education might include several facets of the linkage of
population and education. While most literature on the subject is concerned with the impact of population growth on
school enrollments, a number of other and more subtle concerns might be considered, such as the effects of education on
fertility, mortality, and migration. Although it is not within
the scope of this book to treat this topic in detail, brief comments are offered on two aspects of the relationship of education and demography: (1) the impact of a society's population
on education and (2) the effect of education on fertility rates.

It is obvious, perhaps, that the age structure, size, and
growth of a society's population directly affect education. If,
for example, the child population is growing at a more rapid
rate than the growth rate of educational plant and personnel,
then the enrollment ratios, literacy rates, median school years
completed, and other measures of educational attainment will
tend to fall. Pressure on the schools to accommodate more
pupils through larger classes or double sessions may nega-
tively affect the quality of instruction.

For some countries to achieve primary school expansion at
such a pace as to include 100 percent of the relevant population would be a big task indeed. The school-age population is
typically growing more rapidly than the population as a
whole. Moreover, because of the high demand for schooling,
enrollments are growing at a faster rate than are school-age
populations. The strain on school systems is increased even
further for expenditures per pupil have generally been on the
rise.

---

[23] Goslin, *School in Contemporary Society*, p. 47.

The rate of population growth in the United States is higher than in much of Europe and lower than that typically found in Asia and Latin America. The most obvious impact of population growth on education has been cost. The immediate post-World War II period in the United States saw a "baby boom" that has already materially affected university enrollment; given a minimum of federal support, in keeping with American tradition, the expense of expanded plant and staff has fallen on the states and local school districts.

Nevertheless, the educational attainment of the American population has shown a steady increase over the last several decades. Table 4 provides data on the quantitative trends in schooling for white and nonwhite young adults. Qualitative distinctions in schooling are not indicated, of course, by these figures.

TABLE 4

Median Years of School Completed for Persons 25–29 Years of Age, by Color, 1940–67

Year	Total	White	Nonwhite
1940	10.3	10.7	7.0
1950	12.1	12.2	8.7
1960	12.3	12.3	10.8
1967	12.5	12.6	12.1

SOURCE: Conrad Taeuber, "Population: Trends and Characteristics," in *Indicators of Social Change,* ed. Eleanor Bernert Sheldon and Wilbert E. Moore (New York: Russell Sage Foundation, 1968), p. 38.

However, the situation is more complicated than this, for the population growth has not been distributed evenly among school districts. Migration has been largely in the direction of metropolitan areas. Essentially this has meant that the outer urban and suburban communities have acquired a disproportionate share of the pupils. In addition to the occurrence of differential growth rates between metropolitan and rural areas, however, residential patterns have affected the nature of schooling. While the slogan "slums and suburbs" grossly oversimplifies the trends in residential patterns in the United States, the inner cities are essentially populated by minority groups and poorer whites. This fact has not only broken down the comprehensiveness of student bodies, and therefore school programs, but has raised fundamental questions about the purposes of the schools. The school in America, as in every society, is called upon to assist in inculcating certain values and attitudes in the young. Obviously in the essentially white middle-class suburbs there is less possibility of conflict between community-held values and those of the greater society. However, some portions of the urban minority groups—e.g., blacks, Mexicans, and Puerto Ricans—reject many of the values they perceive to be prevalent in the greater society. Schools, they argue, must be locally controlled and must function to enhance the values and the self-concepts of their clientele. Schools, as the slogans go, must teach that "Black is beautiful," "Chicano is beautiful," and so forth. Obviously, the frustrations felt by members of minority groups and the resulting pressures for educational change are not merely reactions to population movements; nevertheless, such shifts have exacerbated the problem.

But what is the effect of education on population change, particularly what is the effect of education on fertility? There appears to be some relationship between educational level and receptivity to programs of fertility control. A number of successful fertility-control programs have been reported in Japan, Korea, Taiwan, and other areas where the literacy and educational levels of the populations involved were relatively high. On the other hand, unsuccessful programs have been reported in certain areas of low literacy, such as portions of India, Pakistan, and the United Arab Republic.[24]

---

[24] One study of Korea suggests that a successful program of adult education aimed directly at reducing fertility would be a better investment than physical investment or general educational expansion. It is argued that, in the Korean context, additional workers add little or nothing to the national product and

The association between educational level and receptivity to these direct programs is striking; moreover, the strong relationship appears to hold true in both rural and urban areas. (This condition is significant because the urban life style—learned largely through such informal channels as the neighborhood and peer groups—would be expected to favor the limiting of family size.) Some evidence also exists that the general educational level of a nation is inversely associated with fertility, irrespective of ideological or religious influences. Clearly, however, "intervening variables," such as religion, intelligence, family structure, etc., could be the crucial determinants of success or failure of programs of family-planning education. Among particularly devout groups, ideological and religious factors may, of course, be significant. Studies in the United States, for example, show that Catholics who attend parochial school from the primary level through college tend to have larger families than Catholics whose education is secular. In this case some selection probably occurred—the more religiously oriented Catholics being drawn in disproportionate numbers into the Catholic educational system—but formal education undoubtedly acted as reinforcement.[25]

Westoff and Potvin summarized their American research on the effects of higher education on attitudes toward family planning, as follows:

> 1. Protestant, Jewish, and Mormon women, and students with no religious preference all experience an increase in the proportions intending to plan their families, but the differences for the most part are

---

therefore a smaller work force would not, in itself, significantly reduce the total product created over a given period. A successful fertility-reduction campaign would thus allow a total product (growing because of general economic growth) to be distributed among fewer persons, thus increasing per capita income. See John Isbister, "Family Planning and Economic Growth in Developing Countries," in *Background Papers* (Geneva: International Conference on Family Planning Programmes, 23–27 August 1965), pp. 4–19.

[25] See Charles F. Westoff, "Family Growth in Metropolitan America," in *Research in Family Planning*, ed. Clyde V. Kiser (Princeton, N.J.: Princeton University Press, 1963), p. 189.

slight and could easily be due to factors other than the college experience.

2. Although Catholic women also become more inclined to plan, there is a considerable amount of variation by types of schools attended.

There does appear to be some secularizing effect of a nonsectarian education on the graduates of Catholic high schools. . . .

3. The entire difference between Catholic graduates from nonsectarian high schools who attend Catholic colleges and those who attend nonsectarian colleges is selectivity, evidenced by sharp initial differences in the first year.[26]

Thus, the many ramifications of the relationships of education and population may be of crucial concern to nations at various levels of development and industrialization. Rapid population growth and a young population structure may place a heavy burden on educational facilities. However, population control may be no less important to developed nations as they seek to promote ever-higher standards of living and to conserve scarce resources.

3. *Quantitative changes in education are also being strongly influenced by the phenomenon of increased social demand—a condition widespread among contemporary societies.* Rising expectations among the parents and the youth of less developed societies, stimulated by glimpses of the wealthier outside world or by the privileges of the small educated groups at home, have given rise to an intense desire for education. In the more advanced societies, increased affluence and the propensity to view education as a requisite for respectable status and a good job have also increased the demand for education. In the contemporary United States, for example, the legacy of an advanced education is seen as perhaps the greatest gift possible to one's children.

---

[26] Charles F. Westoff and Raymond H. Potvin, *College Women and Fertility Values* (Princeton, N.J.: Princeton University Press, 1967), pp. 58–59.

The postindustrial society is, then, an education-centered and a knowledge-centered society. The production and distribution of knowledge are taking an increasing share of the nation's oragnizations and industries. The largest of the knowledge industries is the educational system, whose recent historical growth is partly indicated in table 5.

Increases in educational expenditures are natural accompaniments of enrollment growth. The gross expenditures on education in the United States have grown from $234 million in 1900 to $2.556 billion in 1930, to $18.622 billion in 1960 to $58.5 billion in 1969. During this period there has, of course, been a radical expansion of enrollments. Nevertheless, the expenditure per pupil has also been on the rise, thus suggesting, even after discounting the effects of inflation, a growing faith in education as a national asset.

With such growth in educational expenditures, much attention has recently been given to the possibilities for increasing the efficiency of American school systems; that is, the following question is being raised: How is it possible for students to acquire more knowledge in the same number of years of schooling or acquire the same amount of knowledge in a lesser number of years? Later in this chapter the possibilities of increasing educational efficiency will be discussed in some detail.

4. *Associated with the increased demand for education is an egalitarian overtone—at times a dominant force, at times merely a subtle pressure.* In much of Europe and North America, for example, many of the "educational reforms" have been a direct outgrowth of social reform aimed at extending social opportunities. That is, an extended period of participation in a common educational culture has increasingly been seen as prerequisite to social justice. Nations, particularly the more industrialized ones, are giving much attention, then, to the notion of equality of educational opportunity.

Most industrialized nations are increasingly reluctant to pay the social price of early selection in education. Compulsory and unselective education is being extended into second-

TABLE 5

School Enrollments in the United States, 1945–70

Year	Enrolled Millions
1945	25.5
1946	27.2
1947	28.7
1948	29.5
1949	30.3
1950	30.3
1951	30.9
1952	32.5
1953	34.4
1954	36.1
1955	37.4
1956	39.4
1957	41.2
1958	42.9
1959	44.4
1960	46.3
1961	47.7
1962	48.7
1963	50.4
1964	51.7
1965	53.8
1966	55.1
1967	56.5[a]
1968	57.9
1969	58.6[b]
1970	59.2

SOURCE: Adapted from Beverly Duncan, "Trends in Output and Distribution of Schooling," in Sheldon and Moore, *Indicators of Social Change*, p. 609.
[a] U.S. Department of Health, Education, & Welfare, *Digest of Educational Statistics 1969 and 1970* (OE-10024), p. 2.
[b] U.S. Department of Health, Education, & Welfare, *Progress of Public Education in the U.S.A. 1968–69* (OE 10005-69A).

ary education. However, equity in terms of participation rates of children from different social origins may be promoted only temporarily by elimination of financial or even aptitude criteria for selection. For example, the so-called secondary modern school of England in terms of the social status of its students is similar to the English senior elementary schools of pre-World War II. In the United States the junior colleges and first university years perform a selection function similar to that of the high school of former years. And while the percentage of youth graduating from high school in the United States has increased dramatically over the past few decades, the proportion of high school graduates entering college and proportion of college entrants receiving degrees has demonstrated only modest growth.

Moreover, a kind of track system is being enhanced because the higher-quality institutions are expanding their enrollments at a slower rate than those of lesser quality. This is most clearly the case in postsecondary education. Thus, even should the U.S. government decide to provide heavy subsidization for higher education rather than rationing it to the middle class through a price mechanism, inequities stemming from socially induced learning advantages would still persist. At the earlier educational levels, qualitative differences are also apparent, and with the greater social emphasis on educational attainments those with a poor start in the educational race will find themselves with an increasing handicap. The question has arisen, at least in the highly industrialized societies, whether it is desirable to introduce (or reintroduce, since ascriptive criteria were common in selection procedures until contemporary times) nonintellectual criteria for school selection.

There may, of course, be a conflict between the goals of equity and efficiency in the operation of schools. The precise nature of the conflict, however, is yet to be fully explored. Scarce resources may dictate that educational decision makers should seek an optimum relationship between educational expenses and productivity or economic growth. However, in advanced societies it is often assumed that policies of equity lead to fuller utiilzation of human resources, greater participation in the polity, higher morale, and so forth. In this sense, an equitable society is a highly productive society.

Moreover, the implications of the questions and issues concerning inequality when seen in the broader social context have ideological overtones. Essentially, there are two views:

1. As societies industrialize, extremes in inequality are brought closer together and there is a greater concentration around the median. The assumption is that modern mass consumption and employment patterns foster this concentration. With regard to education, it is assumed that higher education levels and the resulting skill components acquired by the laboring work force progressively erode earlier inequalities.

2. An interpretation that has Marxist overtones but also some support among non-Marxist scholars suggests that in an industrial society increased productivity leads to increased exploitation and accumulation of wealth by the few.

If the first view is assumed to be the correct one, then social investment such as in education may be used as a mild corrective. This view has tended to persist outside the socialist world but is currently being subjected to reevaluation.

Returning to manifestation of inequalities in the lower schools, it is clear then that even when the length of exposure to schooling is the same for different social groups disparities in educational opportunity persist. The difference between suburban schooling and slum schooling in the United States has been examined at length in recent years. Conant in 1961 called attention to the "totally different kinds" of public schools that serve the city and the suburbs.[27] A few years later Keppel noted:

> The wealthier, better-staffed school districts are the ones with the language laboratories, science equipment, planetariums, mathematics laboratories, green-

---

[27] James Bryant Conant, *Slums and Suburbs* (New York: McGraw-Hill, 1961).

houses, integrated textbooks (but often little integration), testing services, public address systems, and the like. It is not only that educational leaders with more original ideas serve in the wealthier districts, or that the less imaginative serve in poor districts, but rather that the ability or lack of ability to buy is also a factor —for even salesmen and distributors steer clear of those districts with which they cannot "do business." [28]

The persistence in the United States of any significant difference in the quality of education between school districts runs counter not only to egalitarian ideals but also to the law of the land.[29] It has been suggested that at least three basic legal and public themes in American tradition relate to the issue of equality of educational opportunity.

The first is the general statement of the equal protection clause of the Fourteenth Amendment to the Constitution of the United States:

No State shall . . . deny to any person within its jurisdiction the equal protection of the laws.

The second is the Supreme Court's specific interpretation of the equal protection clause in *Brown* v. *Board of Education:*

The opportunity of an education . . . , where the state has undertaken to provide it is a right which must be made available to all on equal terms.

Lest "equal" be construed too rigidly, the third theme, as stated by Benson, applies throughout:

The one universally accepted criterion of a public activity is that it affords equal treatment to equals. With respect to schooling, this implies that any two children of the same abilities shall receive equivalent forms of assistance in develop-

---

[28] Francis Keppel, *The Necessary Revolution in American Education* (New York: Harper and Row, 1966), p. 77.
[29] U.S. Supreme Court, May 17, 1954, 347 U.S. 483,74 S.Ct. 686,98 L.Ed. 873.

ing those abilities, whatever their parental cir-
cumstances are.[30]

5. *The dynamism of technological and social change, the
pressures (in both developed and less developed nations) for
more education for more children, the desire to make education's impact greater on the economy and society, and severe
budget constraints signify an urgency to promote innovations within the educational system and even to seek alternative models to the existing system.* Reimer, for example,
taking a global view of educational problems condemns the
existing educational systems as follows:

> Today's school system requires basic reform or replace-
> ment for the following reasons:
> 1. Two-thirds of the world's population cannot be pro-
>   vided education at present unit costs.
> 2. The school system fails in its attempt to educate most
>   students of the lower class. They drop out before they
>   become literate.
> 3. The school system also fails in part to educate most of its
>   nominally successful students, stultifying rather than nur-
>   turing their life-time capacity and desire for learning.[31]

Illich views the school as it exists today as being completely
incapable of meeting contemporary educational problems.
"This is a time of crisis in the institution of the school, a
crisis which may mark the end of the 'age of schooling' in
the Western world." Illich, speaking at a university com-
mencement in Puerto Rico, further argued that the school
in the Western Hemisphere is now identified with education
as "the church once was with religion" and that "it will soon
be evident that the school is as marginal to education as
the witch doctor is to public health."

---

[30] Charles S. Benson, *The Cheerful Prospect: A Statement on the Future of
Public Education* (Boston: Houghton Mifflin, 1965), p. 62.
[31] Everett Reimer, "Alternatives in Education," in Adams, *Education in
National Development*, p. 85.

For purposes of clarity, further elaboration of this position is necessary. Illich argues that school systems are untenable for both economic and social reasons. Current arrangements of financing schooling "lead to regressive taxation in that the people who get a secondary education receive much more money back than their parents proportionately paid in taxes." [32]

Since there appears to be no way of avoiding such a costly arrangement and since the privileged are the more likely to succeed academically (and thereby reap the rewards from schooling) other, less institutionalized means of education should be sought. The nature of alternatives to schooling is not clear, however. Computer terminals in homes and shopping centers, study groups in the corner tea room or drugstore, and job-related training may provide partial substitutes for schools. On any hand, the deschooling of society is a giant-size undertaking, and what grows from the ashes of the schools cannot be guaranteed to be an improvement.

While some may feel that Illich paints an overly forbidding picture of the current educational scene, many observers believe certain drastic educational changes are in the wind. Perhaps the major areas of change can be classified under three separate but not unrelated headings:

1. Teacher roles
2. Efficiency in the management of the system
3. Alternative educational models

1. The teacher in the past has been a "teller," and has been assumed to be the principal source of information for learners. At least in the more progressive school districts of the United States the teacher is now seen as becoming a "coordinator of learning resources" or a "learning facilitator." Some observers predict that the teacher soon will not teach the main body of subject matter—at least not in such

---

[32] Ivan Illich, "Toward a Society Without Schools," *Center Report* 4, no. 1, Center for the Study of Democratic Institutions, p. 3.

skill subjects as mathematics and language—because various types of technology will perform this task. Thus the teacher of the future, in addition to being a content specialist, must become more of an organizer of a variety of learning resources. While such predictions may be accurate, the general lack of receptivity to technology thus far by the schools suggest that this change in role may be a long time in coming. More discussion of teacher roles and education as an occupation will be found in later chapters.

2. Efficiency relates to productivity and productivity in any enterprise or "production process" is the relationship between input and output. Clearly this is a difficult concept to apply to the educational system. What precisely is meant by educational input? By educational output? Do these concepts include affective as well as cognitive learnings? How can we attribute new characteristics of graduates to the school process? How can we measure the variegated dimensions of input and output?

These are important questions and cannot be easily brushed aside. Nevertheless, the concepts of productivity and efficiency (the output per unit input) are currently receiving much attention by educational policy makers, scholars, and lay critics. Given the recent developments in the "management sciences," such attention is unlikely to wane in the near future.[33]

One critic of American education argues that more efficient schools (through a better use of technology, paraprofessional help, and a lengthening of the school year) could teach in five or ten years what is now taught in twelve years. He outlines the possible harmful consequences of the present system.

I. Effects upon the *untalented* and *uninterested* students

---

[33] More elaborate analyses of productivity and efficiency in education can be found elsewhere. See, for example, Daniel Rogers, "Efficiency in Education," and Manuel Zymelman, "Education, Manpower and the Labor Force" in Adams, *Education in National Development*, pp. 47–65, 98–117.

1. They learn no more than they would have learned in less time.
2. They acquire a stronger distaste for education and an antagonism toward intellectual values.
3. They acquire poorer habits of work because, with the curriculum spread over more years, they have less to do per year and per week and get accustomed to more loafing than they could otherwise; these habits may lower their productivity for many years, perhaps for their entire working lives.

II. Effects upon the *talented* and *interested* students
4. Their motivation and industry is lessened as the competition in the classrooms and for honor rolls is reduced.
5. Their preparation for colleges and universities suffers because standards of achievement are inevitably lowered if the student body includes the less able and less ambitious.
6. Their educational opportunities are reduced by the spreading of the curriculum over more years, which becomes unavoidable with the forced inclusion of the weaker students; "skipping" of grades is no substitute for a curriculum designed to "stretch" the mind.
7. Their prospective productivity in mathematical and scientific studies is jeopardized by the delay in the completion of their studies beyond the age period in which peak capacity is reached in these subjects and the greatest contributions are likely to be made.

III. Effects upon *all* students
8. The greater emphasis upon athletics—usually associated with an academically "slow" curriculum—in a group composed of a greater percentage of intellectually poorer students

distorts the value system of the community, generally lowering the prestige of academic and intellectual achievement.

IV. Effects upon current output

9. The reduction in the labor supply effected by keeping unwilling students in the classrooms and away from the labor market causes a current loss of output, an immediate sacrifice of national product quite apart from the long-run effects upon productivity listed in the first eight points above.

10. The need for additional teachers implies another encroachment upon current output. (If the supply of teachers is highly inelastic and the use of teachers for the added classes encroaches upon the availability of teachers for earlier grades, the resulting deterioration of teaching in all grades is another factor with deleterious effects on all students.) [34]

A reduction in the time required to achieve educational goals might be achieved through (a) setting fewer or lower educational goals; (b) setting few or lower goals for the ancillary functions of schools, such as custodial care and indoctrination; (c) achieving goals more efficiently. Of these possibilities, all appear quite feasible except the lowering of educational goals—society is demanding higher, not lower, levels of skills and knowledge of its citizens.

Reduction of unit costs might be attained through use of paraprofessional personnel to perform certain tasks, by relying more on materials for self-instruction, and by achieving "economies of scale" through use of media. The future is likely to see more innovations and experimentation in each of these areas.

---

[34] Fritz Machlup, *The Production and Distribution of Knowledge in the United States* (Princeton, N.J.: Princeton University Press, 1962), pp. 128–29.

Inputs per student may be reduced or the number of students served may be increased by similar means. Again the use of media becomes an obvious choice, although other possibilities also exist. Utilization of technology plus greater reliance on structured means for older pupils to teach younger pupils (particularly in less affluent societies) may double or treble the acceptable pupil-teacher ratio.

An international comparison of achievement in mathematics has added new support to criticisms of the quality and efficiency of American education. This research study, conducted in twelve countries under the International Project for the Evaluation of Educational Achievement (IEA), has been widely interpreted as a condemnation of mathematics teaching in American schools. The main purpose of the IEA project was to "investigate the outcomes of various school systems by relating as many as possible of the relevant input variables (to the extent that they could be assessed) to the output assessed by international test instruments." [35] In terms of the aims of the project, it is further stated:

> In the discussions at an early stage in the project, education was considered as a part of a larger social-political-philosophical system. In most countries, rapid changes are occurring such as revolutionary modifications of the industrial technical apparatus, patterns of living, geographical and social mobility attitudes toward the role of science in society, and especially the relative role of humanistic and scientific learning. Any fruitful comparison must take account of how education has responded to changes in the society.[36]

In spite of such cautionary statements, however, as soon as the research results had indicated that thirteen-year-olds in the United States were lower in mathematics achievement than were thirteen-year-olds from any of the other twelve

---

[35] Torsten Husen, ed., *International Study of Achievement in Mathematics.* (New York: John Wiley, 1967), p. 30.

[36] Ibid., p. 30.

nations studied, a considerable fuss and cry was raised concerning the lack of academic standards in the American schools.

3. The typical educational response to societal demand for new skills and greater knowledge has been proliferation of courses and extension of the period of schooling. Moreover, the financing and control of education and the structure of the teaching-learning process remained little altered. Now, however, models that drastically alter these traditional patterns are being suggested. (For a more extended discussion of such models, see chapter 9.) By way of illustration, one conceptual scheme that has received considerable recent attention suggests an open-market arrangement for the buying and selling of educational goods and services.

In this regard, a number of proposals that might be subsumed under the term *voucher systems* have been put forward. These vary from recommendations that private contracts provide all school services to the contracting of specific limited services. Friedman, for example, a distinguished economist, argues that education which is assumed to have high neighborhood benefits, e.g., general education for citizenship, should be financed by the government but vocational and professional education should be privately financed by the families concerned. Thus vouchers would be distributed based on the cost per child of that amount and kind of education deemed beneficial to society. This portion of a child's education would be regulated and financed by the government. Friedman also argues, however, that parents should be given the opportunity to select the school of their choice.[37]

Thus far, only a few experiments have been undertaken for the direct purchase of professional services. However, a variety of other drastic innovations have moved from the drawing board—or, more likely, from ad hoc professional discussions—into operation in experimnetal schools.

The names of some of the experimental schools suggest

---

[37] Milton Friedman, "The Role of Government in Education," in *Perspectives in the Economics of Education*, ed. Charles S. Benson (Boston: Houghton Mifflin, 1968), pp. 132–42.

their orientation: Student Development Center, All Together Free School, Workshop School, Involvement Education. Of these it has been said:

> They represent a fairly wide spectrum of educa-
> tional thought, with a heavy sprinkling of super-Sum-
> merhills. About half of them are inner-city schools—
> approximately 80% are designed to accommodate stu-
> dents from pre-school through high school. Organiza-
> tion, curriculum, and financing vary widely.[38]

Replies from a survey of four hundred innovative schools
offer further insight into the spirit of these schools:

> We believe in the right of every individual to be free
> to experience the world around him in his own way.

> We encourage kids to live their own lives. Classes
> are not compulsory; self-government runs the school.

> We believe that in a loving, accepting environment
> in which emotional needs are met, children will feel
> free to grow; and that feeling free, they *will* grow, *will*
> follow their natural curiosity, *will* do whatever they
> find necessary to meet their needs.

> Philosophy: A cross of Skinner and Neill and Leary
> and IWW. The school is an integral part of a farm
> commune research organization crazy house.[39]

Most, but not all, of these innovations lie outside the
public schools. Within the Philadelphia school system one
much publicized reform has been described as the "school
without walls." The director of this innovative program
notes:

> It is true that we teach some unconventional sub-
> jects, but the study groups are mostly small, under 10

---

[38] Donald W. Robinson, "Alternative Schools: Challenge to Traditional
Education," *Phi Delta Kappan* 50, no. 7 (March 1970): 375.

[39] The above are quoted in Robinson, "Alternative Schools," p. 374. Original source was a survey conducted by Leonard Solo and Stan Barondes of the
Teacher Drop-Out Center (Amherst, Mass.: University of Massachusetts).

students, and the old ways of classroom teaching just do not make any sense. So students and faculty are re-defining what we mean by teaching and learning. Our faculty members teach, but when they do, it is not in a classroom; it is in the city, in an office building, in City Hall, in the street, depending on what they are teaching.[40]

Summary

Education occupies a central place in the several "revolutionary" changes that characterize the contemporary world. Each of these changes has made new demands on educational systems and offered new challenges. Educational systems in turn have not been passive institutions to be buffeted by the winds of change. Many of the ideas and motivations for technological and social change undoubtedly have germinated and been nurtured in formal school settings. Yet educational institutions generally have not been in the forefront of these changes; indeed, some would argue that they have been among the most serious obstructions.

The centrality of an educational system in meeting both the technological demands and the equity considerations of modern (and "postmodern") society has made education a focal point of discussion, debate, and controversy. Some observers in the United States appear to be willing to scrap much of the existing structure and content of education. When, for example, Margaret Mead was asked, "Is there any single thing in the present educational system worth keeping?" she is reported to have replied, "What about some of the buildings?" [41] Probably few educators, citizens, or students would take as extreme a stand. Nevertheless, in comparison with the past, a larger proportion of all of these groups appears to be willing to consider radical educational innovations.

---

[40] Ibid.
[41] Reported in Roy A. Carr and Gerald C. Hayward, "Educating by Chit," *Education and Urban Society* 2, no. 2 (1970): 180.

References

Anderson, Robert H. *Teaching in a World of Change.* New York: Harcourt, Brace and World, 1966.

Daedalus. "Toward the Year 2000." Summer 1967.

Galbraith, John Kenneth. *The New Industrial State.* Boston: Houghton Mifflin, 1967.

Goodlad, John I., ed., *The Changing American School.* Sixty-Fifth Yearbook of the National Society for the Study of Education, part 2. Chicago: University of Chicago Press, 1966.

Jencks, Christopher, and Riesman, David. *The Academic Revolution.* Garden City, N.Y.: Doubleday, 1968.

McLuhan, Marshall, and Leonard, George B. "The Future of Education: The Class of 1989." *Look* 31,4 (21 February 1967): 23–25.

Rossi, Peter H., and Biddle, Bruce J., eds. *The New Media and Education: Their Impact on Society.* Garden City, N.Y.: Doubleday Anchor, 1967.

Sheldon, Eleanor Bernert, and Moore, Wilbert E., eds. *Indicators of Social Change.* New York: Russell Sage Foundation, 1968 (particularly chapters 1, 5, 12).

Discussion Questions

1. What are the major demands on the following generated by or accompanying technological change?

    a. Curriculum

    b. Teacher competence

    c. Clientele of the schools

    d. Instructional innovations

    e. Attitudes about change

    f. Occupational requirements

2. What major demographic changes are occurring in American society today? Explain the impact of these changes on schools.

3. What distinctions may be made between educational media and educational technology?

4. What impact has the changing structure of the labor force (a pyramidal shape through a diamond shape to an emergent inverted pyramid) had on the educational system?

5. What evidence can you give to support the statement that the United States is becoming a "knowledge-centered" society?

6. Which educational innovations and experimentations appear to offer the most promise in producing the kinds of talent needed in a technological society? In reducing educational expenditures? In equalizing educational opportunity? In counteracting alienation and loss of community?

the education
process
and its
social environment

2

Part 2 deals with the way in which schooling and informal instruction support, or are in conflict with, the demands of modern industrialized society. How does the school in its structure reinforce the values in the outside society? How may a lack of congruence between school and society be reinforced? With advanced industrialization, has the role of teacher changed? And particularly, what is the nature of the conflict and the alienation of youth generated by contemporary society?

Chapter 3 takes a broad and generally abstract view of social learning outside and inside the formal school system. For the sake of perspective and contrast, variations in socialization patterns are examined in the less-developed as well as in the industrially more advanced societies. Chapter 4 enlarges upon a theme introduced in chapter 3, namely, the students, their adjustments, frustrations, and visible alienation.

CHAPTER THREE

Socialization, Schooling, and Education

The maintenance of social order presumably demands some measure of consensus among the members of a society about the goals to be sought, the means that may be employed to obtain them, and the norms governing social interaction. This consensus rests upon a shared set of beliefs and symbols acquired through the process of socialization. Socialization, then, may be viewed as the means by which an individual is integrated into his society and involves the adaptation of the individual to the fellow members of his group, which, in turn, gives him status and assigns to him the roles he plays as an adult.

Yet considerable ambiguity persists in usage of the term socialization. Anthropologists, for example, prefer the terms enculturation and acculturation. *Enculturation* describes the process of learning through which man achieves competence in his own culture in all its uniqueness. *Acculturation* occurs when groups from different cultures come into continuous firsthand contact, resulting in changes of the original culture of both groups. While Whiting has advocated the replacement of the term socialization by enculturation or even child-rearing,[1] Clausen has argued that these and other frequently suggested alternatives may be encompassed by the concept of socialization which he defines as:

> [the] learning that prepares the individual for membership in his society or in particular groups within the society. Socialization is thus the generic concept that embraces child-rearing, education, enculturation, role-learning, occupational preparation, preparation for marriage and parenthood, and, indeed, all social learning that is relevant to one's group membership and life transitions.[2]

Some sociologists might feel uncomfortable with the sweeping definition above. However, perhaps most would agree that socialization requires the inculcation of certain commitments and the development of certain skills and behavior. The emphasis is on the social purpose of the process, and the nature of the specified requirements is set by the society.

However, the conformity to societal norms and values is not taken for granted but is regarded as an adaptive process that is explained in terms of continuing integration of individual behavioral dispositions with the needs of social structure. Personality and social structure are conceived as separate but interdependent systems that must be in balance in order to maintain social equilibrium.

The major guides to behavior acquired by any individual in the process of being socialized involve certain images of roles that are related to the major positions or statuses he expects, or is expected, to occupy at various times in his life. Some psychologists have suggested that socialized individuals tend to make their behavior conform to those models of decorum and conduct sketched on their social memories

---

[1] John W. M. Whiting, "Socialization: Anthropologic Aspects," in *International Encyclopedia of the Social Sciences,* vol. 14 (New York: Macmillan and Free Press, 1968), pp. 545–51.

[2] John Clausen, "Recent Development in Socialization Theory and Research," *Annals of the American Academy of Political and Social Science,* no. 377 (1968): 139.

early in life. Moreover, "this is true even though the final details are acquired only with the actual status and the final manner of comportment in these roles depends largely on interaction with other persons." [3]

Socialization may be viewed as taking place on both a formal and an incidental learning level through the influence of societal agents such as family, church, and social class. Schooling represents a formalization of the socialization process, usually directed specifically toward the young. Schooling entails planned learning by certified specialists who ideally can provide the kinds of experiences that will enable their charges to play their roles successfully. In this light, schools may be said to have two primary functions. The first is instructional and involves the transmission of knowledge, values, and norms, along with the appropriate motivation necessary to prepare the young for adult roles. The second is the selection and allocation of individuals to channels leading to specific statuses. Thus an elementary school student will be socialized in school in terms of his role and status as a student, but he will also be learning, to some extent, the skills basic to his future occupational and societal roles, as well as role expectations for himself and others in adult society. Furthermore, he will be learning these things both in the formal classroom situation and within the context of the informal interaction taking place with his fellow students and his adult associates in the school.

Distinctions Between Informal Social Learning and Formal Education

Rather obviously, in quantitative terms most learning takes place through relatively unstructured, informal relationships. Yet the distinction between formal and informal learning may not be as sharp as often implied. On the one hand, it

---

[3] Melvin Tumin, "Competing Status Systems" in *Development and Society,* ed. David E. Novack and Robert Lekachman (New York: St. Martin's Press, 1968), p. 230.

might be said that all people are teachers inasmuch as they transmit behavior patterns and languages. At the same time it could be argued that even in a formal school setting the major portion of learning takes place through informal relationships. Further, as with the family—and to a lesser extent, occupational and voluntary social groups—the school setting is one in which the teaching roles are performed by older people.

Yet, significant distinctions exist between informal social learning and formal education. In the family children first learn the nature of authority and how to respond appropriately to it. But the school extends the notion of authority to a broader range of adults and routinizes relationships between subordinate and dominant statuses. Schools provide more diverse relationships and offer models less homogeneous than those found in the family. The school has more tangible goals than the family and a more regularized system of evaluation. And the school presumably seeks to differentiate learning requirements, not only on the basis of sex and age, but also along the lines of ability and interest. Thus, formal education tends to be built on a model that assumes that only a portion of the children can or should learn certain types of behavior.

The pattern of socialization within the school has sometimes been viewed as being less consistent and less efficient than the methods operating in the larger society. Brookover and Erickson, for example, argue that the school, unlike informal groups, does not make "consistent use of reward and punishment for appropriate and expected behavior." These authors further offer the hypothesis that "academic behaviors would be learned as effectively as non-academic types if similar patterns of expectation and processes of teaching were employed." [4] This generalization and hypothesis need to be examined further. These authors are evidently arguing that more homogeneity in behavior models, a more consistent

---

[4] Wilbur B. Brookover and Edsel L. Erickson, *Society, Schools and Learning* (Boston: Allyn and Bacon, 1969), chap. 2, p. 32.

use of reward and punishment, and provision of a more continuous and integrated pattern of teaching would result in more successful schools. While one might agree in principle with this argument, it is difficult to envision American schools in the near future undergoing so radical a transformation. Schooling, because of its clientele and because of its multiple functions, provides more diverse relationships than the family. The numerous tangible goals of the schools appear to support a variety of teaching methods and evaluation schemes. Finally, the more transient and time-bound notion of schooling colors relationships between learner and learner and between teacher and learner.

Yet this response is not fully adequate, for there are those who argue that the knowledge and skills taught within the school are of secondary importance. To some observers the most significant objective of schooling is the development of emotional qualities and competencies in broader social roles. In this perspective, the socialization function of the schools differs little in goals from the child-rearing process of the family.

The Social and Educational Contexts of Modernizing Societies

The processes of social change and economic development require new roles and statuses for a large proportion of the members of a society. The introduction of industrialization and application of scientific knowledge makes the family apprenticeship method of skill-learning obsolete. Newly achieved independence requires development of loyalty to a polity that extends beyond the family, clan, or village. Ecological changes, including a movement toward urban concentration, instill new aspirations and question old living patterns. Introduction of Western medicine calls into question the validity of time-honored methods of healing and possibly their ideological bases. More extensive communication systems create new awareness.

Education in most modernizing societies has been an institution serving those small elite groups that have wielded political, economic, or religious power. This phenomenon is in keeping with the differentiation concept (introduced in chapter 1), for the groups that have been the center of the societal-differentiation process are those who would find it most necessary to build educational institutions to provide the skills, attitudes, or social graces through which they could maintain, adapt, or further develop their status and power.

Clearly, the quantity and quality of education vary greatly among the one hundred or so national societies typically referred to as modernizing or developing. As we have seen, numerous scales and indices attest to the wide variations that exist in these nations in terms of literacy rates, enrollment ratios, dropout rates, and proportion of national budget alloted to education. Wide variations may also be found in terms of quality of school personnel (measured by years of formal training required of teachers and administrators) as well as in quality of physical plants and instructional materials.

In the classrooms, teachers are likely to be ill-educated but trained. The textbook and the syllabus circumscribe the content of learning and are nearly the exclusive focus of teacher and pupil activities. Through the medium of a teacher, facts and ideas proceed from the textbook to the chalkboard to the pupil's copybook. At a later date this material will be the subject of an examination. The basic limitation of this approach lies not in its tediousness but in its meaninglessness. The school world sets its standards of accuracy, consistency, and relevance in terms not of the world outside but in terms of the symbols locked in books.

More importantly, considering broad socialization goals, education in the modernizing nations, at least beyond the 3 Rs, largely remains the privilege of the elite. The contributions made by secondary education to the success of social change and economic development are considered pivotal by many serious studies of education and modernization. This level of schooling is relied upon by many developing nations to provide skills, attitudes, and leadership in the modernization process. But access to this level is limited and may be associated closely to the extent of paternal education, social class, and place of residence.

The relationship between education and socialization in modernizing societies may differ in two major ways from that found in either traditional or modern societies. First, the schools in modernizing societies may be required to provide images of major roles which are in contrast with, or at least not universally represented by, other socializing agents. For example, the role and status of a responsible citizen of a new self-governing nation-state require a pattern of behavior that is different from that of a citizen whose responsibility and participation in decision making was limited to his clan. Social scientists claim that effective socialization in these new statuses will depend on the ability of individuals to perceive themselves as players of these new roles (empathic capability, see chapter 1) and at the same time as no longer playing the roles attached to traditional statuses.

A new self-image and greater empathy depend in part on new kinds of information. Particularly perhaps in the less industrialized societies, schools, as sources of information and as means for acquiring it, have a number of advantages over other institutions. These include:

1. The danger of incorrect information is greatly reduced.
2. The probability of making incorrect inferences from experience is reduced.
3. Information concerning values and norms is acquired more quickly and more efficiently than by means of inferences from experiences.
4. A broader range of information concerning contingencies than is available in everyday life can be presented, and thus behavior patterns may be changed.[5]

Second, schools may be required to effect the inculcation of new norms and delineation of new roles with greater

---

[5] Don Adams and Joseph P. Farrell, eds., *Education and Social Development,* mimeographed (Syracuse University, 1965), chap. 7.

rapidity than is required in traditional or modern societies. By way of illustration, the lag between patterns of education and emerging ideological persuasions may be seen in recent developments in a number of African nations. President Julius Nyerere of Tanzania, for example, commenting on past elitist educational patterns noted: ". . . colonial education induced attitudes of human inequality, and in practice underpinned the dominance of the weak by the strong, especially in the economic field." [6]

Nyerere describes the socialist society he envisions for Tanzania, and its supporting educational system:

> . . . the educational system of Tanzania must emphasize cooperative endeavour, not individual advancement; it must stress concepts of equality and the responsibility to give service which goes with any special ability, whether it be in carpentry, in animal husbandry or in academic pursuits. And, in particular our education must counteract the temptation to intellectual arrogance; for this leads to the well-educated despising those whose abilities are non-academic or who have no special abilities but are just human beings. Such arrogance has no place in a society of equal citizens." [7]

The socialization process of education may be also identified in the creation of what have been termed "broker" roles within the society. Simply described, those members of modernizing societies who have achieved new roles and statuses may become models or interpreters of new attitudes to their less-educated associates or communities. Some studies have indicated that socially mobile sons of peasant families may instill previously unknown aspirations for social mobility among neighbors; that teachers, doctors, and local-level government officials may serve to interpret, on an informal basis, national-level political ideologies and loyalties, style-of-life practices, and aspirations to their communities.

---

[6] *Nationalist,* Dar es Salaam, Tanzania, 10 March 1967.
[7] Ibid.

The above paragraphs suggest some of the possible ramifications of socialization emanating from the educational systems in the process of modernization. The implication has been that these characteristics are positive in the sense that they promote economic and social change, which is presumed to be a goal of these societies. However, it should be recognized that efforts of education to support the increasing differentiation of roles and statuses carry with them many tensions, conflicts, and strains.

For example, new expectations for social mobility or higher status may be unrealistic in the given social structure and thus lead to frustration or anomie for a large portion of the population. Second, the schism created by the education of an elite few may decrease rather than increase national unity. The socialization provided by schools in modernizing societies may in effect be supporting two conflicting purposes. When schools introduce new skills, specializations, and their supportive role commitments to their students, they create greater opportunities for social mobility. However, when these opportunities are offered primarily in the form of access to higher levels of education, even on the basis of merit, the children of the urban middle class tend to be the ones who benefit. Moreover, educational systems, by various administrative and programmatic devices, segregate students along academic, social, and racial lines. New values and attitudes that are assumed to be part of the socialization process in the educational experience will be transmitted to those portions of the population who are least in need of them. Meanwhile, the children of rural, poor, or otherwise underprivileged groups are further separated from their educated counterparts. Thus the principle of provision of educational opportunity on the basis of measured merit actually may operate against the creation of national solidarity or integration. On the other hand, opportunities provided on the basis of some other criterion may slow down economic devleopment. Herein lies a major dilemma, for the policy maker may have to choose between goals of social equity or economic efficiency.

Schooling and Socialization in the Postindustrial Society

Ten separate socialization agents or populations of agents have been identified in modern and postindustrial societies:

1. Mass media
2. The subculture of parents
3. The subculture of like-age and older peers
4. The formal education system, public and private
5. The churches, with their programs for children and youth
6. The leisure-time agencies, with their recreational, cultural, and character-education programs
7. The social-control and protection agencies, such as the police, courts, traffic-safety agents, etc.
8. The therapeutic, special-correction, and resocialization services, such as counselors, remedial clinics, and programs for the handicapped
9. Employment offices and work supervisors who hire the young and supervise them on their paid jobs
10. Political leaders who have an interest in involving the young in political activities such as civil rights protests.[8]

The focus here is on the educational system, although attention is also given to the effects of the family and peer groupings on the lives of the young. Particularly emphasized are the nature and extent of the interactions among these socialization agents, and their degree of reinforcement and conflict.[9]

---

[8] John A. Clausen, ed., *Socialization and Society* (Boston: Little, Brown, 1968), p. 335.

[9] The mass media, television, radio, comic books, and movies, undoubtedly are very significant in the socialization of the young in advanced societies. Yet the nature of their influence is largely suppositional. The content and personnel found in the mass media clearly have wide interest and prestige in society. By their content alone, media depict many social roles. The duties of the sheriff, waitress, doctor, and government spy are now known by even the youngest children of the household. The mass media offer models of behavior—heroes, superheroes, villains, beautiful-people models, in-people models, models of squares, rebels, foreigners, and so on.

Familial and Societal Norms

The first and perhaps the most important socializing agency for the child is the family. Here the child forms intense and enduring emotional attachments. The family filters the outside world for the child. Only certain stimuli, values, friends, and TV programs are allowed to enter the child's world. The child learns behavior appropriate to his status, according to his age and sex within the constraints of family preferences.

The child-rearing patterns in the American family have been significantly altered during the last few decades. Parents are seen as becoming (1) more permissive; (2) more affectionate; and (3) increasingly more willing to utilize psychological techniques of discipline, e.g., withdrawal of love, etc. These changes are most evident among middle-class families. Bronfenbrenner, in speculating on the implications of the new patterns of socialization in the family, suggests that while certain old problems may have been ameliorated, new ones have emerged. For example, children from middle-class homes do tend to excel in the more "desirable" characteristics such as self-control, achievement, responsibility, and leadership. However, high achievement motivation flourishes in a family atmosphere of "cold democracy," and children from

---

What is the scope and nature of the influence of these media on children? Empirical studies in this area tell us far less than we would like to know. We know, for example, that in the United States children, on the average, spend more time watching television between the ages of six and eighteen than they do in school. Judging from the apparent success advertising has had through all mass media, one might assume that the overall impact of media on children's behavior would be great indeed.

It might be hypothesized that (1) the strength and direction of the influence of media are likely to depend on the child's level of maturity—children of different ages react differently to similar television programs; (2) the particular preferences and reactions depend upon the child's interpersonal relationships; and (3) the perception and influence of media themes are related to the social background of the child. See Frederick Elkin, *The Child and Society* (New York: Random House, 1960), pp. 73–74. For a more recent but also inconclusive study, see *Television and Growing Up: The Impact of Televized Violence*, Report to the Surgeon-General, U.S. Public Health Service (Washington, D.C.: G.P.O., 1972).

achievement-oriented homes tend to be more aggressive, tense, domineering, and cruel.[10]

Parsons views the school in the United States, or more specifically, the elementary school class as performing the following socialization functions: (1) an emancipation of the child from primary emotional attachment to his family; (2) an internalization of a level of societal values and norms that is a step higher than those he can learn in his family alone; (3) a differentiation of the school class in terms of actual achievement and of differential *valuation* of achievement; and (4) from society's point of view, a selection and allocation of its human resources relative to the adult role system.[11]

Schooling, through explicit instruction and through other experiences, contributes to the identification of social norms, accepting them, and behaving in accordance with them. Dreeben discusses the manner in which schools assist students in acquiring the four norms: *independence, achievement, universalism,* and *specificity*.[12] These norms, as we have already noted, are frequently associated with the process of modernization. Here, however, we will limit discussion to the school's contribution to the learning of norms of achievement and universalism in industrialized societies. The former in particular is generally considered central to the value system of American society.

How does the school assist individuals (or groups) in conforming to achievement norms, that is, accepting the obligation to master tasks according to standards of excellence? Presumably parental attitudes and behavior toward children lay a foundation for the level of motivation to achieve that a child brings to school. The structural characteristics of schooling build upon this foundation. Dreeben suggests the following distinctive structural features of schools:

[10] Urie Bronfenbrenner, "The Changing American Child—A Speculative Analysis," *Quarterly of Behavior and Development* 7 (1961): 73–84.

[11] Talcott Parsons, "The School Class as a Social System: Some of the Functions in American Society," *Harvard Educational Review* 29, no. 4 (Fall 1959): 297–318, reprinted in *Socialization and Schools* (compiled for *Harvard Educational Review*, 1968).

[12] Robert Dreeben, "The Contribution of Schooling to the Learning of Norms," *Harvard Educational Review* 37, no. 2 (Spring 1967): pp. 211–37.

1. Responsibility for the control of schools and for instruction in the classroom rests in the hands of adults who are not the kinsmen of pupils.

2. Children leave the household daily to attend school and return at the close of the day; that is, they continue their active membership and participation in the family.

3. Schools are distinguished structurally according to levels; despite the similarities between elementary and secondary levels, there are conspicuous differences involving:

  (a) variation in the heterogeneity of the student body related to school-district size;
  (b) degree of differentiation of the teaching staff based upon subject specialization;
  (c) presence or absence of formal provision for tracking pupils based largely on past academic achievement;
  (d) variation in the number of pupils that each teacher confronts daily.

4. Pupils progress through school grade by grade at yearly intervals, each time severing associations with one set of teachers and establishing associations with a new set (unlike the family, where children's relationships with parents usually do not follow a sequential pattern of severance and reestablishment).

5. Pupils move through school as members of age-equal cohorts (unlike the family, in which the age dispersion of children is characteristically larger than that of the classroom).

6. Classrooms, like families, consist of adult and nonadult positions, but the former have a much larger nonadult membership.[13]

Within the school, both instructional and extracurricular activities tend to be structured to require evaluation and comparison of the student. Classroom experiences involve a variety of tasks, frequently within an assignment-performance-evaluation sequence. Indeed, the school class becomes differentiated along a continuum of achievement. Dilemmas

---

[13] Ibid., p. 25.

and conflict arise because the pupils must compete and be compared with their classmates academically but depend upon their friendship in out-of-school activities. As Dreeben notes: "The classroom thus provides not only the achievement experiences itself but by-products of it . . . "[14]

Pupils learn to live with both success and failure, but the latter creates special problems of stress. A minority of pupils has few experiences of failure, while a minority has few experiences of success. The majority of pupils probably "wins some" and "loses some." Note, however, the handicaps of children from the lowest social strata, who often have a few adult models of regularity, routine, and responsibility, the behavior patterns that are demanded by schools from the very earliest grades.

In a setting where achievement is the norm, failure would seem to present special problems. That is, experience in failure may help pupils adjust to the real world, yet each new failure may be nonetheless damaging. Settling for second best (or fourth or tenth) is difficult under the principle of achievement. And do the schools adequately prepare pupils to substitute one set of goals for another and to maintain self-respect in the face of diminished expectations?

Dreeben comments:

> The school provides a wider variety of achievement experiences than does the family but at the same time has fewer resources for supporting and protecting pupils' self-respect in the face of failure. As pupils proceed through successive school levels, the rigors of achievement increase, at least for those who continue along the main academic line. Moreover at the secondary levels the number of activities governed according to the achievement principle increases as does the variety of these activities. As preparation for adult public life in which the application of this principle is widespread, schooling contributes to personal development in assuring that the majority of pupils not only will have performed tasks according to the achieve-

---

[14] Ibid., p. 38.

ment standard but will have had experience in an expanding number of situations in which activities are organized according to it.[15]

The learning of universalistic norms may accompany the acquisition of achievement norms. In both academic and extracurricular activities pupils are treated by others as members of categories, e.g., second grade, Algebra I class, or baseball team. In these settings, in contrast to the familial situations, they are confronted with similar tasks and learn to accept similar treatment within a given category. Indeed, considering the size of the class and the narrow age range of children, the teacher has much less chance than a parent to make particularistic interpretations.

The tracking, or grouping, arrangement whereby pupils of similar capabilities receive instruction from a variety of teachers provides an excellent opportunity to learn the principle of universalism. Typically in the United States secondary school pupils are grouped, partly through self-selection, into a program, e.g., college preparatory or general, and frequently in more refined gradations on the basis of teacher evaluation. If it may be assumed that the criteria applied to evaluate performance are roughly constant across tracks and subjects, the meaning of universalism, or categorization, becomes apparent.

Universalism implies equity or fairness. Here, again, the contrast between family and school becomes apparent. Within the school, grading in academic work and punishment of offenses are expected to be unrelated to personal characteristics of the pupil. That is, equivalent accomplishments (or misdeeds) receive the same teacher response. Within the family, however, judgments about equity are influenced by such factors as age, health, past performance, and so forth.[16]

---

[15] Ibid., p. 39.

[16] An elaboration of the school experiences that facilitate or inhibit learning is not within the scope of this chapter. For some further sense of the forces and conditions that affect the child's motivation and ability to learn, the student is recommended to Goodwin Watson, ed., *Change in School Systems,* particularly chapter 5. In this reference, Jung et al. distinguish "five levels of human phenomena that condition how effectively human and mate-

Industrial society appears to be achievement based, and conducive to, if not dependent upon, the acceptance of universalistic norms. To the extent that society permits men to rise or fall on the basis of their performance and schools permit pupils to succeed or fail on the same criterion, a congruence exists. And, we are arguing, to a degree this is indeed how things happen. Yet two caveats need to be inserted. First, educational credentials in schools and in society are often assumed to be a proxy for performance capability. Second, in a more direct way, ascriptive and particularistic criteria influence one's educational and life chances. Chapters 5 and 6 further treat these points.

Schooling and the Establishment

But are schools really powerful agencies for socialization? And if so, for which students are they most successful? If schools socialize so well, why the generation gap and various forms of student rebellion? Is the socialization that takes place within the academic context part of the same cloth as that which is generated through activities more directly under the control of the children and youth? We could continue at length to pose questions in this vein. Given the state of the art, they would, alas, only serve to frustrate the author and the reader alike.

Yet, perhaps three further points can be made in elaboration.

First, the description offered thus far presents a view of

rial resources are utilized to create learning experiences for children." These are: (1) "the pupil as a self, and individual psychological and biological unit in the learning experience"; (2) "the classroom peer group as a subculture of child clients"; (3) "level of others—*direct workers*—who interact with pupils in creating learning experiences," e.g., teachers, parents and peers; (4) "those who directly facilitate or inhibit the efforts of the direct workers," e.g., principals, curriculum specialists, and other teachers; (5) "persons who influence the nature of the school system as an organization," e.g., superintendents and school board members.*

* Charles C. Jung, Robert Fox, and Ronald Lippitt, "An Orientation and Strategy for Working on Problems of Change in School Systems," in *Change in School Systems*, ed. Goodwin Watson (Washington, D.C.: NEA Cooperative Project for Educational Development, 1967), pp. 69–70. See also the model of a "good" learning process on p. 76.

schooling that is too antiseptic, too rational, too conflict-free. Observations of elementary school classrooms suggest that teachers may engage in as many as a thousand interpersonal interchanges each day. Such a large number of pupil-teacher contacts understandably results in inconsistencies in teacher behavior. The nature of these many interchanges cannot be anticipated, and therefore many are not subject to advanced planning. It has frequently been noted that the frenetic activity of a teacher is divided between two curricula: the usual academic one and a hidden one of rules, regulations, and routines. But a third curriculum is also present, consisting of affective and social concerns generated by a given child in a given social milieu. Contradictions and conflicts are bound to be fostered, partly resulting from our lack of understanding of the process of socialization and partly because of the spontaneity of classroom situations.

Second, the schools, irrespective of the extent of their influence, tend to socialize in terms of a set of norms and values held by a particular segment of society. The description we have offered above of schools and teachers reinforcing universalistic and achievement norms suggests in American society that the educational system supports what might be called the superordinate society, or perhaps more narrowly the "Establishment," or the "ruling classes." Do those blacks, Indians, Puerto Ricans, and members of other minority groups who have initiated separate or supplementary schools seek the same social learnings, the same values, and the same norms?

The liberal credo has been that socialization through schools and other agencies along the lines we have described was the aim for all. Extending compulsory schooling and providing racial integration were seen as two major efforts to maximize the effects of schools in appropriate directions. The liberal view did not deny that privileges continued to accrue disproportionately to certain segments of the society but held that such inequity would be erased with time. Many members of minority groups shared, and continue to share, these hopes. Recently the view, which might be seen as central to the great American dream, has been strongly challenged.

Within the classroom, universalistic and achievement norms are encouraged, partly because the teacher acts as an appropriate model. But, for example, how "fair" is the teacher? Is the middle-class teacher equally objective in his treatment of girls and boys, poor and rich, black and white? Teachers reward the behavior they prefer, and as many studies indicate they tend to prefer (1) those pupils who are more conforming and less assertive; and (2) those pupils who exhibit the dress, manners, and norms of the middle class.[17]

A third point in need of elaboration, if not modification, relates to the socialization that takes place in peer and age groupings to generate a distinctive group culture. As has been noted, the content of socialization goals varies with age level. With younger children in American society, the focus appears to be on achievement motivation, regularity, self-determination, obedience, neatness, and a sense of membership in the classroom group. For adolescents, more attention is centered on the management of sex and aggression.

It is the purpose of this section to focus directly on some of the problems and requirements of socialization beyond childhood, particularly on the distinctive, powerful, and rebellious youth culture.[18] Chapter 4 extends, in less abstract terms, the argument presented here.

---

[17] One study * on the preferences of student teachers concludes:

> The results provide striking support for the hypothesis that student teachers prefer pupils whose behavior reflects rigidity, conformity, and orderliness or dependency, passivity and acquiescence rather than pupils whose behavior is indicative of flexibility, nonconformity, and untidiness or independence, activity and assertiveness.

* Norma D. Feshbach, "Student Teacher Preferences for Elementary School Pupils Varying in Personality Characteristics," in *The Experience of Schooling*, ed. Melvin L. Silberman (New York: Holt, Rinehart and Winston, 1971), p. 82.

[18] At the adolescent level, particularly, conflict between pupils and school administrators and teachers may be manifested even in matters of personal dress, appearance, and the like. One author has commented that such conflicts have been explained (to him) in a wide variety of ways, including: 1. Beatle haircuts (also eye make-up, sloppy clothes, short skirts, and so on) destroy the image of the school which the administration wants to create in the public eye.   2. The school legitimately stands *in loco parentis*, but this position is being challenged (hence is reactively asserted by administrators). 3. Adults feel jealous of (or guilty about) adolescents' management of sex

In a rapidly changing society or even in the most traditional society the socialization that an individual receives in childhood is inadequate to prepare him fully for the tasks of adult life. Much has been written about the potency and durability of socialization during childhood, and scholars generally emphasize the difficulty in altering basic behavioral patterns acquired when young. The focus of socialization of the young may be well placed; however, egalitarian societies must attempt to ameliorate inadequacies of early social learning. Moreover, the advanced industrial society, with its associated shifts in occupational requirements and geographical and social mobility, typically demands many adjustments in career patterns and life styles. As societies progress toward higher levels of industrialization, there is more likelihood of discontinuities between what is expected in the successive roles of an individual. Increasingly, then, socialization must become a process found throughout the life cycle.

It is sometimes said that adolescence is a stage of life at which a person is changing from predominate membership in the family to predominate membership in society. Yet, this characterization seems inadequate, if not untrue, in the advanced industrialized societies today. Both the family and the adult society appear to have relinquished some of their drawing power to preadolescent youth. Working mothers and smaller family units, among other factors, have contributed to a lessening of the impact of the family on the socialization of the young. The importance of attaining status within the peer group provides substitute allegiances, commitments, and psychological support. As the culture of the youth group asserts itself, its distinctiveness from that of the adult society

---

between puberty and marriage.   4. Intergenerational value conflicts are at work.   5. Presentations of self that are erotic or violent interfere with the learning process.   6. The school is expected to be a bastion of morality, strengthening superegos as much as possible.   7. Being neat, formal, and so on must be taught to children if they are to take their place in society; casual clothing also implies that no serious attention to learning is taking place.   8. A competitive, win-lose, negotiative relationship has developed, rather than a cooperative, problem-solving one.   9. School administrators are playing Delilah to the teen-agers' Samson.*

* Matthew B. Miles, "Some Properties of Schools as Social Systems," in Watson, *Change in School Systems*, pp. 6–7.

becomes clear and in a somewhat circular fashion becomes reinforced.

But our concern here and in the following chapter is not to probe in detail the many causes and the complex process of socialization within youth culture. Our interest is more narrow. The previous sections were primarily concerned with the involvement and contribution of schooling to the socialization process. The emphasis particularly, but not exclusively, was on the socialization and schooling of young children. Here we wish to highlight the issues and challenges for teachers created by an increasingly powerful youth culture that sees itself not only different from, but often in serious conflict with, adult society. Some of the questions that must be dealt with include:

To what extent can the schools take the blame or credit for the characteristics of youth culture and the disenchantment of many youth? What is the bearing of socialization patterns on the current unrest of youth found in many contemporary societies? On student revolt? On the generation gap? Has the alienation and protest of today's youth been a result of earlier socialization practices? Can the dissatisfaction of present-day youth be blamed on leftist teachers in the secondary schools and universities? (Or can the problems of or with youth be traced to Dr. Spock?) [19]

---

[19] Note, for example, the variety of hypotheses, often contradictory, that have been offered to explain the political activism of youth: 1. Student political activism is a special manifestation of adolescent rebellion. The greater the intergenerational differences and the greater the overall intensity of adolescent rebellion, the greater the likelihood of political activism. 2. Adolescent rebellion takes political form primarily when the student perceives political values as salient to the parents or other authorities against whom rebellion is directed. 3. The more group self-consciousness among young people and students, the greater the probability of student political activism. 4. Education itself produces a critical outlook that stimulates political complaints and political activism. 5. The more idealistic the students and the more oriented to absolute ends, the greater the tendency toward political activism. 6. Strong commitment to the nation coupled with weak commitment to mediating institutions such as government, parties, and voluntary associations, produces political activism on the part of students. 7. The greater the concern with matters of courage and manhood, the greater the political activism of male students. 8. The greater the self-esteem of the student as a student, the less the political activism. 9. The greater the sexual and other personal frustration of the student, the greater the tendency

Some scholars have suggested that the search by youth for its own norms, values, and styles is partly a reaction to restrictive and dull schooling. On the other hand many political leaders, particularly, appear to believe that the peculiar habits of youth are the direct result of sins of omission, e.g., lack of discipline or of commission, for example, leftist teaching in the schools.

In exposing students to a wide range of man's thought, schools have probably assisted in the growth of radical beliefs leading to political protest. This may be particularly true in the upper branches of education. Yet, in general, a better case can be made for the schools as agents of conservatism. In rather strong language Jules Henry states:

> The gathering of the mind while we "set the spirit free" or the fettering of the spirit as we free the mind is an abiding paradox of "civilization" in its more refined dimensions. . . . The schools are the central conserving forces of the culture. . . . It stands to reason that were young people truly creative the culture would fall apart, for originality, by definition, is different from what is given, and what is given is the culture itself. From the endless, pathetic "creative hours" of kindergarten to the most abstruse problems in sociology and anthropology, the function of education is to prevent the truly creative intellect from getting out of hand.[20]

But the shackling of the mind and spirit is not unique to schools. And certainly this generation of schools is not so much worse in this respect than the last as to have produced a distinctively strong and rebellious youth culture. Moreover, accusations that the schools "fetter" the mind smack somewhat of intellectual snobbery. Schools, to be sure, tend to be

toward political activism.   10. The less hampered the student is by practical concerns, such as earning a living or bringing up a family, the greater the tendency toward political activism.*

* Frederick W. Frey, "Political Science, Education and Development," in *The Social Sciences and the Comparative Study of Educational Systems,* ed. Joseph Fischer (Scranton, Pa.: International Textbook, 1970), pp. 405–406.

[20] Jules Henry, *Culture Against Man* (New York: Vintage, 1965), pp. 285–86.

dull and uncompromising places for the most creative minds, but the phenomenon of the youth culture encompasses a wide range of capabilities. It is not exclusively a rebellion of the rich, the poor, the bright, or the dull. We are interested in a phenomenon that is not merely visible among a few children from certain "kinds" of families and environments. Unrest and alienation and lack of intergenerational dialogue to some extent represent a worldwide condition and would appear to include millions of youth.

As Margaret Mead has pointed out, two decades ago the central problem with which young people were concerned (at least in the United States) was that of identity. Today the concern is with commitment—"to what past, present, or future can the idealistic young commit themselves." [21]

Commitment cannot be to the values and ideals of the older generation, for the rapidity of technological change and the accompanying social change have created an irreversible division between young and old. Mead notes, "Even very recently, the elders could say: 'You know, I have been young, and *you* never have been old.' But today's young people can reply: 'You never have been young in the world I am young in, and you never can be.' " [22]

How young people feel is graphically expressed in an essay by a fifteen-year-old boy from Texas:

> There is a mass confusion in the minds of my generation in trying to find a solution for ourselves and the world around us.
>
> We see the world as a huge rumble as it swiftly goes by with wars, poverty, prejudice, and the lack of understanding among people and nations.
>
> Then we stop and think: There must be a better way and we have to find it. . .
>
> My generation is being used almost like a machine. We are to learn set standards, strive for better education, so we can follow in our elders' footsteps. But why?

---

[21] Margaret Mead, *Culture and Commitment* (New York: Natural History Press, and Doubleday, 1970), preface, p. ix.
[22] Ibid., p. 63.

If we are to be a generation of repetition, the situation will be worse. But how shall we change? We need a great deal of love for everyone, we need a universal understanding among people, we need to think of ourselves and to express our feelings, but that is not all. I have yet to discover what else we need, nor have I practiced these things as fully as I should. Because, when I try, I'm sneered at by my elders and those who do not hear, or look at it with a closed mind. . .

Sometimes I walk down a deserted beach listening to the waves and birds and I hear them forever calling and forever crying and sometimes we feel that way but everyone goes on with his own little routines, afraid to stop and listen for fear of cracking their nutshell.

The answer is out there somewhere. We need to search for it.[23]

But less than any preceding generation will today's youth "follow in their elders' footsteps." The elders still may hold most of the keys to power, and some reform, e.g., the end of the draft and a lowering of voting age, is possible only with their goodwill. And, of course, this is a source for disenchantment for the articulate and rebellious young people who are saying, in effect, "You adults shall no longer limit our future."

The models for youth, then, are largely to be found not among adults, but within their own generation. A few youths invent a new cultural mode and this spreads through a socialization network that is beginning to encompass the whole world. Yet, this picture can be exaggerated for (1) youth culture is not altogether uniform; and (2) the influence of home and community remains visible.

Moreover, two important segments of society—the "liberal intellectuals" and those who in the United States have been dubbed the "silent majority"—appear to have overreacted to the more visible and more noisy of the young. The former group has tended to overly romanticize contemporary youth while the latter has reacted with great suspicion and distrust.

---

[23] Essay by Shannon Dickson, quoted in ibid., pp. 76–77.

Long hair and rags do not necessarily make the young Christ-like in any significant way nor do these affectations necessarily suggest irresponsibility and immorality. The rhetoric of "relevance" and "involvement" may be as hollow from the mouths of youth as it is from the public relations personnel of giant corporations. And is there any reason to demand consistent, predictable behavior, either radical or conservative, of the young when adults so freely indulge in inconsistency?

Summary

Socialization as a process of acquiring new skills, values, and commitments encompasses the activities of many institutions. If we were fully able to identify the precise contributions of formal education to this process we would have unraveled much of the mystery of schooling. Lacking such profound insight, we are often forced to rely on supposition generated by inconclusive research and "expert" opinion. Knowing something of the changing behavior of children and youth, the structure of school activities, and the preferences of teachers, we often assume a linkage that has not been demonstrated in any scientific way.

Yet in highly industrialized societies the schools are clearly perceived as central to the socialization process. The norms that schools appear to foster, such as independence, achievement, and universalism, are those frequently demanded in the greater society toward the ends of efficiency and equity. The congruence between the norms of school and society is visible, regardless of the traditional or progressive character of the school system in question. New uses of teachers and innovations in instructional design largely act in altering the "delivery" of the norms without substituting new norms. However, both ends and means of formal education are being subjected to unprecedented debate, and the dilemmas and conflicts must not be slighted. Chapter 4 addresses itself to some uncertainties and issues faced by teachers and students in the contemporary United States.

References

Brookover, Wilbur B., and Erickson, Edsel L. *Society, Schools and Learning.* Boston: Allyn and Bacon, 1969.

Clausen, John A., ed. *Socialization and Society.* Boston: Little, Brown, 1968.

Dreeben, Robert. *On What is Learned in School.* Reading, Mass.: Addison-Wesley, 1968.

Silberman, Melvin L., ed. *The Experience of Schooling.* New York: Holt, Rinehart and Winston, 1971.

Socialization and Schools, compiled for *Harvard Educational Review,* 1968.

Discussion Questions

1. What advantages do you find in the concept of *socialization* as opposed to *enculturation?*

2. How may the relationship between education and socialization alter as societies modernize?

3. How have child-rearing patterns changed between your generation and that of your parents?

4. How did the structure of activities of the elementary and secondary schools you attended foster achievement norms? To what extent did the evaluation procedures promote universalistic norms?

5. What are the distinctive features of contemporary youth culture? How are these features reinforced?

6. What has been your experience in "the shackling of the mind and spirit" by schools?

CHAPTER FOUR

Students and Schools

Toward the close of the preceding chapter it was asserted that one of the major socialization problems faced in education systems in postindustrial societies is that of dealing with the youth subculture. Article after article, volume after volume, have been devoted to descriptions of, and prescriptions for, the problems of adolescent rebellion in contemporary America. No attempt will be made here to review that literature or to offer any new analysis of the "problem of youth." What will be attempted is to point out again a few of the major aspects of the problem and to suggest how some educational practices exacerbate rather than ameliorate the situation.

The Problem: The Teen-Age Revolution

Youth in revolt has become a favorite topic among those concerned with education, and one frequently hears tautological assertions to the effect that rebellious adolescents are making schools bad and bad schools are making adolescents rebellious. What is meant by those who assert that the young are in revolution? And when the young see themselves as being in revolt, what reasons do they give and to what extent do they see schools and educators as the enemy? These are serious questions that beg for the attention of educators. There is no claim that what follows is the truth about these matters; it is but one attempt to conceptualize some of the problems and an invitation for the reader to consider, argue, and to join the inquiry.

A rather widespread view, perhaps heard less today than in the recent past, holds that there is no new or novel problem with today's youth. Believers in this view argue that there is really nothing to be said, that the notion of teen-agers in revolt is but a modern version of an age-old conflict between adults and those soon to become adults. The problem, some have pointed out, was reflected in a comment attributed to Socrates:

> Our youth now loves luxury. They have bad manners and contempt for authority. They show disrespect for their elders and love idle chatter instead of exercise. Children are now tyrants—not the servants of the household. They no longer rise when their elders enter the room. They contradict their parents, chatter before company, gobble up their food, and tyrannize their teachers.

Thus that which has been called the "generation gap" is seen as something with a long history, not a phenomenon peculiar to the mid-twentieth century. There is at least an element of truth in this view. In every generation the young seem to have the capacity and willingness occasionally to enrage adults. But it may also be that adults, when enraged by youth, compare the behavior of those young people with their own youthful behavior as they recall it. And, as is suspected by the young and known by the old, the youthful good deeds of the elders have had plenty of time to grow. To take our clue from Will Rogers, we might say that the young are not what they used to be and probably never were. Thus there has undoubtedly always been both "intergenerational conflict" and a tendency of some older members of the society to forget or minimize that conflict in their own youth.

Yet the present concern with youth in rebellion cannot be so easily dismissed. Major social changes have occurred, bringing about modifications in the form, and increases in the intensity, of the conflict between the young and the old. The there-is-nothing-new-under-the-sun view of the values and behavior of youth does not, upon examination, seem adequate.

A second commonly heard view can be labeled the prophet-of-doom-position. This is the argument that the behavior, the values, and the growing power of the young are signs of decadence and are reason for despair. It is a claim that our society is breaking down in the sense that the young have not been and are not being "socialized" properly; thus the youth of today have not been equipped with the values and attitudes that will allow them to perform adequately as adults. There are always, of course, prophets of doom. And in their view, too, is at least some truth: The changes we are witnessing in our young threaten some values and institutional practices that, if not cherished in the past, have nevertheless been accepted. Yet there is good reason to believe that the dire predictions of the prophets of doom will turn out, as Mark Twain commented on his reported death, to be greatly exaggerated. Problems can be great without being insoluble, and they can be insoluble without being catastrophic.

A third common view is held by a few of the young themselves and by a sizable number of apologists for youth. This view attributes to youth a kind of superior wisdom. Rather than thought of as the spoiled generation, the young are viewed as the unspoiled. Not threatened by a lack of material goods, they have transcended materialism and have attached themselves to a new humanism. They are seen as socially sensitive and aware, suspicious of those who are of the "Establishment," and capable of reordering the society so that it reflects rather than merely verbalizes democratic values. In this view, too, we can find some elements of truth. Some concerns, such as economic security, have been paramount with many older people in our society and yet are of little concern to many of the young. True also is the fact that many young people are less willing than their elders to compromise on human concerns in the society. And without doubt some wise young men and women have a valuable perspective on social and human problems—a perspective not shared by many older members of the society. But whatever the truth in this view, there seems to be no extensive evidence at present to suggest that, in addition to a different perspective on our myriad problems, the young have a *superior* perspective. Certainly the wisdom of the young should be sought, but that is because wisdom should be sought no matter where it may be found. And wisdom is too scarce to suppose that it is the special province of any group.

These three views have been treated here in simplistic fashion. Each could be formulated more completely, and their adherents specifically identified. The purpose here, however, is simply to outline the views in order to make explicit the assumptions underlying this chapter. Thus we have asserted that there has always been adolescent-adult conflict, but it is also true that the current conflict has taken on new forms and greater intensity. We have claimed, too, that the conflict is serious, but it would be an error to join the prophets of doom in bemoaning what they take to be an advancing stage in the decline and fall of our culture. And, finally, we have argued that the young have valuable contributions to make, contributions that need not wait until they have joined the "older generation," but there is no indication that a greater wisdom has been bestowed upon them than upon those of more advanced age.

If we are agreed that we are witnessing some important changes in our young, how are we to understand those changes? The magnitude of the changes perceived is reflected by the common use of the phrase "the youth revolution." In a sense this terminology is misleading, not because the *extent* of the changes does not warrant the term *revolution,* but because that term may suggest that the young have somehow decided to initiate changes in a long-standing status quo. If we must use revolution terminology, then what we are witnessing in our youth is not so much revolution as counter revolution. The young are not so much rejecting a long-standing status quo relationship with adults and adult-dominated institutions as they are in counter revolt against revolutionary changes in the wider society.

Many of these changes have been discussed in chapters 2 and 3 and will not be discussed in detail here. Suffice it to say here that there have been changes in the society, which, from the point of view of the adolescent, have placed him in a difficult position. These changes have resulted in a situation in which the adolescent is not so much a child as adolescents before him have been, but neither is he as close to adulthood. In times past one went fairly directly from childhood to adulthood: the period of adolescence was brief. A person in the past, we might notice, had little time to be what we today call a "teen-ager" (indeed, even this term was not used as it is today until well within this century). Today, because of changes in the society, the young are often encouraged more strongly and earlier to stop being children. Yet at the same time they are denied adult status longer and longer. Their counter revolution, it might be argued, has been a response to this dilemma. Not having identity as either child or adult, they have responded by asserting and developing an identity of their own. But they have been forced into this position, and we ought not be surprised that they have become a self-conscious group within our society, a group that sets some of its own goals, rewards, and punishments. We ought not be surprised, that is, when a youth subculture develops. Thus there is a sense in which the counter revolution seems to have been successful. And to the extent that it has been successful, educators, along with other adults, are, as someone has said, "spies in the country of the young." (Pressing this metaphor a little further, it might be well to notice that *their* intelligence forces have, in the past, been much better than ours.) As spies, perhaps we need to look a little more carefully at this country in which we spy, at the pressures faced by youth as they react to the society of adults.

It was asserted earlier that in many cases we encourage the young more strongly and at an earlier age to stop being children.[1] It has been pointed out frequently in educational writings that the tasks generally set before children are those of acquiring adult behaviors and competencies. These tasks are set at an early age and are clear to children, even though we may deny that adult behaviors are our goals. We may *say* that we want children to be simply children, or that we want them to enjoy their childhood while they can, but other actions and other words often contradict this. Most of us have said to a small boy suffering some small hurt, "Be a little man!" And of the teen-ager whose behavior annoys us we demand, "Don't be childish!" Our praise for children, in schools and out, is frequently the result of the child's meeting or progressing toward adult behavioral standards. (Little League baseball is often mentioned as a case in point, but there are a host of other examples.) In short, we say early and often to the young, "Stop being a child!" Adolescents do, with respect to this command at least, obey their elders.

But the adolescent does not become an adult merely because he ceases to be a child. When do we, in contemporary American society, grant full adult status? In *one sense,* the answer to this question does not seem to have changed greatly in the last century. When a person becomes economically self-sufficient, when he enters the labor market as an adult, when he becomes independent of the family—then he is considered an adult. What *has* changed, of course, is that this sort of independence is now postponed, that adolescents find it increasingly difficult to fill these criteria of adulthood. It is not so long ago that a person fifteen or sixteen years old was considered an adult. Today we postpone the independence of adulthood. We employ various means, intentionally

---

[1] Stages of physiological development are also being changed. Probably due to medical and nutritional improvements, the average age at which puberty sets in has been lowered considerably. Thus, in addition to the social and psychological pressures, physiological changes affect youth at an earlier age than among previous generations.

or unintentionally, to keep the young dependent. One major means of doing so is the school: as long as young people are in school, we tend to regard them as something less than adult. And we demand that the young stay in school for increasing periods of time: we insist that all should remain in high school, that all who are able stay in school through college, and that an increasing number remain through professional or graduate school. This, of course, keeps the young out of the labor market and, occasionally, off the street. It continues their dependence on family and other adults, both economically and psychologically. This is not to say that the reasons for keeping youth in schools are not persuasive or that it would be better to return to former times when advanced schooling was for the few, and the factory and farm were for the many. The point is rather that one of the effects of continued schooling for the many has been continued dependence of the young, and that this continued dependence becomes a burden for these young.[2]

The result of this prolonging of dependence is a sizable, and growing, proportion of our population that is viewed as composed neither of children nor of adults. Whether called teen-agers, adolescents, the younger generation, or simply youth,[3] these young people have come to constitute a self-conscious group, demanding and getting certain rights and privileges, setting some of their own goals and systems of rewards, and apparently rejecting much of the adult society

---

[2] In a sense a part of this problem is that we have failed to make the role of student an acceptable adult role in our society. Whatever the reason for this, the problem promises to be even greater in the years ahead as the need for retraining and other kinds of continuing education increases. What we need to recognize is that we are beyond that point in our history when schools and schooling are for the young alone. The first large group to suffer from our failure to recognize this fully are the young adults presently in our secondary schools and colleges.

[3] Some of the terms have become misleading. "Teen-ager," for example, may suggest that the upper age limit for membership is twenty. But again we are in effect extending the age at which one becomes adult, and the college-student slogan "You can't trust anyone over thirty!" gives a better indication of the age at which almost all have emigrated from the "country of the young."

that in so many ways rejects them. The transition from childhood to adulthood, at one time quite rapid and based largely on physiological maturation, is now a rather lengthy period in a person's life. Complex social and economic considerations help to account for this, but no explanation of how the situation came to be will resolve all the educational problems that have resulted.

What problems does this present to those engaged in the schooling of the young? The major problem is that in this increasingly long transition period the young person is in the school, and the institutionalized aspects of the transition itself is increasingly supervised and certified by school personnel. We have already alluded to value conflicts in the school, conflicts between lower-class and middle-class values, conflicts between one racial or ethnic group and another, or conflicts between "traditional" and "emergent" values in our culture. All these conflicts are real enough, but there is yet another major conflict: the conflict between the values, beliefs, and attitudes encouraged by the youth subculture and those reflected in the practices of schooling. It is frequently the school that bears the brunt of the attack by the young as they seek to define their role in the society. What is it that schools do that enrages the young, that they see as threatening and destructive? The answer is by no means clear, but some central features and problems appear to play an important part. Let us turn now to some of those features.

Any person who has reflected upon his schooling can undoubtedly list a variety of problems that are perennial. Included on such a list would be the inappropriate or unnecessary or simply obsolete aspects of the curriculum and the lack of competent teachers. But dull teachers and "irrelevant" subject matter, although important, do not account for all the contemporary concern of youth with matters of schooling. These are age-old problems, not new or novel ones. However, there have been some striking changes in schooling, which have raised new problems and made old problems take on a new importance. Two major changes to be discussed here are: (1) the increased importance attached to schooling in contemporary America; and (2) the school's role in the occupational training and the "credentialing" of students. (These were discussed briefly in chapter 3 as the "allocation" function of the schools.)

The Increased Importance of Schooling

It is common for educationists to assert that those outside the educational institution place too little value on formal schooling. Yet, as a society, we have greatly increased the emphasis on schooling and in so doing have created an educational problem of great magnitude. The growing concern with schooling is reflected, for example, in the fact that today more and more people are writing, debating, and sometimes rioting over what is happening or failing to happen in our schools. Why is it that we hold schooling in such high regard? What educational problems, if any, result from attributing great importance to formal schooling? There are a number of possible answers to these questions, not all of which can be considered here. Nevertheless, we should at least remind ourselves that increased attention to formal schooling and increased importance of education are not at all the same thing. Certainly one could take the position that we need more and better education without subscribing to the view that those institutions called schools represent the only possible means to such education. Schooling represents a particular way of educating, not the only way. We could place increased emphasis on education while *decreasing* the emphasis on formal schooling. Thus, when we place more importance on formal schooling we have not only elected to increase and improve education, but we have, in effect, selected a particular option with which to accomplish that task.[4]

In most contemporary societies there is an emphasis on

---

[4] This "option" has been vigorously denounced by some critics. See, for example, Ivan Illich, *Deschooling Society* (New York: Harper & Row, 1971).

formal schooling as the means of acquiring increased education. From the point of view of the clients of the schools—the students—we have created a situation in which we (1) recognize virtually no alternative or legitimate escape from schools; (2) recognize no excuse for students who find themselves failures in the schools; and (3) allow the judgments about students made by school personnel within the school (supposedly based on academic performance) to be used to justify crucial out-of-school decisions that greatly affect the lives of students. Let us look further at these problems resulting from our emphasis on formal schooling.

Today schools and schooling are more important than in the past, not just for those who succeed (by the standards set by the school) but also for those deemed failures in the academic enterprise. It has been widely accepted that academic success is a good predictor of success in society, at least when success in society is defined in terms of higher social status and a greater share of wealth. Similarly, it is believed that failure in school is a good predictor of failure in the society. The reasons for the acceptance of these beliefs are complex. The result is a sense in which it can be justifiably said that a young person is unlikely to escape the effects of schooling. The school is encountered before taxes and death, but it has become in the lives of youth another example of the inevitable. In the school the young person is judged, and the judgments made are often based in part on nonacademic considerations. Once made, these decisions follow the person long after he has ceased to be a student. Of course there are conditions under which one can remove himself or be removed from the school. Some graduate, others drop out, and still others are expelled. But "escaping" the school is not sufficient for one to escape the judgments made about him by teachers and administrators.

Thus, there are two factors here. First, the young cannot avoid the school; they must, for a time at least, attend. Second, they cannot escape the judgments made about them by school personnel, even after they have escaped the physical confines of the school. If but *one* of these things were true, the problem of youth would be less severe. Being required to "go through" school would be much less threatening to the student if he could choose to leave behind the judgments of the school people when he left the school. And the problem of being unable to escape school judgments would probably be less disturbing if the schooling itself were a matter of choice. However, the combination of the two factors makes the school an institution with great power over its clients' lives. That those clients respond, sometimes in fear, sometimes in anger, and sometimes in apathetic resignation, ought not surprise us.

In contrast to earlier periods of our history, the school is now virtually the only promised route to upward mobility. It is the new "frontier," where each is sent and each is judged. The judgment of how well the student can cope with the school-frontier, it seems to be assumed, is an adequate appraisal of the merits of the student. Hence evaluations made by educators are used to assess the merits of the student even after he leaves the school to take an "adult" position in the society.[5]

Much of what is called school reform is based on the claim that what is supposed to be done is not being done well; e.g., mistakes are being made in the judgments of merit. Schools are reformed by changing them so that they do better what they are already doing. Such reform, if it does nothing else, has the effect of removing the "bad school" excuse. Making schools better *in this sense* may lead to higher student achievement or higher College Board scores or happier parents and teachers. But such reform can hardly be expected to lower the anxiety or reduce the threat felt by students.

The comments above should not be taken as simply a criticism of compulsory schooling. Indeed, the fact of *legal* compulsory schooling may be of little actual importance.

---

[5] Employers who, for purposes of hiring, use "performance criteria" *rather than* formal educational credentials represent an exception to this over-generalization.

Given our present emphasis on formal education, doing away with the legal requirements of school attendance would not necessarily ameliorate the problem. To be sure, some would leave the school earlier, but this would mean only that they would be labeled as failures at an earlier age. There are many factors other than legal requirements which make schooling virtually compulsory, e.g., tying entrance into occupations to completion of some level of formal schooling. We should notice also that what we are discussing is not simply a problem of miseducation. Of course schooling *is* required by law, and schools frequently *do* engage in miseducation, but the problem here centers not on those truths but on the fact that "life chances" are increasingly determined in schools. Hence schooling is a deadly serious business for the young. Success in school breeds success outside school, and school failure virtually guarantees that other failures will follow.

For the student, the problem becomes even worse when he is encouraged to see school judgments as judgments of himself *as a person* and not merely judgments about how well he performs on school tasks. Thus he may come to see himself not just as a *D* student in solving quadratic equations or dissecting a frog, but as a *D* human being. And although it is probably unintentional, we too often encourage this sort of evaluation both inside and outside our schools. Dropouts, for example, are too often encouraged to believe that if they are unemployed it is because they are not worthy of holding jobs and that they are not worthy of holding jobs because they have not finished high school. Seldom do we help them recognize that in our economy it is often the case that we have more workers than jobs and hence *some* workers will be unemployed no matter what their educational background.

Thus school judgments, no matter how accurate, are sometimes misinterpreted, or are used in place of other judgments. When this occurs, it seems clear that the consequences for the person judged can be destructive indeed. Educators are fond of arguing that one major task of the school is that of helping students achieve a sense of personal identity and worth. If that is a goal, much that happens within the school and much that is done with the information schools provide militates against achieving that goal.

Whatever the role of the school in giving the student a sense of personal worth, the school performs another major task. That is the task of training for and allocating to occupations. The relationship between schooling and occupation will be discussed at length in chapter 5. Here we focus only on how the performance of the school is likely to be perceived by student-clients.

Occupational Training and "Credentialism"

Some have argued that schools in our society have become the preemployment arm of industry, that they have become obsessed with the allocation function, and that as a result liberal, or liberating, education has been sacrificed. Whether or not this is true, it appears that failure in schools, *no matter what the content of the schooling,* works against the person in the allocation process. If the student decides to become a nuclear physicist, schooling offers the appropriate training. Success in the schools will speed the student toward his goal, while failure in the school will prevent him from reaching that goal. But suppose the student wants to be an insurance salesman or a store manager. Then the relationship between his schooling and job aspiration may not be as direct. Nevertheless, like the student who wants to be a physicist, this student's chances are best if he succeeds in school, and failure in school may prevent him from entering his chosen occupation. School failure is important today no matter what the content of the schooling. And although there are many occupations where one may need little formal schooling to perform satisfactorily, he may need many years of successful schooling to *get* the job.

What does all this mean? It suggests that although those trained through formal schooling to perform high-level technical skills may constitute a kind of "diploma elite" or "meritocracy," not *all* those in high-status positions or desired occupations gained entrance by learning complex skills and technical knowledge in schools, colleges, and universities. Rather, many succeed in gaining admission to the higher-status occupational groups because they have been successful in schools, *even though the content of the schooling is irrelevant to the job.* And many may have been denied access to jobs on the grounds of inadequate performance in schools, even when they might perform the job skills more proficiently than the person who succeeds in school and gets the job. Thus, it may be argued that schools contribute to an emphasis on ascription rather than achievement. That is, schools emphasize academic achievement as they define that achievement. Of course, as was pointed out in chapter 3, "academic achievement" may encompass far more than the subject matter covered by the formal curriculum. Nevertheless, this achievement in school comes to be used by the broader society as a fair appraisal of a person's ability to function well in a nonschool context. If the person achieves in school, merit is ascribed to him; if a person fails to achieve in school, merit is denied him and he may not be allowed to demonstrate merit in performing some desired out-of-school tasks. In short, academic achievement has become in some cases only another kind of ascription in the allocation process.

There are, of course, many cases in which the merging of training and allocation functions in the schools makes sense, for the content of the schooling is based, in part at least, on occupational preparation. But there remain many occupations for which educational, or intellectual, achievement, at least as it is formally defined and judged, is neither necessary for nor relevant to those occupations for which people are screened on the basis of school success. When a person is judged and allowed access to one of these occupations solely on the basis of success in school, then academic achievement has begun to function as an ascribed characteristic.

If academic achievement were recognized as a composite of judgments about how well the student conforms to the norms of the institution as well as how well he acquires particular skills, then perhaps the allocative function of the schools could be better understood. We need to be clearer about what should and should not be claimed about a person on the basis of what he does in school. Not to be clear about this is to place our youth in an unnecessarily threatening position. For example, within the school the student cannot escape the allocation process. He may, of course, be free to choose between a "general" or "liberal" education on the one hand, and professional or vocational education on the other. But whatever his choice, he will face the allocation process. School success will help him speed to other successes, no matter what the content of the schooling.[6] And failure will follow him quite as tenaciously. Many students are deluded,[7] many hurt. Many withdraw, rejecting both those who operate the schools and the society that would use schools in this way. And many of our attempts to improve schools—to make them continue to serve the same function more efficiently—can hardly be encouraging to students. Schools that are improved in this sense, after all, will become more threatening, not less so. More efficient schools will remove the only defense, other than withdrawing or revolting against the schools, that is available to today's student: the claim that schools frequently make serious errors in their judgments of students.

---

[6] This needs some qualification. Success in school does increase the likelihood of success in the world of work. But in recent years it has become painfully evident to those with high levels of formal education that they are not immune to suffering as the result of changes in the economy. In the 1960s many spoke of the insatiable need for talent in the technological state. In the early 1970s many highly trained scientists and engineers found themselves unemployed. Thus it has become clear that formal education does not guarantee success or even employment. It remains true, however, that failure in schools goes far toward guaranteeing failure outside the school. Success may not come as a result of schooling, but it almost certainly will not come without schooling.

[7] Perhaps the most deluded of all is the college student who, voicing the ideals of liberal education and damning the growing vocationalism on college campuses, proceeds to graduate school, undergoes some of the most narrow of all training and then moves, Ph.D. in hand, to another campus as a professor.

Summary

We have argued in this chapter that the contemporary conflict between youth and adults is genuine conflict, that it is a more intense conflict than in the past, that it is not a sign of decadence nor reason for despair, and that, finally, it is not evidence of the superior wisdom of either the young or the old. Changes in the society, we said, have presented the young with problems. They have responded and are responding to these problems in ways that threaten many of their elders.

The "youth revolution," it seems, is at least partially the result of our extending adolescence by postponing full adult status. This presents a particular problem to schools, for during the "extended youth" of today's young, they are in the schools. And the schools, for other reasons, have come to function in a way that extends and worsens the problems of the young. Schooling cannot, we asserted, be escaped by the young. Not only are young people required to spend time in schools, but they are also judged by the school. And the school judgments are then used to make crucial decisions about the "life chances" of students.

Accordingly, the school has become, from the point of view of the young, a very powerful and threatening institution. Not all youth respond in the same way, however. Many learn to accept—or at least cope with—the institution. Others try to withdraw or to pretend that they do not care, or to give up and simply let those who control the schools do what they may. Still others will neither accept nor give up, but choose to fight. Educators will have to learn to deal with all these responses. This may mean that the educator's life, from time to time, will not be a pleasant one. But then he will have many of the nation's youth as company.

References

Altbach, Philip G., and Laufer, Robert S. *The New Pilgrims: Youth Protest in Transition.* New York: David McKay, 1972.

Clark, Burton R. *Educating the Expert Society.* San Francisco: Chandler, 1962.

Coleman, James S. *The Adolescent Society.* New York: Free Press of Glencoe, 1961.

Friedenberg, Edgar Z. *Coming of Age in America: Growth and Acquiescence.* New York: Vintage Books, 1965.

Goodman, Paul. *Compulsory Mis-éducation* and *The Community of Scholars.* New York: Vintage Books, 1966.

Hodgkinson, Harold L. *Education, Interaction, and Social Change.* Englewood Cliffs, N.J.: Prentice-Hall, 1967.

Sexton, Patricia Cayo. *The American School: A Sociological Analysis.* Englewood Cliffs, N.J.: Prentice-Hall, 1967.

Shostak, Arthur B. ed. *Sociology and Student Life.* New York: David McKay, 1971.

Silberman, Melvin L., ed. *The Experience of Schooling.* New York: Holt, Rinehart and Winston, 1971.

Discussion Questions

1. To what extent are the problems faced by the young in American society similar to those problems faced by:
    a. blacks, Chicanos, American Indians?
    b. the elderly?
    c. welfare recipients?
    d. women?

2. What steps might we take as a society if we wish to make education more important but schooling less important? Is it possible for a society to make formal schooling more important but education less important?

3. Should schooling credentials be demanded for some occupations but not for others? If so, what criteria would you suggest for deciding which occupations should limit membership to those with proper schooling credentials?

4. We hear a great deal today about the dangers of invasion of privacy. Do you regard the use of school records by those outside the school as an invasion of an individual's privacy? Why or why not?

5. With the lowering of the voting age to eighteen, the youth of America have increased greatly their political power. Would granting students increased power within schools and colleges solve the problems discussed in this chapter? Why or why not?

education,
occupation,
and the
social structure

3

In Part 3 we are primarily concerned with the relationships between schooling and the world of work and between schooling and equality of opportunity. How, for example, does the educational system adjust to changes in occupational needs? Many parents think of schools almost exclusively in terms of future jobs and future status. It is generally assumed that higher levels of education result in better jobs and more prestige for the individual. How does increased schooling affect performance on the job? Do members of different social and racial groups with equivalent educational level have equivalent job opportunities? Chapter 5, particularly, will elaborate and qualify this generalization.

Chapter 6 attempts to correct the many oversimplifications associated with discussions of equality of opportunity within the educational system and within society. Concern for equity is a major influence on educational policy throughout the world. Distinctions in definitions of equality may be subtle and must be carefully analyzed before the implications for educational change become clear.

CHAPTER FIVE

Schooling, Manpower, and Occupation

Learning an occupation is one of our most important activities after childhood. This learning consists, at a minimum, of acquiring job-related skills and developing acceptable employer-employee and employee-employee relationships. The situation is complicated, however, by modernization and technological change, which give rise to increasing division of labor and specialization.[1] Thus, modernization increases the number of occupational choices available and may, under

---

[1] The possible dangers of overspecialization have been the concern of philosophers and humanists for years. Buckminster Fuller, in contrast to many observers, suggests that the computer may counteract this danger:

I'm quite confident now that we are going to have to be really on our own. I would be very worried about the whole thing if it were not for biology and anthropology and the fact that all human tribes and all biological species become extinct through over-specialization. Specialization is inbred at the expense of general adaptability. When you've lost adaptability, then you are extinct. Man was becoming more and more specialized and developing enormous capability to produce energy, with nobody to coordinate him.

We were becoming so specialized that we were about to lose, when suddenly one of our civilization tools, the computer, which is an extension of our brain and can operate faster than our brain, came into being. I'm quite confident that the great antibody to our specialization is the computer. The computer and what we call automation are about to take over the specialization and force man back to his innate comprehensive role—to be really the humanist.*

* R. Buckminster Fuller, "Commitment to Humanity," *The Humanist* (May–June 1970): 33.

the push of egalitarian pressures, at the same time allow the individual more freedom of choice. Even after the initial occupational choice has been made, the problem has not been eliminated, for a person entering the work force will need to be retrained several times during his work life. In this chapter attention will be largely focused on the changing occupational structure (with heavy emphasis on the United States) and on the implications of such change on the inputs and output of the educational system.

Perspectives on Occupational Structure

Technological innovation, urbanization, and bureaucratization—among other forces—have given character to the changing occupational structure. These forces have been at work for some time in the more industrialized nations but are only now beginning to influence the nature of work in the less-developed nations. The latter tend to have a large percentage of their labor force in agriculture, and not only a relatively small number of persons in the technical and professional pursuits but also a limited variety of highly specialized occupations. Moreover, the nations at the earliest stages of development typically have very limited human resources and very limited capacity to absorb highly educated or skilled persons. Most developing nations have invested heavily in education only to learn that employment possibilities tend not to keep pace with expansion of educational output.

Concern for a match between employment possibilities (to a considerable extent a function of development) and the number and kind of graduates from the educational system is, of course, not limited to the less developed nations. This is a problem at all levels of development; witness, for example, the perennial but fluctuating unemployment in the United States. Moreover, in the industrialized nations, the advent of automation has created new instabilities in occupational structure and new problems in educational planning and vocational guidance.

Let us now focus directly on the changing occupational structure in the United States and its implications for education. The following offers a historical perspective on the development of the contemporary highly differentiated occupational structure:

> In early America, and in fact, in all of the plow-culture societies that dominated the world until the Industrial Revolution, most men were farmers. At the time of the American Revolution some nine out of every ten citizens were part of a farm family, and on the farm one does not go out to work; one's work is right there, and one spends most of life with the family and a relatively small number of neighbors. Even in the towns, many of the shops were family ventures. A common pattern in the small cities throughout the world of plow agriculture was to have the shop in one part of a building and the dwelling quarters for the family and assistants in another part of the same edifice. . . .
>
> The large number of institutions and associations through which the modern American seeks to satisfy his needs and the diversification and functional specialization of industry are both the results of a long process of social evolution. The evidence available indicates that men began their history with practically nothing but their bodies and minds and perhaps the use of sticks and stones for weapons and tools. Slowly and irregularly they made discoveries and accumulated inventions—both material and nonmaterial. They invented new tools, new languages, and new systems of social relations. The most basic process appears to have been the invention of tools and methods of production, including the development of power machinery and, recently, automation. As productive techniques improved and knowledge of them accumulated, larger numbers of human beings could exist. Larger aggregates of people tend to produce social systems with more institutions and associations. Larger communities also make more feasible the specialization of production, because larger markets mean that the production

of a specialized workman can easily be disposed of in trade for things produced by others. This specialization tends to result in production for sale and thus to promote trade, which in turn encourages specialization and probably invention. All these factors and many others have interacted upon each other in the long history of human productive effort.

This long slow irregular process seems on the whole to have gathered speed as it has gone along. Apparently there is a tendency for technical inventions to snowball. Within the last three centuries, even within the last decade, a veritable explosion has taken place, which has pushed the movement toward multiple organizations and industrial specialization to extremes never before known. It seems safe to say that never before in all the history of human kind has there been a relatively self-sufficient civilized country in which less than 10 per cent of its productive workers were engaged in farming. Nor has there been another nation in which such a vast number of people lived by contributing such minute specialties to the common productive scheme—and inedible specialties at that. Just imagine the confusion if oil drillers or airbag strippers or college professors or even cotton farmers had to live solely on things produced by themselves and their families.[2]

Additional data may be offered to supplement this picture and bring it up to date. In 1900 six occupational categories— engravers, locomotive engineers, brick masons, blacksmiths, metal molders, and shoemakers—accounted for one out of every four craftsmen in the United States. In 1967 they accounted for less than one in twenty. On the other side of the coin, in recent years new occupations have been appearing in large numbers. In July 1971, for example, the Sunday *New York Times* carried notices of employment opportunities for

---

[2] Charles B. Spaulding, "Occupations in American Society," in *An Introduction to Industrial Sociology* (San Francisco: Chandler, 1961), chap. 2, pp. 19–22.

such workers as systems engineers, computer programmers, planning managers, and digital specialists, occupations which were practically non-existent a decade earlier. The history of occupations in the United States shows both slow, persistent modifications and rapid, short-term shifts. The kinds of occupational change and the rapidity of the changes depend upon the differential impact of technology, war, peace, changing public and private tastes, and a number of other factors that make prediction of occupational structure an extremely hazardous activity. This uncertainty in turn frustrates the creation of educational policy designed to link education to the changing demands for knowledge and skills.

A more detailed picture of the future occupational results of changes currently taking place in the United States—and in other technologically advanced nations—requires answers to such questions as the following:

1. What is the extent to which technological innovation and elaboration will be applied to our full range of social problems?
2. Does cybernation—the use of automation and computers —imply that not only the unskilled but also many "brain-users" will become superfluous? (Since computers can design most of the objects we need, only the talent of those creative persons who might be called "designers" will be in great demand in the future.)
3. Does cybernation, because of its implications for rapid changes in job skills and because of its promise of increased leisure, mean the end of work as the focus of life for an increasing number of people?
4. Will biological engineering be practiced on any significant level to, say, alter the genetic code in the direction of increased intellectual potential?
5. Will social engineering be practiced on any significant level in the form of highly explicit educational planning, either in educational selection or in specifying acceptable output?

The Manpower Link Between Education and Work

Given the pressures for greater educational efficiency and effectiveness in the more developed as well as in the less developed societies, a great effort has been made over the last several years to quantify relationships between educational output and the skills needed by a particular economy or needed to attain an anticipated future economic level. Thus the concepts of human resource planning and manpower planning have evolved, and attempts to forecast manpower needs for particular nations have proliferated. More detailed discussion of the manpower and other approaches to educational planning will be offered in chapter 8. The comments here serve merely as an introduction to that topic within the context of this chapter.

The term *manpower* is used to denote the labor force, its size, and skill composition. Increasingly, in contemporary times the characteristics of available manpower (females are included) are considered to be the crucial element in a nation's economic health. A healthy and skilled labor force is viewed as a requisite for an industrializing society, and programs to foster such a desirable state occupy high-priority status among national goals in both the less developed and the highly developed societies.

Educational prerequisites are typically associated with most categories of manpower. Therefore, it is usually argued that the educational system has a major role in the allocation of young adults to various levels and kinds of occupation. Brookover describes this allocation process as follows:

> This allocation function begins in the early elementary grades and continues throughout the child's school career. The accumulation of teacher evaluations and student performance largely determines the level and type of education which each child will receive. This, in turn, structures the range of social statuses and occupations in which a person may perform as an adult. This process of allocation as performed by the school

involves both the system of grading and testing and the selection of curricula in which the student receives his formal education. The grading and testing process determines to a large measure both the level of education a student is likely to receive and the curricula to which he will be assigned. The student with low grades and low aptitude and achievement test scores in the elementary school is not likely to go much beyond the minimum required level of secondary education. Such students will receive a minimum amount of general education and are likely to be guided into vocational programs which provide minimum training for occupations requiring less skill and lower educational prerequisites. In a similar fashion, students with higher grades in various elementary and secondary school subjects and comparable aptitude and achievement test scores will be guided into higher levels of education. This allocation of the educational system has become much more complicated as a result of the ever-increasing proportion of the labor force which requires higher levels of education. Not only must a school assist in selecting mechanics and doctors by grading, promoting, or failing, and counseling, but a much higher proportion must be directed into the college and graduate levels of education and allocated to the various positions requiring such education.[3]

The following simple figure may help elaborate the main relationships existing between occupational structure, manpower needs, and educational demands. As this conceptualization suggests, the educational system prepares skilled and educated persons who may be thought of as forming a manpower system. Some of this manpower will return to run the educational system while other manpower will become inputs to a wide variety of industry systems. The dotted lines indicate that interindustry manpower flows exist and that the

---

[3] Wilbur B. Brookover and Sigmund Nosow, "Education for a Changing World of Work," U.S. Department of Health, Education, and Welfare, *A Sociological Analysis of Vocational Education in the United States,* appendix 3 (Washington, D.C.: U.S. Government Printing Office, 1963), pp. 32–33.

industry system, through identification of its manpower needs and so forth, may influence the functioning of the educational system. These seemingly simple relationships, however, may become complicated in a number of ways. For example, the educational system is not the only producer of qualified labor. Indeed, many persons question whether producing qualified labor should be viewed as an important educational function. Furthermore, as we will examine subsequently, the degree and manner in which schooling is capable of qualitatively altering the labor force is a matter of considerable controversy.

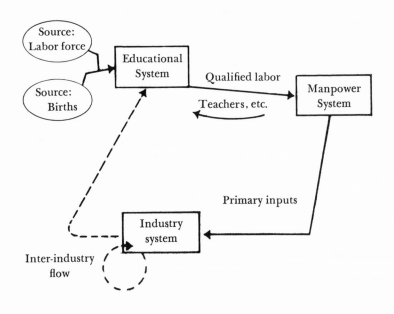

FIGURE 3

Education, Manpower, and Industry Systems

Trends in Occupational and Industrial Change

We have previously depicted the changing occupational structure as moving from one with a great proportion of unskilled workers to one with a great proportion of skilled workers. It is time now to elaborate on this crude description. Tables 6 and 7 provide perspective on the changing occupational structure and describe the estimated growth (or decline in the case of agriculture) in employment groups through 1970. Table 8 provides some comparative insight into the variations in occupational structure among nations. The greater proportion of workers in those occupations associated with advanced education or technical training among the more advanced nations is most apparent.

A number of major results of these occupational and industrial shifts are visible. First, as tables 6 and 7 indicate, there has been a tremendous change in the industrial distribution of the employed population. In about 1950 the service-producing sectors moved ahead of the goods-producing sections for the first time, and by the middle of the 1960s the former employed nearly 15 million more persons than the latter. Second, reflecting this shift, the number of white-collar occupations increased rapidly and by the early 1960s exceeded their blue-collar counterparts by several million. The white-collar occupations now include more than two out of every five workers. The farm group, on the other hand, has moved during the twentieth century from first to last place in the overall standings.

The two groups that played the major role in the increase of white-collar workers are the professional and clerical groups. By the early 1960s more than one out of every ten workers was a professional or technical person. Moreover, associated with the growth in numbers of professionals is the expanded demand for those workers identified as semiprofessional, paraprofessional, or technicians. The single fastest-growing category, however, has been the clerical occupations.

Another significant characteristic of the changing work scene is the associated population mobility. The working life of an individual is being characterized more and more by occupational and geographical mobility. Tables 9 and 10 show the extent of job change for working males in the United States. Distinct differences in mobility patterns may exist, however, between social classes.

TABLE 6

Major Occupational Groups of Employed Civilian Workers, United States, 1910, 1950, and 1959

Major Occupational Group	MILLIONS OF PERSONS			PERCENTAGE		
	1910	1950	1959	1910	1950	1959
Total	35.5	56.2	65.0	100.0	100.0	100.0
Professional, technical, and kindred workers	1.6	4.9	7.2	4.6	8.7	11.1
Managers, officials, and proprietors:	8.7	9.3	10.0	24.5	16.6	15.4
Farmers and farm managers	6.1	4.3	3.1	17.3	7.7	4.8
Managers, officials, and proprietors, except farm	2.6	5.0	6.9	7.2	8.9	10.6
Clerical and kindred workers	2.0	6.9	9.1	5.5	12.3	14.0
Sales workers	1.8	3.9	4.3	5.0	7.0	6.6
Craftsmen, foremen, and kindred workers	4.1	7.8	8.4	11.7	13.8	12.9
Operatives and kindred workers	5.0	11.9	11.6	14.1	21.1	17.9
Service workers	3.4	5.7	8.1	9.6	10.1	12.5
Laborers:	8.9	5.8	6.3	25.0	10.4	9.7
Farm laborers and foremen	4.7	2.4	2.5	13.4	4.3	3.8
Laborers, except farm and mine	4.1	3.4	3.8	11.6	6.1	5.9

SOURCE: Charles S. Spaulding, *An Introduction to Industrial Sociology* (San Francisco: Chandler, 1961) p. 28. Original source: The figures for 1910 and 1950 have been taken from Gladys L. Palmer and Ann R. Miller, "The Occupational and Industrial Distribution of Employment, 1910–1950," in *Manpower in the United States*, ed. William Haber et al. (New York: Harper and Brothers, 1954), chap. 6, with the permission of the publisher. The 1959 data are from U.S. Bureau of the Census, *Current Population Reports: Labor Force*, series P–57, no. 202 (Washington, D.C.: May 1959), p. 16. Totals not exact because of rounding.

TABLE 7

Major Industry Groups of Employed Civilian
Workers, United States, 1910 and 1950

Major Industry Group	MILLIONS OF PERSONS		PERCENTAGE	
	1910	1950	1910	1950
Total	35.6	56.2	100.0	100.0
Agriculture, forestry, and fisheries	11.0	7.0	31.0	12.4
Mining	.9	.9	2.8	1.7
Construction	2.2	3.5	6.1	6.2
Manufacturing	7.3	14.8	20.5	26.3
Transportation, communications, and other public utilities	3.1	4.4	8.7	7.9
Wholesale and retail trade	4.2	10.7	11.8	19.1
Finance, insurance, and real estate	.6	2.0	1.6	3.5
Business repair services	.3	1.4	.8	2.6
Personal services	3.5	3.6	9.8	6.3
Entertainment and recreation services	.2	.6	.5	1.0
Professional and related services	1.7	4.8	4.7	8.5
Public administration	.6	2.5	1.7	4.5

SOURCE: Spaulding, Introduction to Industrial Sociology, p. 28. Original source: Palmer and Miller, "Occupational and Industrial Distribution."

TABLE 8

Occupational Structure of the Total Labor Force
and Output per Worker, by Country

	Year	Productivity U.S.$	Percentage					Total
			0	1	2	3	4-9	
U.S.A.	1960	7,080	10.8	8.3	13.3	8.9	58.7	100.0
Canada	1961	5,120	9.7	6.3	12.9	8.9	62.1	100.0
Sweden	1960	3,410	11.6	2.0	8.5	9.5	68.4	100.0
Norway	1960	2,930	8.1	3.2	7.0	7.6	74.2	100.0
France	1961	2,820	9.7	2.0	7.1	9.1	72.2	100.0
U.K.	1961	2,670	8.7	2.7	13.1	9.8	65.8	100.0
Costa Rica	1963	1,090	5.2	1.3	5.2	8.0	80.2	100.0
Greece	1961	890	4.0	0.5	3.6	9.8	82.1	100.0
Peru	1961	740	3.7	1.3	3.3	7.7	84.0	100.0
Japan	1960	730	4.9	2.3	10.4	10.4	71.8	100.0
Portugal	1960	660	2.8	1.3	4.5	6.4	85.0	100.0
Egypt (UAR)	1960	520	3.2	1.1	3.7	8.2	83.9	100.0
Korea	1962	250	2.4	1.3	2.6	8.3	85.5	100.0
(Rep. of) India	1961	160	2.8	0.6	1.6	4.2	90.8	100.0

0 = Professional, technical, and related workers
1 = Administrative, executive, and managerial workers
2 = Clerical workers
3 = Sales workers
4-9 = All others

SOURCE: Yearbook of Labour Statistics (Geneva: International Labour Office, 1965).

TABLE 9

*Work Life and Job-Changing Expectancies
for Males, 1960–61 (at Beginning of
Age Interval)*

Age	Work Life Expectancy	Expected Number of Job Changes during Remaining Working Life	Job Life Expectancy
10–24 years	42.6	6.6	5.6
25–34	37.9	4.8	6.5
35–44	28.6	2.7	7.7
45–54	19.7	1.4	8.1
55–64	11.9	0.6	7.2
65 and over	6.3	0.2	4.7

SOURCE: S. H. Garfinkle. "Job Changing and Manpower Training," Manpower Report to U.S. Department of Labor, Office of Manpower, Automation and Training (Washington, D.C.: June 1964), p. 2.

TABLE 10

*Percentage of Male Workers Not Continuing on
One Job into the Second Year, by Age, January 1963*

Age	Percentage
25–34 years	55
35–44	60
45–49	58
50–54	60
55–59	58

SOURCE: Calculated from table 2, p. 4, in Garfinkle, "Job Changing and Manpower Training."
NOTE: The figures exclude men leaving jobs because of death.

One observer notes:

> The lower the individual on the occupational ladder,
> the more likely he is to move around horizontally with-
> out ever climbing the ladder. The jobs that he gets and
> holds are often unrelated to the jobs he has held and
> he tends not to hold them long.[4]

Education and the Economy

An extended discussion of the relationships between education and jobs leads naturally to a consideration of linkages
between education and the economy. Such questions arise as:
What is the contribution of education to economic growth?
What are the comparative returns from education and other
investments? To the society? To the individual? Curiosity in
these directions coupled with the growing costs of education
have stimulated a number of economists to focus their attention on the investment benefits of education or, using the
analogy of physical capital, "human capital."

Inquiries in the economics of education have tended toward several directions. Simple correlational studies of educational indices and measures of economic growth frequently
indicated a high statistical association. That is, changes in
measures of educational development, such as educational enrollments, tend to be associated with changes in economic
measures such as GNP per capita. Intercountry comparisons
along these lines have been useful in gaining perspective on
the range of educational efforts among countries at various
stages of development. Yet several problems beset this approach: the obtaining of comparable data on the indices
used; the unavailability of highly discriminating educational
indices; the failure to take into consideration the question of
time lag (presumably the contributions of education are
greater some years after it has been acquired) and question-
able utility of the approach for planning—since it leaves un-

---

[4] Quoted in Seymour L. Wolfbein, *Education and Training for Full Employment* (New York: Columbia University Press, 1962), p. 59.

answered the basic question of cause. Moreover, the range of the statistical association between education and growth rates among nations suggests that further study of this relationship is in order.

A second approach attempts to focus directly on the social or individual returns acquired from education. The results, if not the methodology, of these efforts are widely familiar in educational circles because of the popularization of findings that indicate how expected lifetime earnings increase with the completion of additional schooling. As is well known, variance in the earning power of people with different educational backgrounds is frequently great. Becker, for example, after extensive empirical investigation, concluded that "even after adjustment for differential ability, the private rate of return to a typical white male college graduate would be considerable, say, certainly more than 10 per cent." [5] However, there is immense technical difficulty in measuring the costs of schooling—not only in terms of buildings, instruction, and so on, but also in terms of what the student might have been earning had he not been in school (income foregone). And what is the relationship between advantages received by the individual and those accrued to society? Is proof that personal income increases with education also proof that national productivity increases? Apparently not always, for among other things, relating earnings to productivity assumes that higher earnings are received by persons with special skills that enable them to make a larger economic contribution. Such may not always be the case, as for example, when a skilled group is able to exercise market control.

Furthermore, even the relationship between personal income and level of education is cloudy. Does income increase proportionately with each year of schooling? Clearly it does not. Diplomas and degrees add more to the increment of income than warranted by the additional time spent in earning them. By way of extreme example, note the happening of a few years ago when many law schools began replacing their

[5] Gary Becker, *Human Capital* (New York: Columbia University Press, 1964), p. 88.

bachelor of law degree with a doctorate. Although their preparation has not been changed, the graduates under the new system automatically start at a higher civil-service classification if they work for the federal government than did graduates under the old system.

Other factors further complicate the picture. Discrimination on the basis of sex, race, and other factors makes the relationship between education and income less than straightforward. And how does one explain the differential earnings between, say, orthodontists and other specialized dentists with similar length of training?

A third technique used in gauging the contribution of education to economic growth has been called the residual approach. This method "consists of taking the total increase in economic output of a country over a given period of time, identifying as much of the total increase as possible with measurable inputs (physical capital and labor being the two inputs usually chosen), and then saying that the residual is attributable to the unspecified inputs." [6]

Schultz, who has been involved in pioneering efforts in studying the contribution of education and economic growth, offers the following analysis of U.S. data:

> Between 1929 and 1957, the real income of the United States doubled, increasing from 150 to 302 billion dollars in 1956 prices. The proportion attributed to human effort appears not to have changed appreciably between these two dates. If we take the share earned by labor to have been 75 per cent, its contribution increased from 112.5 to 226.5 billion dollars over this period. The labor force in 1929 consisted of 49.2 million persons, resulting in an earned income of $2,287.00 per member of the labor force. If the earnings per person were held constant, the labor force of 68.0 millions in 1957 would have earned 155.5 billion dollars. Labor, however, earned 226.5 billion dollars

[6] William G. Bowen, *Economic Aspects of Education* (Princeton, N.J.: Princeton University Press, 1964), p. 10.

or 71 billion dollars more than it would have had the earnings per person in the labor force not risen. How much of this 71 billion dollars is attributable to more education? [7]

Schultz then answers his own question by concluding that the increase in the education per person of the labor force between 1929 and 1957 explains 36 to 70 percent of the otherwise unexplained increase in earnings per worker.

While this approach strikes at the heart of the problem, in that it focuses on the educational contribution to the total national economic output, severe difficulty arises over the concept of *residual*. From the description of the approach quoted above, it can be seen that the residual might well be attributable to factors other than education. Since the residual could reflect a variety of economic and social factors, one author appropriately referred to it as a "measure of our ignorance." [8]

The explanation of *how* education contributes to the economy gives rise to wide conjecture and little in the way of hard evidence. The following represents a partial list of contributions as suggested in pertinent literature:

1. The educational system is the prime producer of the quantity and quality of skilled manpower needed in the economy.
2. Education, particularly at the higher levels, produces new techniques and ideas that may be directly utilized to modify the technology or organization of productivity.
3. Education increases a person's ability to learn, thereby making educated labor more malleable and retrainable than uneducated labor.
4. Education gives the future worker the discipline and attitudes (including a commitment to universal and

---

[7] Theodore W. Schultz, "Education and Economic Growth," in *Social Forces Influencing American Education,* National Society for the Study of Education Yearbook 1961 (Chicago: University of Chicago Press, 1961), pp. 79–82.

[8] Moses Abramovitz, *Resources and Output Trends in the United States Since 1870* (New York: National Bureau of Economic Research, 1956), p. 11.

achievement norms) that are congruent with the objectives of modern industry.

Do educational systems indeed function in this manner? Are such attributes and products the result of discernible curricula, teaching procedures, and the like? The following sections constitute a partial response to these questions.

Educational and Training Needs

The data presented on occupational trends indicate a shift toward jobs that require more education and training. An occupational structure with job patterns emphasizing professional, technical, and skilled workers requires a higher level of education than an agricultural and manual oriented economy. The changing demand for education is reflected in intergenerational differences in educational attainment.

As table 10 indicates, persons in the labor force by 1970 already showed a median educational attainment well beyond that typically required for completion of high school; indeed, by 1970 the median years of education for professional and managerial occupations were nearly the number required for a college degree. Thus, historically, all segments of the work force—indeed, the whole American population—are receiving an increasing amount of formal schooling.

The deviation in median years of schooling of "Negro and other races" (table 12) from the general labor force is worthy of note. Negroes and other minority groups tend to have a higher educational achievement than the median for the population in the higher-status occupations. These data support the frequent charge that "if you're black (or Puerto Rican or Indian or a woman), you've got to be better to make it." That is, minority groups have been required to over-educate themselves for the jobs with more prestige. Recent efforts of government and industry to meliorate this situation may be having an effect in making the educational levels of the groups comprising the labor force more similar. Data in the 1970s may alter the historical trends suggested in a comparison of tables 11 and 12.[9]

The fact that higher educational levels are generally associated with those occupational groups showing rapid expansion is usually taken to mean that an ever higher educational level is needed to perform the tasks of modern industry. As a corollary, it is frequently argued that those who have not obtained at least a high school diploma have neither the training nor the capacity for performing adequately in the modern economy. These views argue for more and more formal education for more and more people.

The advocates of manpower planning wittingly or unwittingly tend to support these trends. If occupations can be translated directly into explicit educational requirements, then the need for education, in these limited terms, is clearly defined. As a new occupational structure appears the requisite level and kind of schooling can be redefined. But, is there a difference between the amount of schooling and training needed for the job as opposed to the level of education demanded by the employer? Moreover, what is the changing mix of general education, vocational and professional education, and nonschool training.

Some studies suggest that there is indeed a significant difference between the educational level needed for adequate job performance and that preferred by employers. Jaffe examined just this relationship using the following rationale:

> . . . if modern technology requires well-educated
> workers, as some advocates claim, we should find that
> in those industries in which there have been very great

---

[9] The growing popularity of the junior college will probably add to the rising educational requirements for jobs. In 1966 there were more than a million students enrolled in more than 800 public and private junior colleges located in 49 of the 50 states. The enrollment predictions for 1970 are for 6 to 8 million students. It is estimated that by 1980 there will be 25 million youth of college age.*

* Charles C. Collins. *Junior College Student Personnel Programs: What They Are and What They Should Be* (Washington, D.C.: American Association of Junior Colleges, 1967), p. 1.

TABLE 11

Median Years of School Completed by the Employed Civilian Labor Force 18 Years and Over, by Sex, Occupation Group, and Color, Selected Dates, 1948–70. Total Population

Sex and occupation group	March 1970	March 1969	March 1968	March 1967	March 1966	March 1965	March 1964	March 1962	March 1959	March 1957	October 1952	October 1948[1]
TOTAL												
BOTH SEXES												
All occupation groups	12.4	12.4	12.3	12.3	12.3	12.2	12.2	12.1	12.0	11.7	10.9	10.6
Professional and managerial workers	14.9	14.9	14.8	14.7	14.6	14.2	14.0	13.9	13.5	13.2	12.9	12.8
Professional and technical workers	16.3	16.3	16.3	16.3	16.3	16.3	16.2	16.2	16.2	16+	16+	16+
Managers, officials, and proprietors	12.7	12.7	12.7	12.7	12.6	12.6	12.5	12.5	12.4	12.4	12.2	12.2
Farmers and farm laborers	9.3	9.3	9.1	8.9	8.8	8.7	8.7	8.7	8.6	8.5	8.3	8.0
Farmers and farm managers	(2)	(2)	(2)	9.1	8.9	8.8	8.8	8.8	8.7	8.6	8.5	8.2
Farm laborers and foreman	(2)	(2)	(2)	8.6	8.6	8.4	8.5	8.5	8.3	8.2	7.5	7.6

Clerical and sales workers	12.4	12.4	12.4	12.5	12.5	12.5	12.5	12.5	12.5	12.6	12.6	12.6
Clerical workers	(²)	12.5	12.5	12.5	12.5	12.5	12.5	12.5	12.5	12.6	12.6	12.6
Sales workers	(²)	12.3	12.4	12.4	12.5	12.5	12.5	12.5	12.5	12.6	12.6	12.6
Craftsmen, operatives, and laborers	9.0	9.2	9.7	10.0	10.4	10.7	10.8	11.0	11.1	11.2	11.4	11.6
Craftsmen and foremen	9.7	10.1	10.5	11.0	11.2	11.5	11.7	11.9	12.0	12.0	12.1	12.1
Operatives	9.1	9.1	9.5	9.9	10.1	10.5	10.6	10.7	10.8	11.0	11.1	11.3
Nonfarm laborers	8.0	8.3	8.5	8.6	8.9	9.3	9.5	9.5	9.5	9.8	10.0	10.5
Service workers	8.7	8.8	9.0	9.7	10.2	10.5	10.8	10.9	11.0	11.1	11.3	11.7
Private household workers	(²)	8.1	8.3	8.4	8.7	8.8	8.9	8.9	8.9	(²)	(²)	(²)
Other service workers	(²)	9.2	9.6	10.3	10.8	11.0	11.3	11.4	11.5	(²)	(²)	(²)
MALE												
All occupation groups	10.2	10.4	11.2	11.7	12.1	12.1	12.2	12.2	12.3	12.3	12.3	12.4
Professional and managerial workers	12.6	12.8	12.9	13.2	13.5	13.6	13.9	14.3	14.4	14.5	14.6	14.6
Professional and technical workers	16+	16+	16+	16.4	16.4	16.2	16.4	16.4	16.3	16.4	16.4	16.4
Managers, officials, and proprietors	12.2	12.2	12.4	12.4	12.5	12.6	12.6	12.7	12.7	12.8	12.8	12.8
Farmers and farm laborers	8.2	8.4	8.4	8.6	8.7	8.7	8.7	8.7	8.8	8.9	9.0	9.1
Farmers and farm managers	8.3	8.5	8.6	8.7	8.8	8.8	8.8	8.9	9.1	9.7	9.8	9.3

Sex and occupation group	March 1970	March 1969	March 1968	March 1967	March 1966	March 1965	March 1964	March 1962	March 1959	March 1957	October 1952	October 1948[1]
TOTAL												
MALE												
Farm laborers and foremen	8.9	8.4	8.3	8.2	7.9	8.0	8.2	8.3	7.7	7.4	7.2	7.8
Clerical and sales workers	12.7	12.7	12.6	12.6	12.6	12.6	12.6	12.6	12.5	12.5	12.4	12.4
Clerical workers	12.6	12.6	12.6	12.5	12.5	12.5	12.5	12.5	12.5	12.4	12.4	(2)
Sales workers	12.8	12.8	12.8	12.8	12.7	12.7	12.7	12.7	12.6	12.5	12.5	(2)
Craftsmen, operatives, and laborers	11.8	11.6	11.3	11.2	11.1	11.0	10.8	10.4	10.1	9.7	9.1	9.0
Craftsmen and foremen	12.1	12.1	12.0	12.0	11.8	11.7	11.5	11.2	11.0	10.5	10.1	9.7
Operatives	11.5	11.3	11.1	11.0	10.9	10.8	10.7	10.2	10.0	9.6	9.0	9.1
Nonfarm laborers	10.5	10.0	9.8	9.5	9.4	9.5	9.3	8.9	8.5	8.5	8.3	8.0
Service workers	12.0	11.7	11.6	11.4	11.3	11.1	10.6	10.3	10.1	(2)	(2)	9.0
Private household workers	(2)	(2)	(2)	(3)	(3)	(3)	(3)	(3)	(3)	(4)	(4)	(2)
Other service workers	(2)	(2)	(2)	11.5	11.3	11.2	10.6	10.4	10.1	9.0	8.8	(2)
FEMALE												
All occupation groups	12.4	12.4	12.4	12.4	12.3	12.3	12.3	12.3	12.2	12.1	12.0	11.7
Professional and managerial workers	15.5	15.5	15.5	15.3	15.3	15.0	15.0	14.7	14.0	14.4	14.0	13.7

Professional and technical workers	15.9	16+	16+	15.9	16.1	16.1	16.2	16.2	16.2	16.2	16.2	16.2
Managers, officials, and proprietors	12.1	12.2	12.3	12.2	12.4	12.4	12.4	12.5	12.4	12.5	12.5	12.6
Farmers and farm laborers	7.4	8.0	[2]	8.7	8.9	9.0	9.0	10.2	10.7	10.8	11.3	10.3
Farmers and farm managers	7.8	8.5	[4]	8.5	9.0	9.1	9.0	9.6	[3]	[2]	[2]	[2]
Farm laborers and foremen	7.3	7.9	8.7	8.8	8.9	9.0	9.0	10.4	10.7	[2]	[2]	[2]
Clerical and sales workers	12.4	12.4	12.4	12.4	12.5	12.5	12.5	12.5	12.5	12.5	12.5	12.5
Clerical workers	[2]	12.5	12.5	12.5	12.5	12.5	12.5	12.5	12.5	12.6	12.6	12.6
Sales workers	[2]	12.1	12.0	12.2	12.1	12.2	12.2	12.2	12.3	12.3	12.3	12.4
Craftsmen, operatives, and laborers	9.1	9.4	[2]	9.8	10.0	10.1	10.2	10.5	10.6	10.7	10.9	11.1
Craftsmen and foremen	10.4	11.5	11.3	11.2	11.2	11.2	11.8	12.1	11.5	12.1	12.2	12.1
Operatives	9.0	9.3	9.3	9.7	9.9	10.0	10.1	10.4	10.5	10.6	10.7	11.0
Nonfarm laborers	[4]	8.5	[4]	[3]	10.0	[3]	9.6	[3]	[3]	10.7	10.9	11.2
Service workers	8.5	8.8	9.0	9.5	10.2	10.4	10.6	10.7	10.8	10.9	11.2	11.5
Private household workers	[2]	8.1	8.3	8.4	8.7	8.8	8.9	8.9	8.9	8.8	8.9	9.1
Other service workers	[2]	9.7	10.2	10.5	11.1	11.2	11.4	11.5	11.5	11.6	11.9	12.0

SOURCE: *Manpower Report of the President,* April 1971 (U.S. Dept. of Labor, 1971), p. 247.
[1] Data for 1948 do not include persons 65 years and over.
[2] Not available.
[3] Median not shown where base is less than 100,000.
[4] Median not shown where base is less than 150,000.

TABLE 12

Median Years of School Completed by the Employed Civilian Labor Force 18 Years and Over, by Sex, Occupation Group, and Color, Selected Dates, 1959–70. Negro and Other Races

Sex and occupation group	NEGRO AND OTHER RACES [1]								
	March 1970	March 1969	March 1968	March 1967	March 1966	March 1965	March 1964	March 1962	March 1959
BOTH SEXES									
All occupation groups	11.7	11.3	11.1	10.8	10 5	10.5	10.1	9.6	8.6
Professional and managerial workers	15.8	15.7	16.1	16.0	16.1	16.1	15.4	14.7	15.1
Professional and technical workers	(2)	(2)	(2)	16.3	16.5	16.5	16.2	16.2	16.2
Managers, officials, and proprietors	(2)	(2)	(2)	12.2	12.4	11.8	10.7	11.0	8.4
Farmers and farm laborers	6.1	6.7	6.6	6.2	5.9	5.5	6.1	5.9	5.5
Farmers and farm managers	(2)	(2)	(2)	6.7	(3)	5.9	5.9	5.6	5.2
Farm laborers and foremen	(2)	(2)	(2)	6.0	5.8	5.3	6.2	6.0	5.7
Clerical and sales workers	12.6	12.6	12.6	12.5	12.5	12.6	12.5	12.4	12.5
Clerical workers	(2)	(2)	(2)	12.5	12.6	12.6	12.6	12.5	12.5
Sales workers	(2)	(2)	(2)	12.3	12.2	12.3	12.2	12.0	(3)
Craftsmen, operatives, and laborers	10.5	10.4	10.2	9.9	9.6	9.7	9.6	8.8	8.2
Craftsmen and foremen	(2)	(2)	(2)	10.2	10.5	10.4	10.6	9.0	9.3
Operatives	(2)	(2)	(2)	10.4	10.1	10.2	10.1	9.3	8.7

Nonfarm laborers	6.8	8.1	8.4	8.6	8.6	8.6	(2)	(2)	(2)
Service workers	8.8	9.2	9.3	9.8	9.7	9.8	9.8	9.8	10.3
Private household workers	7.8	8.3	8.6	8.9	8.6	8.5	(2)	(2)	(2)
Other service workers	9.8	10.2	10.0	10.4	10.6	10.7	(2)	(2)	(2)
MALE									
All occupation groups	8.2	9.0	9.7	10.1	10.0	10.3	10.7	10.8	11.1
Professional and managerial workers	14.8	12.8	15.4	16.0	15.7	14.6	15.4	15.0	14.6
Professional and technical workers	16.2	16.2	16.5	16.6	16.6	16.2	16.5	16.6	16.6
Managers, officials, and proprietors	(3)	10.7	11.0	11.5	12.1	12.1	12.3	12.4	12.4
Farmers and farm laborers	5.3	5.6	5.9	5.2	5.6	6.1	6.1	6.3	6.6
Farmers and farm managers	5.0	5.2	5.3	5.8	(3)	6.6	(2)	(2)	(2)
Farm laborers and foremen	5.5	5.7	6.2	(3)	5.5	5.8	(2)	(2)	(2)
Clerical and sales workers	12.4	12.4	12.3	12.5	12.5	12.4	12.5	12.5	12.6
Craftsmen, operatives, and laborers	7.9	8.6	9.4	9.6	9.4	9.5	10.0	10.2	10.2
Craftsmen and foremen	9.2	8.9	10.5	10.3	10.2	10.1	10.5	11.0	10.5
Operatives	8.4	8.9	10.0	10.0	9.9	10.0	10.4	10.6	10.6
Nonfarm laborers	6.7	8.1	8.3	8.6	8.5	8.6	8.9	8.8	9.2
Service workers	9.6	9.4	8.9	10.0	10.2	10.3	10.3	10.2	10.5
FEMALE									
All occupation groups	9.4	10.5	10.8	11.2	11.2	11.6	11.8	11.9	12.1
Professional and managerial workers	15.6	16.2	15.5	16.3	16.3	16.3	16.5	16.2	16.3
Farmers and farm laborers	(3)	(3)	(3)	(3)	(3)	(3)	(3)	(4)	(4)
Clerical and sales workers	12.5	12.5	12.6	12.6	12.5	12.6	12.6	12.6	12.6

NEGRO AND OTHER RACES [1]

Sex and occupation group	March 1970	March 1969	March 1968	March 1967	March 1966	March 1965	March 1964	March 1962	March 1959
FEMALE									
Craftsmen, operatives, and laborers	11.6	11.2	11.2	11.1	10.9	10.6	10.7	10.0	9.5
Service workers	10.2	9.7	9.6	9.6	9.5	9.7	9.5	9.2	8.6
Private household workers	8.7	8.4	8.4	8.5	8.6	8.9	8.6	8.3	7.8
Other service workers	11.2	10.9	11.0	11.0	10.8	10.7	10.8	10.7	10.0

SOURCE: *Manpower Report of the President*, April 1971 (Washington, D.C.: U.S. Government Printing Office, 1971), p. 247.

[1] Data by color not available prior to 1959.
[2] Not available.
[3] Median not shown where base is less than 100,000.
[4] Median not shown where base is less than 75,000.

increases in output per worker the educational level of the workers generally should have risen significantly. Conversely, in industries which experienced little, if any, increase in output per worker, presumably there was no "need" for the employed workers to have an increased amount of schooling.[10]

Jaffe arrived at the following conclusions based on data from the 1950 and 1960 censuses:

1. Virtually every occupational group experienced an (educational) increase during this period. Yet, "as of 1960, at least half of the employed were 'dropouts,' persons who had not graduated from high school."
2. ". . . there is little, if any, relationship between changes in output per worker and changes in educational levels. This generalization holds true for men and women and for clerical and sales workers as well as manual workers." [11]

There appears to be substantial, although not overwhelming, evidence that at least in many occupations diverse educational backgrounds may have little relation to performance. One study, for example, was conducted in 1967 on the productivity, turnover, and absenteeism of 585 former and present female workers in a Mississippi textile company. Results indicated that educational level was inversely related to performance.[12] Berg reports: "The education of high producers did not differ from that of low producers to any statistically significant degree, although the less productive ones were slightly better educated." [13] A second and comparable study in a southern U.S. hosiery-manufacturing plant produced similar findings. Berg comments: "Productivity and

---

[10] A. J. Jaffe, "Education and Automation" (Paper presented at the annual meeting of the Population Association of America, Chicago, Ill., 23 April 1965), pp. 35–36.
[11] Ibid., p. 37.
[12] Ivar Berg, Education and Jobs: The Great Training Robbery (New York: Praeger, 1970), p. 86.
[13] Ibid., pp. 87–88.

turnover were related to age, family stability, and a number of intraorganizational factors but they were *not* associated with educational achievement among day-shift workers; education was *inversely* related to both measures of performance among employees on the night shift in this company." [14]

The studies reported above were conducted on blue-collar workers; however, supporting research is available on technicians and white-collar workers. Data on professional and managerial workers do not appear to warrant hard generalization. In this group higher educational level often means higher income, yet educational achievement and evaluation of performance or potential do not appear to be closely associated.

These inferences are drawn from the results of a large number of empirical studies. Problems in sampling, comparability, and the limitation of empiricism itself argue for caution in making conclusions concerning education and job performance. At a minimum, however, doubts are reinforced regarding the benefits of education assumed by employers.

A high level of education among the population may, of course, be supported for other than occupational reasons. Indeed, as will be shown in chapter 6, in the United States and in other industrially advanced nations the human needs for increased productivity are not always the most influential determinants of educational policy. Secondly, although higher educational levels may not be *needed*, the fact remains that within a given industry and occupation those with higher educational achievement typically earn more. And irrespective of the undergirding rationale, pronounced discrimination in favor of the better educated persists in hiring practices.

It could also be argued that extending the years in school is a reflection of economic rationality in which people can indulge once they no longer have to worry about where the next meal is coming from. By postponing earnings for a few

---

[14] Ibid., p. 88.

years, they acquire higher earning power for the rest of their lives. There is no doubt that lifetime earnings rise with education. If, in addition, working life span also rises, the return on the investment in education, made by postponing the start of income by a few years, rises exponentially. In other words, extending the years of schooling is rational economic behavior. It "maximizes profits" far more effectively than anything the shrewdest businessman could ever have worked out.

There may be one more explanation of this sharp increase in years of schooling. People physically may not be able to stand a working life of fifty years. It may simply be too long. A part of the gain in working life span is therefore offset by postponing entrance into the labor force to a later age. Schooling is not seen primarily as desirable in itself nor as a means to a better livelihood. It is seen very largely as a way of "keeping the kids off the street," while still keeping them out of the labor force for a few years.[15]

Implications for Educational Change

The specific implications of occupational and industrial trends for formal schooling and for out-of-school training programs are subject to controversy. At a fairly high level of generality, considerable agreement may be noted. There is, for example, little disagreement that school curricula should reflect changes in scientific and technological thought. Secondly, there is recognition of the need at a general policy level for better coordination of the agencies that directly affect employment, e.g., the school, Selective Service agencies, state employment offices, training and retraining units of industry, and so on. Third, vocational counseling in the schools is being subjected to reanalysis. During the last several years attention to vocational counseling has been on the decline, influenced evidently by pressures on counselors to emphasize

---

[15] Peter F. Drucker, *The Age of Discontinuity* (New York: Harper and Row, 1969), pp. 283–84.

assistance to the college-bound youth. Presumably, college or "personal adjustment" counseling is more prestigious than vocational counseling. Fourth, there is increasing agreement that the sequence of schooling, then work, requires modification in the face of technological demands. Flexibility is required in the length of education and training programs and in the time of entry to such programs. The importance of training programs external to formal schooling is likely to increase. Along these lines Drucker observes:

> We need continuing education, that is, frequent return of the experienced and accomplished adult to formal learning . . . it makes absolutely no sense to attempt to give the youngster everything he will need. Indeed, it becomes absurd. He does not yet know what knowledge he will need ten or fifteen years hence. What he does know increasingly is that he needs things that are not yet available.
>
> If educators give any thought to the question, they assume that we should have both ever-extended schooling and continuing education. But the two are actually in opposition. Extended schooling assumes that we will cram more and more into the preparation for life and work. Continuing education assumes that school becomes integrated with life. Extended schooling still assumes that one can only learn before one becomes an adult. Continuing education assumes that one learns certain things best as an adult. Above all, extended schooling believes that the longer we keep the young away from work and life, the more they will have learned. Continuing education assumes, on the contrary, that the more experience in life and work people have, the more eager they will be to learn and the more capable they will be of learning.[16]

In many areas of school policy, however, controversy persists regarding appropriate priorities. Partly the problem lies

---

[16] Ibid., p. 324.

in the fact that educational and training programs may contribute in many different ways to industrial needs and occupational preparation. Advocates of extended basic or general education argue that in a period when specific skills required in any sector are changing rapidly, this kind of education promotes adaptability of workers. Others viewing the large amount of unemployment among unskilled youth recommend a vocational education in the form of specific training in skills. In spite of some evidence that vocational school (secondary school level) graduates obtain employment more quickly than graduates of general secondary schools, there appear to be strong reservations among many educators, economists, and employers about recommending extensive vocationalization of secondary education. One view of the relation of general and vocational education which is receiving considerable support from both vocational and general educators is described in the following:

> Readjustment to new occupations involves the development of a set of attitudes toward change as well as high levels of knowledge and basic academic skills. An understanding of the changing nature of the labor force and flexibility in attitudes toward work will greatly facilitate the process of retraining which will be necessary for large proportions of our working population in the years ahead. This suggests that the major part of our education for vocations should not be oriented to training for a specific occupational career. Rather, the vocational educational program should be designed to prepare youth for a continuing program of adult education throughout life. Vocational education which is designed to prepare an individual for a particular occupation before he completes his pre-service education may serve as a handicap rather than advantage to a large segment of the working force. Although workers in high-level professional jobs such as medicine, scientific research, and other fields may remain in essentially the same occupation throughout their lifetime, the rapidly changing technology in these fields

also necessitates a continuing education program. Fewer workers can look forward to a lifetime career in which the knowledge and skills which qualify them for a specific occupation in their youths will serve throughout their working life. An understanding of this fact and an education which prepares the individual for a continuing occupational growth and willingness to acquire new skills is probably the best vocational education that can be provided in our pre-service school program.[17]

Thus justification for extended general and liberal education may be found on either "practical" or humane grounds. Silberman puts it like this:

Students need to learn far more than the basic skills. Children who have just started school may still be in the labor force in the year 2030. For them, nothing could be more wildly impractical than an education designed to prepare them for specific vocations or professions or to facilitate their adjustment to the world as it is. To be practical, an education should prepare a man for work that does not yet exist and whose nature cannot even be imagined. This can be done only by teaching people how to learn, by giving them the kind of intellectual discipline that will enable them to apply man's accumulated wisdom to new problems as they arise, the kind of wisdom that will enable them to recognize new problems as they arise.

Education should prepare people not just to earn a living but to live a life: a creative, humane, and sensitive life. This means that the schools must provide a liberal, humanizing education. And the purpose of liberal education must be, and indeed always has been to educate educators—to turn out men and women who are capable of educating their families, their friends, their communities, and most important, themselves.[18]

[17] Brookover and Nosow, "Education for a Changing World," p. 38.

[18] Charles E. Silberman, "How the Public Schools Kill Dreams and Mutilate Minds," The Atlantic (June 1970): 83–84.

Going beyond such generalizations and attempting to enumerate the more specific implications of the changing world of work for teachers and administrators is both difficult and dangerous. Nevertheless, here are a few tentative conclusions based to a considerable extent on speculation:

1. Increased specialization and differentiation of labor will mean the development of new, specialized positions in education. On the other hand, new synthetic, interspecialty positions will also be created, especially in the managerial and research and development areas.
2. The tremendous demand on the time and energy of professionals in all fields will be reflected in education with the creation of a number of subprofessional and paraprofessional positions.
3. Since increased leisure will largely be the lot of the lesser educated, the lower schools and many private, public, sectarian, and nonsectarian agencies will increase their attention to recreation, "creative" hobbies, and related areas.
4. The planning of education for specific occupations will become even more difficult because of the unpredictability of the occupational effects of rapid technological change.
5. Uncertainty as to precise social and economic needs and conflicting educational demands by various social groups will allow increased experimentation and innovation—although tolerance for experimentation and innovation will be tempered by a higher sensitivity to privacy, which will, at times, frustrate attempts at evaluation.

Education as an Occupation

The occupations associated with education have vastly increased in number over the past few decades. No longer is it possible to rely on the traditional dichotomy of teacher and administrator to describe professional roles in the education system. In keeping with the differentiation of curriculum and the acceptance of new functions within the educational system, a large number of specializations have arisen, such as school psychologist, researcher, reading consultant, school librarian, finance and managerial experts, and a variety of specialists related to particular subject areas.

Concentrating on the precollegiate level, let us examine some of the unique characteristics and peculiar demands of the education occupation (or constellation of occupations). The sheer size of the teaching profession is one of its most distinguishing characteristics. In the United States nearly 2 million persons are engaged in teaching in the public elementary and secondary schools. One-third of all college graduates in the 1960s had been qualified to teach. A second feature of the teaching profession is its large number of females. Although sizable numbers of women are normally associated with teaching throughout the world, few, if any, other nations equal the high proportion of women teachers found in the United States. At the elementary level three out of every four teachers are women, and at the secondary level nearly half of the teachers are women. These two facts—the growth of the occupation resulting from mass education and the large numbers of women associated with it—have strongly influenced the status of the occupation.

We do not have an up-to-date profile of the characteristics of persons entering teaching and other educational careers. Research in the early 1960s does offer some opportunity to compare the college academic performance of those students preparing to teach with that of their classmates. Among the 1961 college graduates in the United States, persons entering teaching had poorer academic records in college than persons entering other occupations. This generalization holds true for both female and male entrants to teaching. Moreover, it appears that the men who left teaching to pursue different work were brighter (as measured by academic standing in college) than those who stayed. Although there is little in the way of supporting evidence generated by formal research, we believe these distinctions, particularly with reference to college attainments, to be less sharp in the 1970s.

In the past, several attempts have been made in the United

States to delineate the competencies and characteristics of American teachers. Frequently in these efforts sets of role definitions were developed and linked to factors of competence. The work of Kinney is somewhat typical. He concluded that all teachers played six roles:

1. *A Director of Learning.* This is the most widely recognized role, requiring ability to plan, administer, and evaluate learning activities.
2. *A Counselor and Guidance Worker.* It is generally recognized today that, to the degree that the school has a counseling program, it is carried on largely by the teachers, and primarily in the classroom.
3. *A Mediator of the Culture.* Our civilization and culture depend on the effectiveness of our schools. They require citizens with the ideals and values peculiar to a democracy, and skilled in the techniques of democratic procedure. In equipping her pupils with these attitudes, ideals and proficiencies the teacher becomes a mediator of the culture.
4. *A Member of the School Community.* In curriculum building, participating in the school government, extracurricular activities, and so on, the teacher is sharing in the responsibilities of the school program.
5. *A Liaison Between School and Community.* As a member of the community the teacher has a responsibility to interpret the educational program to the public. The effectiveness with which this is done determines, in large measure, the degree to which the public understands and cooperates in the educational program.
6. *A Member of the Profession.* Many of the important responsibilities are fulfilled by the teacher, not as an individual in the classroom, but as a member of the organized profession. In general, these include two general functions: Leadership in building the educational program in our society; and safeguarding the quality of membership and welfare of the members of the profession.[19]

---

[19] Lucien Kinney, *Measure of a Good Teacher* (San Francisco: California Teachers Association, 1952), pp. 11–12.

Kinney's list, compiled two decades ago, is of more than historical interest. Although all these roles still persist, nuances of differences have emerged since the 1950s. Teachers are still directors of learning; however, particularly in the larger educational systems, there is an emerging cadre of specialists who may assist the teacher in all aspects of this task. Teachers still counsel and guide; however, in many respects counseling and guidance have become specialized professional functions distinct from classroom teaching. Teachers remain mediators and models of culture. Yet in the 1970s they have to compete in these roles with the mass media which have become vastly expanded and more influential. Teachers obviously belong to a school community and participate in the development of school programs. The extent of such involvement varies greatly, however, depending on the degree of centralization of educational administration and specialization of school personnel. The teacher's role as liaison between school and community has varied in significance according to the status of the teacher and the extent to which education has become a focus of attention for the community. In 1970 it would be more appropriate to title the final role "A Member of the Profession and Union," if such a distinction is meaningful. In many urban areas the American Federation of Teachers has outstripped in membership and in power the local affiliates of the National Education Association. Both teacher groups have become much more aggressive during the two decades on matters of teacher welfare and on pedagogical issues.

Unlike many other occupations, teaching has yet to undergo a full technological revolution. There has been no widespread and rapid increase in teacher productivity—regardless of how productivity is measured. Teaching has been referred to as "man's oldest and most reactionary craft," and as Drucker observes: "Teaching is, in fact, the only traditional craft in which we have not yet fashioned the tools that make an ordinary person capable of superior performance." [20]

_____
[20] Drucker, *Age of Discontinuity*, p. 26.

While it is possible here to comment only briefly and superficially on education as an occupation, given the trenchant criticism recently leveled at teachers, a word in their defense may be in order. Influential contemporary critics of education such as Paul Goodman, Jonathan Kozol, John Holt, and Edgar Z. Friedenberg not only have been harsh in their evaluation of the competence of teachers but frequently have even impugned their motives. Referring to the conclusions that might be drawn from the writings of these authors, Silberman noted, "one might think that the schools are staffed by sadists and clods who are drawn into teaching by the lure of upward mobility and the opportunity to take out their anger . . ." [21]

Certainly there is evidence to suggest that many persons from the lower social classes enter teaching anticipating upward social mobility. Undoubtedly, there are also dull, frustrated, and even sadistic persons who teach. Yet the overwhelming conclusion of those who have the most intimate knowledge of American schools is that in general teachers are intelligent, honest, sympathetic, and committed. As Silberman further points out, the critics often reflect "the general snobbery of the educated upper-middle class toward the white-collar, lower-middle-class world of teachers, social workers, civil servants and policemen." [22]

Indeed, we would argue that in the face of low salaries, low occupational prestige (one study ranked teaching thirty-fifth from the top, just below building contractor and just above railroad engineer), the snobbery and bigotry of many intellectuals, the lack of consultation by administrators on serious matters, the menial tasks imposed on them, the absence of any but intrinsic rewards for a job well done—in the face of these conditions, persons of remarkably high quality make up the teaching profession. Moreover, recent experience of those in teacher education suggests that the quality is improving. More of today's talented youth are seeking teaching appointments than has been the case in the past. To some,

---

[21] Silberman, "How the Public Schools Kill Dreams," p. 90.
[22] Ibid., p. 80.

perhaps, teaching has been a way of avoiding the military draft. But another group (which includes a portion of this first group) has rejected—at least temporarily—many more lucrative opportunities to enter teaching because it appears to be a more moral activity than business and more socially relevant than many of the other professions. Furthermore, this increase in the popularity of teaching, coupled with demographic factors, is beginning to create a sizable surplus in the supply of teachers, particularly in some of the more attractive living areas of the nation. Will an excess in teacher supply drive the quality higher?

Table 13 indicates the past demand and projected future demand for teachers. Teacher demand is affected by the growth of enrollment, the replacement requirements, and new school programs that alter staffing. Because of lowering birth rates in the 1950s and 1960s, school enrollment is already beginning to grow at a slower pace. This part of the demand for teachers is becoming relatively small. The larger part of the demand for teachers has been for replacement of teachers dying or leaving the teaching profession. Table 13 also gives the estimated size of replacement demand. The third factor affecting demand relates to new or expanded programs, emphasis on compensatory education, use of paraprofessional workers, and so forth. Such changes could have drastic effects on the size of the teaching profession; however, they are extremely difficult to predict. Unless educational innovations require large numbers of additional teachers, the demand for teachers to be filled by new college graduates, which peaked in 1966, will continue to decline into the 1970s.

From a different perspective, the proportion of college graduates required to staff the elementary and secondary schools will decline from about 33 percent in 1966 to an estimated 15 percent in 1980.[23]

Thus teaching appears to be one profession where demand can be easily met by the graduates of colleges and universities.

----

[23] John K. Folger, Helen S. Astin, and Alan E. Bayer, *Human Resources and Higher Education* (New York: Russell Sage Foundation, 1970), p. 108.

TABLE 13

Projected Demand for New Elementary and Secondary Teachers, 1959–80 (figures in thousands)

Year	Demand Filled by New College Graduates	Demand Filled by Experienced Returnees	Total Demand	For Enrollment Growth	For Replacement
1959	125	41	166	55	111
1960	134	44	178	63	115
1961	137	46	183	63	120
1962	146	48	194	60	134
1963	156	52	208	80	128
1964	158	52	210	75	135
1965	157	52	209	70	139
Projected					
1966	173	57	230	82	148
1967	170	56	226	70	156
1968	166	55	221	61	160
1969	158	53	211	46	165
1970	161	53	214	46	168
1971	161	54	215	45	170
1972	155	52	207	35	172
1973	157	52	209	35	174
1974	158	52	210	35	175
1975	158	53	211	33	178
1976	147	49	196	15	181
1977	135	45	180	0	180
1978	135	45	180	0	180
1979	135	45	180	0	180
1980	135	45	180	0	180

SOURCE: Projections of replacement needs from U.S. Office of Education, Projections of Educational Statistics to 1975–76. Enrollment-growth projection from Commission on Human Resources and Advanced Education. Projections include the estimated effect of the Elementary and Secondary Education Act of 1965. Experienced returnees are projected at 25 percent of total demand.

But what of the question raised earlier? Will a rise in the quality of teaching be associated with this surplus of persons certified to teach? Given the difficulty of determining the effects of teaching on pupil behavior and achievement, perhaps the question is not worthy of being raised. Yet, though the output or results may remain a mystery, we can predict certain alternatives on the input side. A surplus of teachers may result in even further rigidity in state certification requirements for teaching. This, in turn, could restrict the opportunities of liberal arts graduates, e.g., writers, businessmen, or scientists, to qualify themselves to teach. Whether or not a trend in this direction is good or bad for the quality of teaching is highly debatable. What is clear is that for the first time in decades many educational administrators and school boards will be able to choose among candidates for teaching positions. How they will make such choices and efforts of the educational establishment to assist or frustrate these decisions should provide exciting substance for interested teachers, researchers, and citizens.

Summary

Modern society and economy require a constant development of new occupations and modification or disappearance of old ones. Efficiency demands that the numbers of workers and the qualities of workers be in relative harmony with occupational needs. The part played by formal education in occupational selection and training varies according to the stage of economic development but tends to be particularly significant in industrial and postindustrial societies.

The relation of education and occupation, however, is highly complex. A rising educational level of a population tends to raise the educational requirements for particular jobs; moreover, education influences the distribution of income between occupations. The relation of education and economy, then, is not a mechanical one of educational response to economic demand. Rather, education, to some extent, creates its own demand.

Further, the relationship of education and occupation may be affected by all other major social institutions. The family directly influences the vocational choice of youth and indirectly affects the occupational structure through political, religious, and other organizations. Ideology may affect the prestige of occupations, and various pressure groups can skew supply and demand. Discriminatory practices may effectively close off certain occupations to minority and ethnic groups. Likewise, certain occupations traditionally have been identified as being male or female.

Thus a sort of dilemma is apparent in the United States and other highly industrialized societies. The American egalitarian ethos suggests that we should give high value to the quality of performance. Consistently, however, we have rewarded occupational position far more. Educators have raised the question as to the possibility of restructuring the status system to include nonoccupational systems of esteem that will provide pupils with standards and incentives not related to the job. Many youth who are seeking new standards to guide their commitments and actions are asking the same question. Can success be presented as a concept relevant to many areas of human activity?

References

Berg, Ivar. *Education and Jobs: The Great Training Robbery.* New York: Praeger, 1970.

Brookover, Wilbur B., and Nosow, Sigmund. "A Sociological Analysis of Vocational Education in the United States." In U.S. Department of Health, Education, and Welfare, *Education for a Changing World of Work,* appendix 3. Washington, D.C.: U.S. Government Printing Office, 1963.

Spaulding, Charles B. *An Introduction to Industrial Sociology.* San Francisco: Chandler, 1961.

U.S. Department of Labor. *Manpower Research and Training Under the Manpower Development and Training Act.* Washington, D.C.: U.S. Government Printing Office, March 1964.

Venn, Grant. *Man, Education and Work: Post-Secondary Vocational and Technical Education.* Washington, D.C.: American Council on Education, 1964.

Discussion Questions

1. What is meant by "primary industry"? "secondary industry"? "tertiary industry"? How does the emphasis in an economy shift with advancing industrialization?

2. What have been the major changes in the occupational structure of the United States during the past 100 years?

3. How do changes in the occupational structure affect the demands on the school?

4. What advantages do employees envision from a hiring process that emphasizes educational achievement? Are these views justified? What justification is there for selecting teachers with higher educational qualifications?

5. What are the changing features of education as an occupation?

6. It has been suggested that there is a growing convergence of the training and allocative functions in the school. How is this related to:

    a. Changing manpower needs in the society?

    b. Increasing specialization of curricula?

    c. Increasing division of labor within the educational institution?

CHAPTER SIX

Schooling and the Concern for Equity

One of the major concerns of our contemporary times is with equity. Small and weak nations want parity at world forums with large and powerful nations. Within nations ethnic, religious, and linguistic minorities seek an end to the discrimination practiced by the majority or controlling group. Everywhere the educated young are asking for a larger voice in the institutions that affect their lives. And even the oldest and most fundamental basis for inequality, sex, is being challenged as women strive for equality with men in status, opportunity, and reward.

As we have argued in earlier chapters, modernization and industrialization imply greater social differentiation. Greater differentiation, in turn, provides more bases for allocation of status and prestige. Status distinctions are viewed as evil and invidious by certain ideologies; they are treated simply as a necessary fact of life by others.

However, the nature of systems of stratification has been a subject for continuing debate among social scientists. Two respected writers on the subject conclude: "Social inequality is . . . an unconsciously evolved device by which societies insure that the most important positions are conscientiously filled by the most qualified persons."[1] As Hodgkinson points out, these authors view the stratification system "as operating in an autonomous fashion, guided perhaps by some sort of invisible hand."[2] The precise way in which persons are lured to fulfill necessary tasks or come to occupy particular roles is not clear. But the assumption, in effect, is that every man has his price—a notion some would argue to be implicit in the system of free-enterprise capitalism. And so the basic question persists: Can a society survive without a system of social inequality?

Probably most historians and social scientists are dubious about the possibility in the immediate future of eliminating a hierarchy of prestige among individuals and groups.[3] Nevertheless, it need not be concluded that social inequality is a necessary condition for the continuation of society. The presence of inequality may be more a reflection of the ability of individuals and groups to make comparisons and evaluations of life about them than a manifestation of the fundamental ethics of society. Further, the criteria for making social demarcations and allocating status may vary widely and some standards, e.g., demonstrated talent, may be more socially acceptable than others, e.g., wealth.

Our focus in this chapter is on equity as it is reflected in the interaction of schooling, stratification systems, and social class. More particularly, we will concentrate, though not exclusively, on (1) why some persons or groups have better "life chances" than others; and (2) problems and policies of equalizing opportunity within the educational system and en-

---

[1] Kingsley Davis and Wilbert E. Moore, "Some Principles of Stratificaiton," *American Sociological Review* 10 (1945): 242–49. Also see Kingsley Davis, *Human Society* (New York: Macmillan, 1949).

[2] Harold L. Hodgkinson, *Education, Interaction and Social Change* (Englewood Cliffs, N.J.: Prentice-Hall, 1967), p. 82. The reference to "invisible hand" draws a parallel between this view of stratification and Adam Smith's view of the functioning of the economy.

[3] See, for example, Richard D. Schwartz, "Functional Alternatives to Inequality," *American Sociological Review* 20 (1955): 424–30; Walter Buckley, "Social Stratification and the Functional Theory of Social Differentiation," *American Sociological Review* 23 (1958): 369–75; and B. F. Skinner, *Walden Two* (New York: Macmillan, 1948).

hancing its potential for promoting social mobility. Again, the emphasis will be on the United States, with occasional, though not elaborate, reference to parallel questions or conditions in other societies.

Education and Social Stratification

The notion of social class, at least in a non-Marxian sense, implies that the people (of one social class) see themselves as being different (from the rest). It further suggests that there is observable or perceivable distinguishing behavior on the part of social class members not shared with the rest of society. Clearly, it is possible to conceive of societies as stratified without the strata or layers being social classes. Persons with similar eye or hair color might be said to occupy strata but not to form social classes. However, color of skin might bring us closer to the concept of class, if not caste. Nevertheless, physical distinctions as such are not pertinent to our discussion here, for the focus is only on that vertical hierarchy of strata that take on distinguishing social characteristics.[4]

In the language of the social sciences, those individuals who share a common status form a caste or class. Such social groups may be very explicit and visible, such as the religiously sanctioned castes that have historically existed in India and the color-based castes in the United States. Or they may be more implicit and subtle, as in the class structure of many contemporary societies based on wealth. When we speak of the stratification system in a society we often refer to the nature of its classes (or castes), their hierarchy, and their interrelationships.[5]

---

[4] Even though the terms *social class* and *social status* have been widely used for a number of years by social scientists and, indeed, have nearly become part of household language, debate continues as to the meaning of these concepts. Some scholars even argue that although the concept might be useful in historical studies it has little value "for the clarification of the data on wealth, power, and social status in the contemporary United States and much of Western society in general." Robert Nisbet, *Pacific Sociological Review* 2 (Spring 1959): 11. Particularly, there appears to be difficulty in demarcating class boundaries in the broad middle range of modern societies.

[5] See Kurt B. Mayer, "The Changing Shape of the American Class Structure," *Social Research* 30 (1963): 459.

We are interested not only in the social structure but also in the movement between social classes. The concept of social mobility has undergone little modification since Sorokin's original description:

> By horizontal social mobility . . . is meant the transition of an individual . . . from one social group to another situated in the same level. By vertical social mobility is meant the relations involved in a transition of an individual—from one stratum to another. According to the direction of the transition there are two types of vertical mobility: ascending and descending.[6]

Here our concern is limited to that form of social mobility known as *vertical mobility*. Vertical mobility is typically classified into intergenerational (between father and son or sometimes between grandfather and grandson) and intragenerational (the comparison of the status of the same person at two or more periods of time). A third approach is that of *stratum mobility*, which focuses on positional changes of occupational and social groups, e.g., whether skilled workers have improved their position relatively in society.

The most common indicator of social status is occupational prestige. Other indicators might be occupational skills, occupational income, consumption patterns, aspirations, or indeed any of the measures of stratification. Since a number of indicators are possible, social mobility studies may give rise to some sticky questions. For example, is a movement into the profession of higher prestige, but of less economic security, or lower income, a gain for an individual who moved from an occupation that stands lower in prestige but higher in other respects?

As noted earlier, every society apparently makes some distinction between individuals by ranking them on a scale of value. Such distinctions may rest on a variety of bases: sex, family line, wealth, occupation, talent, and so forth. In a

---

[6] Pitirim A. Sorokin, *Social Mobility* (New York: Harper and Brothers, 1927), p. 133.

primitive society the good hunter might be accorded the most prestige; in an agrarian society such distinction might go to the farmer. In former centuries many nations accorded the highest prestige to the priest or holy men. In China, for centuries prior to 1900, top status went to the scholar, while the merchant, at least in principle, was at the bottom. (Table 14 indicates several of the possible bases for status.)

In preindustrialized Europe social position was frequently perpetuated from generation to generation. The child's possibilities were circumscribed by his family. A boy's future station in life would likely be the same as that of his father. The family, serving both as a production unit and a social organization, delineated his economic responsibilities and bounded his social obligations.

Industrialization, particularly the factory system, undermined the role of the family as the major institution of production and socialization. The means of production became concentrated in the hands of a relatively few persons. Workers relinquished control over their labor in return for salaries. Because of the long hours on the job and the not infrequent replication in the community of the authority structure of the factory, the management group extended considerable influence over the total behavior of the workers.

The new environment created by industrialization gave rise to new social divisions. The new criterion for classification of status was control (or lack of it) over the production process. The social and economic gulf between management and labor or owners and workers tended to be great indeed. Max Weber interpreted the growth of capitalistic business and industry as a reflection of rationality applied to economic activity. As such, in spite of the potential danger of greedy owners or obstinate workers creating an unhealthy social milieu, the trend, according to Weber, should not be viewed as basically unattractive. To Karl Marx, however, the new basis for social division was one further extension of the historical conflict between privileged and oppressed.

TABLE 14

Some Scales of Reward or Status

Item	Stock or State Concept	Flow or Incidence Concept	Conventional Rubric
1	Wealth Assets Property	Income	"Economic" (production)
2	Level of living Possessions	Expenditures Consumption Leisure	"Economic" (consumption)
3	Prestige Honor Reputation, Fame Esteem	Deference Recognition, awards Concern, care, love Moral evaluation	"Social"
4	Education Knowledge Skill	Schooling Training	"Informational"
5	Style of life Status symbols Manners Language	Psychic income Satisfaction Utility Diversion	"Cultural"
6	Power Authority	Influence Decision-making	"Political"
7	Legal status Freedom	Exercise of rights, choice, participation, experience, punishment, deprivation, sanctions	"Civic"
8	Welfare	Life chances	(Composites, summation of 1–7)

SOURCE: Otis Dudley Duncan, "Social Stratification and Mobility," in *Indicators of Social Change,* ed. Eleanor Bernert Sheldon and Wilbert E. Moore (New York: Russell Sage Foundation, 1968), p. 687.

The history of all hitherto existing society is the history of class struggles.

Freeman and slave, patrician and plebian, lord and serf, guild-master and journeyman, in a word, oppressor and oppressed, stood in constant oppression to one another, carried on an uninterrupted, now hidden, now open fight, revolutionary reconstitution of society at large, or in the common ruin of the contending classes. . . . The modern bourgeois society that has sprouted from the ruins of feudal society has not done away with class antagonisms. It has established new classes, new conditions of oppression, new forms of struggle in place of the old ones.[7]

There is general agreement that industrialization has generated changes in patterns of social stratification. But have the evolving higher status positions reflected universal and achievement norms? A case could be made for the argument that industrialization undermined traditional privileges based on ownership of land and even contributed to the demise of social rank justified by divine origin. Yet, to repeat, was a person's position in the hierarchy of status—say in twentieth-century United States—more the result of individual efforts and talents than was one's position in nineteenth-century Europe? More directly pertinent to our central theme, to what extent has education assisted in providing footholds on the ladder to higher social status? Or to what extent has education encouraged social rigidity? In attempting to answer these questions, let us turn to the educational experience of the United States.

The educational response in nineteenth-century United States to the rapid rise of industrialization, particularly the manufacturing and service industries, was growth of the public educational system. There are contrasting views both of the stimuli and the results of this growth. In much of the literature on educational history the expansion of elementary

---

[7] Karl Marx and Friedrich Engels, "The Communist Manifesto," in *Essential Works of Marxism,* ed. Arthur P. Mendel (New York: Bantam Books, 1961), p. 13.

education, the extension of free education to the secondary level, and the state university movement represent progressive and humanitarian policies. More poor could go to school and once there the school could work its wonders—it would maximize the potential of the individual. This image was central to the American dream of evolving a classless, "melting-pot" society. Another view is expressed by Bowles, who sees the increased attention to schooling as serving only the needs of industry:

> Employers in the most rapidly growing sectors of the economy began to require more than obedience and punctuality in their workers: a change in motivational outlook was required. The new structure of production provided little built-in motivation. There were fewer jobs like farming and piece-rate work in manufacturing in which material reward was tied directly to effort. As work roles became more complicated and interrelated, the evaluation of the individual worker's performance became increasingly difficult. Employers began to look for workers who had internalized the production-related values of the firm's managers.
>
> The continued expansion of education was pressed by many who saw schooling as a means of producing these new forms of motivation and discipline . . .[8]

Empirical evidence to substantiate or refute these interpretations awaited the development of social and educational research during the last few decades. The lingering reluctance in the United States to accept the obvious presence of social classes was shattered by a series of community studies of social class structure. Among the early and most significant of these studies were those conducted by W. Lloyd Warner and his associates. Warner used two measures to place community members in social classes: (1) an "objective" measure involving such criteria as occupation, income, neighborhood, and

---

[8] Samuel Bowles, "Unequal Education and the Reproduction of the Social Division of Labor," in *Schooling in a Corporate Society,* ed. Martin Carnoy (New York: David McKay, 1972), pp. 42–43.

type of house; and (2) a measure of the individual's participation in community affairs.

Warner's studies identified a hierarchy of six classes in each of the communities studied. In descending order the names were: upper-upper, lower-upper, upper-middle, lower-middle, upper-lower, and lower-lower. Combining these into three basic levels, Warner concluded that the upper class comprised about 3 percent of the population, the middle class about 38 percent, and the lower class about 58 percent. Since most of these studies were conducted during the 1940s, conclusions regarding the shape of the class structure may have little relevance today. However, the characteristics or culture of the classes and the requisites for mobility between classes may have meaning.[9]

Warner gave considerable attention to the value orientations of each of the classes. A facile depiction of his descriptions has been offered by Kahl as follows: the upper classes, graceful living; the upper-middle class, career; the lower-middle class, respectability; the working class, get by; the lower class, apathy.[10]

Viewing the Warner studies some two decades after they were conducted, Hodgkinson offered these criticisms:

> First, Warner's methods were designed for the investigation of small, relatively closed communities, in which people knew each other and worked where they lived. The highly mobile population of today, with more than one car per family, living in a megapolitan or urban sprawl, contains a far greater fluidity of movement, and a greater flexibility of status judgments than was the case in Warner's small towns. Small, relatively closed communities still exist, of course, and are still being studied, but not as typical of America as a whole.

---

[9] The most comprehensive of these community studies is commonly referred to as the "Yankee City" study. For a single volume summary, see *Yankee City* (New Haven: Yale University Press, 1963). Yankee City is the researcher's name for Newburyport, Massachusetts.

[10] Joseph A. Kahl, *The American Class Structure* (New York: Holt, Rinehart and Winston, 1957), chap. 7, pp. 184–220.

Warner was never able to establish a clustering or central tendency within each of his social classes, which would be necessary to support his belief in a system of relatively closed, autonomous social classes. In every case, on virtually every measure, people spread evenly over his class categories making the cutting edges arbitrary indeed.[11]

Accepting this evidence on the existence of social classes, what can be said about their persistence over time, and the opportunity of individuals to move from one stratum to another? The difficulties in quantifying social stratification are several but the problems of making comparisons among nations are yet more numerous. Without elaborating on the complexities it is important to recognize with two scholars of the field that "any comparisons are at best only approximations." [12]

With this reservation in mind, table 15 may be examined. Mobility is here defined as movement between occupational levels of differing prestige. The index employed in table 15 utilizes the proportion of "occupational inheritance" (the proportion of sons remaining in their stratum of origin) within each stratum of each of the four countries. Great Britain has been used as the base nation. If the occupational inheritance is greater than 100, as with elite inheritance in the United States, then occupational inheritance is greater in the United States than in Great Britain.

Examining the tables further it may be noted:

1. The possibility of sons of elite fathers to inherit their fathers' socioeconomic status is greatest in the United States.
2. Middle-class and skilled sons in the United States have better chances of attaining elite status than their counterparts in other countries.

---

[11] Hodgkinson, *Education, Interaction, and Social Change,* pp. 91–92.
[12] Thomas Fox and S. M. Miller, "Intra Country Variations: Occupational Stratification and Mobility," in *Class, Status and Power,* ed. Reinhard Bendix and Seymour Martin Lipset (New York: Free Press, 1966), p. 574.

3. The semiskilled and unskilled of Japan have more opportunity to attain elite status than their counterparts in
the United States, Great Britain, or The Netherlands.
4. Middle-class inheritance is highest in Japan.
5. Japan also rates highest in unskilled socioeconomic inheritance, with the United States second.

Numerous other conclusions could be drawn from table 15.
Again, however, it should be emphasized, that the results of
available stratification studies are inconclusive. A well-re-
spected study, for example, by Rogoff (using data from an
analysis of marriage licenses issued in Marion County, Indiana) concluded, "No significant changes took place in over-all
mobility rates between 1910 and 1940." [13] Indeed, in the 1940s
many American sociologists argued that the American class
structure was rigid and perhaps becoming more so. Yet such
conclusions were subsequently rejected at a later date. Jackson
and Crockett, referring roughly to the period between 1945
and 1965, found scant evidence that the system of occupational
inheritance was growing more rigid.[14] A study by Blau and
Duncan supports this view by showing that much of the variation in intergenerational occupational mobility is not explained by the father's occupational status. Nevertheless, as
table 16 indicates, movements between father's occupation
and son's occupation in 1962 reflect a persistency between
generations. Thus in table 16 the percentages are higher
around the diagonal running from upper left to lower right,
suggesting a significant degree of occupational inheritance.[15]

In the early 1970s the rigidity argument appears to have
been reopened by young radical social scientists. Nevertheless,
sufficient evidence is still lacking in order to be able to give
unequivocal answers to such questions as: Are social classes
in the United States becoming more rigid? To what extent is

---

[13] Natalie Rogoff, *Recent Trends in Occupational Mobility* (Glencoe, Ill.:
Free Press, 1953), p. 49.

[14] Elton F. Jackson and Harry J. Crockett, Jr., "Occupational Mobility in
the United States: A Point Estimate and Trend Comparison," *American
Sociological Review* 29 (February 1964): 15.

[15] Peter M. Blau and Otis Dudley Duncan, *The American Occupational
Structure* (New York: John Wiley, 1967), p. 29.

TABLE 15

*Comparative Indices of Equality of Opportunity
for Entry into Elite, Middle-Class, Skilled,
Semiskilled, and Unskilled Strata
(Base, Great Britain)*

EQUALITY OF OPPORTUNITY FOR:

	Great Britain	Japan	Netherlands	United States
Elite	100	86	119	124
Middle class	19	34	26	46
Skilled	7	18	24	27
Semiskilled	3	15	7	7
Unskilled	2	15	6	12
$\overline{X}$ (Elite)	26.2	33.6	36.4	43.2
Middle class	100	143	92	137
Elite	88	93	53	70
Skilled	61	59	38	62
Semiskilled	39	61	27	42
Unskilled	36	42	18	37
$\overline{X}$ (Middle class)	64.8	79.6	45.6	69.6
Skilled	100	111	112	81
Semiskilled	84	59	72	56
Unskilled	80	19	69	45
Middle class	76	22	77	22
Elite	29	22	13	23
$\overline{X}$ (Skilled)	73.8	46.6	74.6	45.4
Semiskilled	100	81	148	144
Unskilled	75	19	132	67
Skilled	54	40	69	68
Middle class	36	23	45	30
Elite	16	20	19	12
$\overline{X}$ (Semiskilled)	56.2	36.6	82.6	64.2
Unskilled	100	233	74	144
Semiskilled	57	78	35	39
Skilled	48	44	21	26
Middle class	23	56	14	9
Elite	7	42	2	7
$\overline{X}$ (Unskilled)	47.0	90.6	29.2	45.0

SOURCE: Reinhard Bendix and Seymour Martin Lipset, eds., *Class, Status, and Power* (New York: Free Press, 1966), p. 580.

TABLE 16

Mobility from Father's Occupation to 1962 Occupation for Males Aged 25–64: Outflow Percentages

Father's Occupation	RESPONDENT'S OCCUPATION IN MARCH, 1962																	
	1	2	3	4	5	6	7	8	9	10	11	12	13	14	15	16	17	Total[a]
Professionals																		
1 Self-Empl.	16.7	31.9	9.9	9.5	4.4	4.0	1.4	2.0	1.8	2.2	2.6	1.6	1.8	.4	2.2	2.0	.8	100.0
2 Salaried	3.3	31.9	12.9	5.9	4.8	7.6	1.7	3.8	4.4	1.0	6.9	5.2	3.4	1.0	.6	.8	.2	100.0
3 Managers	3.5	22.6	19.4	6.2	7.9	7.6	1.1	5.4	5.3	3.1	4.0	2.5	1.5	1.1	.8	.5	.1	100.0
4 Salesmen, Other	4.1	17.6	21.2	13.0	9.3	5.3	3.5	2.8	5.4	1.9	2.6	3.7	1.7	.0	.8	1.0	.3	100.0
5 Proprietors	3.7	13.7	18.4	5.8	16.0	6.2	3.3	3.5	5.2	3.9	5.1	3.6	2.8	.5	1.2	1.1	.4	100.0
6 Clerical	2.2	23.5	11.2	5.9	5.1	8.8	1.3	6.6	7.1	1.8	3.8	4.6	5.6	1.0	1.8	1.3	.0	100.0
7 Salesmen, Retail	.7	13.7	14.1	8.8	11.5	6.4	2.7	5.8	3.4	3.1	8.8	5.1	4.6	.1	3.1	2.2	.0	100.0
Craftsmen																		
8 Mfg.	1.0	14.9	8.5	2.4	6.2	6.1	1.7	15.3	6.4	4.4	10.9	6.2	4.6	1.7	2.4	.4	.1	100.0
9 Other	.9	11.1	9.2	3.9	6.5	7.6	1.5	7.8	12.2	4.4	8.2	9.2	4.6	1.2	2.8	.9	.3	100.0
10 Construction	.9	6.7	7.1	2.6	8.3	7.9	.8	10.4	8.2	13.9	7.5	6.2	5.2	1.1	4.3	.8	.6	100.0

Operatives																		
11 Mfg.	1.0	8.6	5.3	2.7	5.6	6.0	1.4	12.2	7.3	3.2	17.9	6.9	5.1	4.0	3.5	.8	.6	100.0
12 Other	.6	11.5	5.1	2.5	6.6	6.3	1.4	7.1	9.3	4.9	10.4	12.5	5.9	2.1	4.2	.9	1.1	100.0
13 Service	.8	8.8	7.4	3.5	6.0	9.0	1.9	8.0	6.4	5.4	11.7	8.1	10.5	2.7	3.3	1.0	.2	100.0
Laborers																		
14 Mfg.	.0	6.0	5.3	.7	3.3	4.4	.7	10.7	6.0	2.8	18.1	9.4	9.4	7.1	5.8	1.7	.9	100.0
15 Other	.4	4.9	3.5	2.5	3.5	8.7	1.7	7.7	8.2	5.7	12.7	10.6	8.1	3.4	9.9	.9	1.1	100.0
16 Farmers	.6	4.2	4.1	1.2	6.0	4.3	1.1	5.6	6.7	5.8	10.2	8.6	4.8	2.4	5.4	16.4	3.9	100.0
17 Farm Laborers	.2	1.9	2.9	.6	4.0	3.5	1.2	6.4	6.6	5.8	13.1	10.8	7.5	3.2	9.2	5.7	9.4	100.0
Total[b]	1.4	10.2	7.9	3.1	7.0	6.1	1.5	7.2	7.1	4.9	9.9	7.6	5.5	2.1	4.3	5.2	1.7	100.0

SOURCE: Blau and Duncan, *American Occupational Structure*, p. 28.
NOTE: The last row in the table gives the percentage distribution of the total labor force in the various occupations. An index of the influence of occupational origins on occupational destinations can be obtained by dividing each value in the matrix by the corresponding figure in the total row. This ratio or index measures the extent to which mobility varies from pure "chance" which would be represented by a value of 1.0. After subjecting their data to this analysis Blau and Duncan conclude: "First, occupational inheritance is in all cases greater than expected on the assumption of independence of origins and destinations. . . . Second, social mobility in nevertheless pervasive. . . . Third, upward mobility . . . is more prevalent than downward mobility . . . and short-distance movements occur more often than long-distance ones." Ibid., p. 36.
ᵃ Rows as shown do not total 100.0 since men not in experienced civilian labor force are not shown separately.
ᵇ Includes men not reporting father's occupation.

America still the land of opportunity? How do mobility rates vary among industrialized nations?

When we turn directly to the interaction of education and social class the situation becomes only slightly clearer. The linkages between education and social mobility depend on a number of factors. Presumably, the proportion of the population that is educated relates to the prestige of those educated. Where higher education is a rare commodity, its recipients may be assimilated into the existing tiny social elite. Such has been the case, for example, in much of Latin America. Likewise, in Western Europe, which exhibits a fairly restricted structure of higher education, those who attend universities anticipate that graduation will place them in select social circles. In the United States, where more than half the persons of university age attend postsecondary education, college and university graduates will occupy a wide range of social and occupational statuses. Most frustrated of all may be university students of certain developing nations, such as the Philippines, Taiwan, and Korea, whose rapidly expanding university systems have far outstripped expansion of technical and professional jobs within the economy. For upward mobility to result, places must be available in the upper strata. Economic structure or a deliberate policy by a dominant elite could prohibit such movement.

But the value placed on a task or role does not depend solely on the relative scarcity of individuals to perform it. The value structure of a society may have deep roots in the history of its people. The overabundance of applicants for white-collar positions in many less developed nations has not always greatly altered the number of aspirants to those positions. Nor did the plethora of lawyers in many Latin nations sharply curtail (at least until recently) enrollments in law schools.

Clearly the people of the world see the educational system as the route to satisfactory jobs. Parents and governments expect education to satisfy the rising expectations of the poor and disenfranchised. From the rural villages of Africa and

Asia to the metropolitan areas of Europe, parents make sacrifices to keep their children in school long enough so that whatever it is that schools give will "stick." Billboards and media in the United States urge young people not to drop out of school and hint at dire consequences, in terms of occupational opportunity, if they do so.

Empirical studies on education and social mobility offer some further insights but fail to present as clear a picture as is desired. After an extensive review of the empirical studies on mobility, Duncan, for example, concluded that while there was no question that the occupational structure has been educationally upgraded, "The inference that educational attainment has been an increasingly important factor in occupational achievement . . . had best be regarded as tentative." [16]

The view of Tumin and Feldman appears to be more representative of that of many contemporary social scientists:

> From the point of view of a theory of stratification, education is the main dissolver of barriers to social mobility. Education opens up the class structure and keeps it fluid, permitting considerably more circulation through class positions than would otherwise be possible. Education, further, yields attitudes and skills relevant to economic development and such development, in turn, allows further opportunity for persons at lower ranks.[17]

One author, however, has forcefully argued that the significance of education in the promotion of vertical mobility tends to be exaggerated. Using data from Sweden, Great Britain, and the United States, Anderson demonstrates that the distribution of schooling is little different among the upwardly mobile sons and the downwardly mobile sons. Ability

[16] Otis Dudley Duncan, "Social Stratification and Mobility," in Sheldon and Moore, *Indicators of Social Change*, p. 687.

[17] Melvin Tumin and Arnold S. Feldman, *Social Class and Social Change in Puerto Rico* (Princeton: Princeton University Press, 1961), p. 7.

and associated motivation, independent of schooling, Anderson concludes, combine to play a more important role.[18]

Even if we accept what appears to be the consensus view that education is a "dissolver of barriers to social mobility," we still may ask for whom and for how many? Do large numbers of the poor, browns, and blacks acquire the sufficient amount of this dissolver? Or should the generalization be worded: For those few persons who are upwardly mobile, education is frequently a contributing factor? Tables 17 and 18, using data from the United States, may shed some light on these matters.

TABLE 17

College Attendance in 1967 Among
High School Graduates, by Family Income [a]

Family Income [b]	Percentage Who Did Not Attend College
Total	53.1
under $ 3,000	80.2
$ 3,000–$ 3,999	67.7
$ 4,000–$ 5,999	63.7
$ 6,000–$ 7,499	58.9
$ 7,500–$ 9,999	49.0
$10,000–$14,999	38.7
$15,000 and over	13.3

SOURCE: U.S. Department of Commerce, Bureau of the Census, *Current Population Report,* series p-20, no. 185, July 11, 1969, p. 6. College attendance refers to both two- and four-year institutions.

[a] Refers to individuals who were high school seniors in October 1965 and who subsequently graduated from high school.

[b] Family income for 12 months preceding October 1965.

---

[18] C. Arnold Anderson, "A Skeptical Note on Education and Mobility," *Education, Economy and Society,* ed. A. H. Halsey, Jean Floud, and C. Arnold Anderson (New York: Free Press, 1961), pp. 164–79.

Table 17 clearly indicates that children whose parents earn higher incomes tend to receive more years of schooling than children whose parents occupy positions lower in the occupational hierarchy. Bowles concludes "If we define social class standing by the income, occupation and educational level of the parents, a child from the 90th percentile in the class distribution may expect on the average to achieve over four and a half more years of schooling than a child from the 10th percentile." [19] While it is fairly common knowledge that "rich kids do better than poor kids" in schools, the magnitude of this advantage is frequently underestimated. Moreover, years of submersion in the culture of the school does not ameliorate the problem. Even among the students who successfully complete high school, the children from poorer families are much less likely to enter higher education.

What about the youth from lower social and economic groups who do succeed in acquiring an advanced education? Do they automatically advance up the social hierarchy? The answer would seem to be: Yes, but. . . . Since the common measure of social class is educational level, those who acquire, say, a university degree by definition may be placed in a certain social class. But since social class is linked to occupation and income we need also to look at the success in these directions of those from the lower social strata.

The situation perhaps is the clearest where race is a factor. Michael Reich concludes:

> . . . exploitation really begins in earnest when the black youth enters the labor market. A black worker with the same number of years of schooling and the same scores on achievement tests as a white worker receives much less income. The black worker cannot get as good a job because the better paying jobs are located too far from the ghetto, or because he was turned down by racist personnel agencies and employ-

---

[19] Bowles, "Unequal Education and the Reproduction of the Social Division of Labor," p. 46.

TABLE 18

Selected Measures of Educational Attainment for Persons 25 Years Old and Over, and 25 to 29 Years Old, by Color and Sex, 1960 and 1940: USA

Age, Color, Sex, and Years of School Completed	1960	1940
	hundred thousands	
25 years old and over		
Less than 5 years of school		
Male:		
white	29.3	47.7
nonwhite	87.7	136.7
Female:		
white	23.5	38.1
nonwhite	62.6	113.3
4 years of high school or more		
Male:		
white	169.7	101.3
nonwhite	98.3	44.9
Female:		
white	182.6	118.7
nonwhite	112.9	51.5
25 to 29 years old		
Less than 5 years of school		
Male:		
white	10.2	15.3
nonwhite	28.8	76.5
Female:		
white	7.3	11.6
nonwhite	16.1	44.7
4 years of high school or more		
Male:		
white	252.6	162.1
nonwhite	166.2	76.7
Female:		
white	260.6	181.3
nonwhite	182.8	89.3

SOURCE: Adapted from 1960 Census of Population, Vol. 1, Characteristics of the Population, Part 1, U.S. Summary, table 241; 1940 Census of Population, Vol. IV, U.S. Summary, table 39.

ers, or because a union denied admittance, or maybe because of an arrest record. Going to school after a certain point doesn't seem to increase a black person's job possibilities very much. The more educated a black person is, the greater is the disparity between his income and that of a white with the same schooling. The result: *in 1966 black college graduates earned less than white high-school dropouts.* And the higher the average wage or salary of an occupation, the lower the percentage of workers in that occupation who are black.[20]

Somewhat similar conclusions are presented by Blair in a comparative study of Mexican-American and European-American incomes and rates of return to schooling. On the basis of data from Santa Clara County (California), he concluded: "getting a high school diploma—or a college diploma —simply does not 'pay off' for Mexican Americans as much as it does for members of the Euro-American majority group." [21]

Even a report by the United States Department of Health, Education, and Welfare, which tends to paint a rosy picture of mobility opportunities in the United States, concludes:

> Most Negro men, regardless of their father's occupations, were [in the early 1960s] working at unskilled or semiskilled jobs—Negro men with the same schooling and the same family background as a comparable group of white men will have jobs of appreciably lower status.[22]

Expansion of educational enrollments and the rising educational level of the population have not equalized educational

---

[20] Michael Reich, "Economic Theories of Racism," in Carnoy, *Schooling in a Corporate Society*, p. 69.

[21] Philip M. Blair, "Job Discrimination and Education: Rates of Return to Education of Mexican-Americans and Euro-Americans in Santa Clara County, California," in Carnoy, *Schooling in a Corporate Society*, p. 97.

[22] *Toward a Social Report* (Washington, D.C.: U.S. Government Printing Office, 1969), pp. 22–25.

attainment among the various social classes. The following headings suffice reasonably well in summarizing the status of inequalities in education: (1) men and women; (2) geographic regions; (3) urban and rural; and (4) color groupings.

1. *Men and women.* The United States ranks very high among nations in terms of the educational opportunities provided for women. In fact, at the precollegiate level, a proportionately larger number of females are enrolled than males. Even in the United States, however, more men than women obtain college degrees.

Data from the United States and a number of European nations support the common assumption that achievement of higher education is frequently based on economic motives among lower-status families while obtaining a college education (particularly for girls) is often based on social motives among higher-status families. Irrespective of the family's financial status, a daughter's chance of attending college appears to be greatly enhanced if her father is well educated. The opposite condition exists for daughters of poorly educated fathers.

2. *Geographic regions.* Wide variation exists in the United States in terms of the educational attainment of the population. The states in the Northeast and in the Far West have the highest educational levels while those in the Southeast have the lowest educational levels. Somewhat similar variations may be seen as in comparing Northern and Southern Europe. Thus, educational attainment parallels indicators of economic development such as per capita income and industrial productivity.

3. *Urban and rural.* Much of the variation in educational attainment within the United States, and within other nations as well, can be attributed to differences in urban-rural composition of the population. The urban, when compared with the rural, style of living apparently requires and motivates a relatively high educational level. Moreover, educational facilities in cities tend to be more prevalent and more

accessible. In the United States, improved transportation and communication, increased geographic mobility of persons, and continual spread in urban influence are lessening the disparities between urban and rural educational levels. Indeed, the urban areas have divided into underprivileged and privileged ecological arrangements, i.e., slums and suburbs.

4. *Color groupings.* Comment has already been made on the persistent difference in educational attainment between white and nonwhite groups in the United States. Some data suggest that there has been a slight narrowing of the educational gap over the last few decades between whites and nonwhites. However, this appears to be largely the result of increased educational attainment of nonwhites at the pre-university levels. There is substantial evidence to suggest that at least until the mid-1960s not only had the nonwhite population been less well educated than the white population, but their net movement into higher education was much less than that of the whites.

Other data could be offered that would further refine the character of inequities in education. Ethnic and religious, as well as racial groups, reflect considerable variation in educational attainment. For example, in the United States Puerto Ricans tend to be at the bottom of the educational ladder, with American Indians and Negroes occupying the next higher rungs. Moreover, Americans of Northern and Western European stock have done better educationally than Americans of Southern European stock. Oriental groups, however, have had a remarkable record of intergenerational upward educational mobility. The educational level of the current generation of young adults of Japanese and Chinese stock compares very favorably with the educational level of any ethnic group. Historically, Protestants have acquired higher educational attainments than Catholics, although intrareligion variations are great.

While inequities in educational attainment appear likely to persist for some time to come, perhaps a little consolation may be taken in the fact that the pattern of distribution of educational attainment is more equal among younger persons. Furthermore, compared to other socioecenomic resources, e.g., income, occupational status, health expenditures, and so on, education appears to be one of the more equally distributed goods.

Selection and Allocation Within the Educational System

Many sorting operations take place within an educational system. The results of these operations not only determine what a student studies but also may directly or indirectly have a bearing on who his friends become, affect his attitude toward schooling, and influence his self-image. Selection and allocation procedures functioning throughout the period of schooling are likely to relate directly to the individual's post-school occupation and status. Let us now look at some of the formal and informal mechanisms that affect a student's educational career and his life chances.

School culture. Imbedded in the school culture are a number of factors that circumscribe educational and vocational choice. Status preferences exhibited by teachers and aspirations of student peers are among the important influencing factors. The extent of such influence may well be largely determined by the homogeneity of the student body. Even in nations such as the United States, where administrative designs are supposed to promote social heterogeneity within the schools, residential patterns and ad hoc pressure groups frequently provide effective counterweights by controlling the socioeconomic background of the school population.

Moreover, in higher education the traditions and prestige of the institution are based significantly on expectations and choice of occupation. In the United States, for example, one does not expect to find a "Harvard man" teaching secondary school. Thus the school provides an aspiration and motivation climate that is usually, but not always, additive to the family environment that sanctions the orientation of individual students.

Selection procedures. The manipulation of access to education is affected directly by the educational structure. As long as schooling above a minimal literacy was restricted to a small minority—as was the case until the twentieth century in the West, and still is the case in a few of the less-developed nations—individual decision (to seek an education) coupled with the school's informal appraisal of talent served the purposes of selection. However, the growth of schooling has been accompanied by a formalization of the selection procedure, as exemplified by the introduction of an increasingly elaborate technology of guidance, tests, and examinations. Some would argue that the technology is little more than a series of devices created by the "haves" to keep most of the "have nots" from getting an advanced education. IQ tests and various achievement examinations are notoriously culture based and strongly discriminate against the ethnic minorities and the poor. Specialists in educational evaluation are well aware of the limitations of the measuring instruments used in the schools and continually urge caution. Yet the technology grinds on.[23]

---

[23] It is perhaps common knowledge that IQ tests are "white, middle-class oriented." However, a ghetto IQ examination (The Soul Folk "Chitling" Test, or the Dove Counterbalance Intelligence Test) has also been developed using the language and culture of urban blacks as a foundation for the test items. The questions on this test include such items as:
 1. "T-Bone Walker" got famous for playing what? (a) Trombone; (b) Piano; (c) "T-Flute"; (d) Guitar; (e) "Hambone"; . . .
 5. If you throw the dice and "7" is showing on the top, what is facing down? (a) "Seven"; (b) "Snake eyes"; (c) "Boxcars"; (d) "Little Joes"; (e) "Eleven" . . . 8. Cheap "chitlings" (not the kind you purchase at a frozen-food counter) will taste rubbery unless they are cooked long enough. How soon can you quit cooking them to eat and enjoy them? (a) 15 minutes; (b) 8 hours; (c) 24 hours; (d) 1 week; (on a low flame); (e) 1 hour . . . 13. Hattie Mae Johnson is on the County. She has four children and her husband is now in jail for non-support, as he was unemployed and was not able to give her any money. Her welfare check is now $286.00 per month. Last night, she went out with the biggest player in town. If she got pregnant, then

The easing of restrictions on the movement from primary to secondary education in the more-developed societies has placed heavy strains on the university preparatory programs and has resulted in added significance for secondary school leaving and university entrance examinations. In an international study of access to higher education, Frank Bowles found four kinds of new requirements that were being superimposed on the more traditional ones:

1. Unstated policies that give preference to candidates whose studies have been broader than required in minimum preparation;
2. Examinations given by institutions of higher education covering more advanced subject matter than the standard examinations;
3. Interviews, informal examinations, and other additional requirements set by specific faculties and departments;
4. Deferred selection after entrance to the institution by examination following a period of general studies in the introductory year.[24]

While the above policies make the actual standard for admission more demanding than the stated requirements, Bowles also found that, particularly in many of the developing nations, informal policies existed that acted to lower the stated requirements. Thus, where there are shortages of qualified students—notably (in many countries) in mathematics, science, and science-related fields—adjustments may be made accordingly.

___

nine months from now, how much more will her welfare check be? (a) $80.00; (b) $2.00; (c) $35.00; (d) $150.00; (e) $100.00 . . .
23. And Jesus said, "Walk together children _____." (a) Don't you get weary. There's a great camp meeting; (b) For we shall overcome; (c) For the family that walks together talks together; (d) By your patience you will win your soul (Luke 21:9); (e) Find the things that are above, not the things that are on Earth (Col. 3:3).
Needless to say, most white high school and university students are not very bright as measured by this instrument.
[24] Frank Bowles, *Access to Higher Education* (New York: Columbia University Press, 1963), pp. 155–56.

Tracking. Tracking or other structural arrangements may be employed to facilitate specialization and to promote or obstruct transfer. A system of tracking or homogenous or interest grouping is common in most societies beyond the years of compulsory education. The rigidity and specificity of the tracks may vary—with a distinct trend in industrialized societies toward allowing easier transfer from one type of curriculum to another.

Herein lies a dilemma and a possible source of conflict. Not only must the "right" students in appropriate numbers be prepared for the "right" vocation, but a level of agreement must be reached regarding the requisites of a vocation. Compare, for example, the postures of the USSR, England, and the United States on this question. The extensive educational effort of the USSR is largely a commitment to that kind of scientific or technological education that will prepare Soviet citizens for well-defined, specialized, vocational tasks. There is little overt controversy regarding the education of generalists as opposed to the education of specialists. Given these conditions, tracking is highly explicit and rather rigid in the USSR—a situation which leads to early circumscription by vocational role.

England, which has a comparatively low density of scientists and professionals, in general offers the most striking contrasts. While, at the secondary and higher levels, England has for decades separated liberal and vocational preparation, the belief in the advantages of narrow vocational specialization has been much less strong. Thus, one finds in the Soviet Union that most managers, administrators, and the like, are technically trained, while their counterparts in England may well hold university degrees in history or literature.

The United States differs from both England and the USSR in that a much higher proportion of youth complete secondary education and enter college. At the secondary and, to some extent, in the immediate postsecondary years, American youth receive a broad, nonspecialized education providing considerable flexibility in terms of job preparation.

Moreover, arrangements for tracking or specialization lead to more of the same. When a secondary school student is placed in a commercial, academic, or any other special program, his future entry into some occupations is encouraged, while his entry into others is impeded. Each level and program in education provides its own credentials for further education and for subsequent work. Also, graduates of the elite educational tracks strive to preserve their educational justification for elitism. Because of the exercise of power by graduates, structural changes leading to further specialization—or even toward less specialization as in certain synthetic experiments in the social sciences—may be frustrated, or at least the achievement of parity by new programs in terms of prestige may be obstructed. There is a direct relationship between the status of an educational institution or an educational program and its occupational relationship. Thus, universities that prepare for higher professions are more prestigious than colleges that do not. Or academic secondary schools that offer a route to higher education are more prestigious than vocational secondary schools, which prepare directly for employment. Status differentials also may be found within an institution, such as between programs of the American comprehensive high school. Moreover, status rubs off both ways: to be defined as a high-status field, an occupation usually must have clearly designated programs of preparation in a university and, conversely, such programs confer relatively high status on graduates in perpetuity.

Equalizing Educational Opportunity

Democratic societies are committed to assuring opportunities for advancement for all segments of their populations. Indeed, many would argue that a prime measure of democracy lies precisely in its ability to distribute goods and services equally among the men and women, urban and rural, and majority and minority groups. As we have seen in all contemporary societies, education is both a reflection of policies of equity and an agency whose purported function is to increase opportunity.

Some perspective on equalizing educational opportunity from the vantage point of the European experience may be in order. The last two decades have been remarkable in educational reform in Europe. Most European educational systems have undergone great expansion; a number of experiments are in progress to make secondary schools more comprehensive in terms of clientele and program; and the notion of *planning* education in order to accomplish national objectives has become popular. Only recently, however, has a concern for equality of opportunity received the spotlight. One manifestation of this may be seen in the experience of the prestigious international group for research and policy studies called the Organization for Economic Cooperation and Development (OECD), which, in the 1960s, devoted an exceeding amount of attention to European educational reform and educational planning.[25]

It is significant that only after a decade of seminars and conferences on the relation of education and manpower, the problems of educational finance and the appraisal of methods of measuring the economic contributions of education, did OECD see fit to consider analysis of formal education in terms of social and educational equity.

As an expression of this change in interest, in 1965 an OECD-sponsored conference was held on "social objectives in educational planning." This conference, in spite of the broader implications of its title, focused largely on a number of case studies pertaining to the degree of equality of educational opportunity in the United States and various European countries. Although it was clear that most papers presented by Europeans defined equality in terms of equal ac-

---

[25] The Organization for Economic Cooperation and Development has the following member nations: Austria, Belgium, Canada, Denmark, France, the Federal Republic of Germany, Greece, Iceland, Ireland, Italy, Japan, Luxembourg, The Netherlands, Norway, Portugal, Spain, Sweden, Switzerland, Turkey, the United Kingdom, and the United States.

cess to education, some probed into the questions of parity in educational participation and in educational success. The findings of the conference have been summarized under these headings:

1. *Expansion of educational opportunity.* "In Europe and the United States educational expansion has not led automatically to more equal participation as between [*sic*] the social strata. . . . However, the evidence from Puerto Rico suggests that newly developing nations need not recapitulate this pattern."

2. *The structure of school systems.* "The shift from a dual system toward comprehensive secondary schools in Europe is expected to increase the participation of working-class students in higher education."

3. *Social class subculture and educability.* "The nature of a modern, industrialized society requires that all children undergo an education which is essentially intellectual in content. . . . " [26]

These conclusions hint at policy—but essentially policy that has been long accepted in the United States. In the contemporary United States the pertinent question becomes: What can be done in equalizing educational opportunities that goes beyond protecting the notion of comprehensiveness and intellectualness of schooling?

Before considering further matters of policy, a closer look at the concept of equity as it applies to education is in order. The term equality of opportunity may have many definitions: Coleman notes four that have emerged in the history of U.S. education:

1. Providing a free education up to a given level, which constituted the principal entry point to the labor force
2. Providing a common curriculum for all children, regardless of background

---

[26] Leila Sussman, "Summary Review by the Rapporteurs" in *Social Objectives in Educational Planning* (Paris: Organization for Economic Cooperation and Development, 1967), pp. 26–27.

3. Providing that children from diverse backgrounds attend the same school
4. Providing equality within a given locality, since local taxes provided the source of support for schools.[27]

Indeed, many of the great educational reforms in late nineteenth- and twentieth-century Europe and America have related to these very points: (1) the length of compulsory education; (2) the type of education received during the compulsory period, i.e., the degree of emphasis on homogeneous and integrative experiences; and (3) the extent of transfer among the selective tracts of postcompulsory education. The democratic and egalitarian ethos and the demands of modern industrial society in Western nations increasingly has been expressed in policy that allows an extended period for students to participate in a common educational culture.

But other definitions of educational equality are emerging. In the United States, in the planning of the design for the study of educational opportunity authorized by the Civil Rights Act of 1964, Coleman notes that five concepts of equality were to be taken into account, three in terms of inputs to the educational system, and two in terms of output.

1. Equality in terms of communities input, i.e., per-pupil expenditure, libraries, quality of teachers, etc.
2. Equality in terms of racial composition, i.e., integrated schools
3. Equality in terms of intangible inputs, such as teacher morale
4. Equality in terms of the effects of school on children of the same background
5. Equality in terms of the effects of the school on children of different backgrounds

The concentration on inputs is still the most common form of equalization. Equality of inputs whether conceived in terms of access or services implies that educational benefits

[27] James S. Coleman, "The Concept of Equality of Educational Opportunity," *Harvard Educational Review* 38, no. 1 (Winter 1968): 11, 16–18.

depend on talent and tenacity. We have already demonstrated that these qualities may be necessary but are not sufficient for educational success.

Equality of outputs focusing on effects has its own built-in assumptions. First, unlike reliance on inputs, equality in terms of output assumes that the educational system can create and control differential rates of learning. That is, the school through differential resource allocation can overcome the effects of home and environmentally induced behavior. Since the poor, black, brown, and women with equal educational credentials are paid less in the United States than white males, the persons from these minority groups must get from the schools more of what it takes to compete in the outside society. This of course raises the question concerning the extent to which the educational system can be realistically expected to counteract the influence of other systems within the society.

Of most interest perhaps to the policy makers is the fact that these concepts of equity have few if any intersections. Equality in terms of community inputs assumes the provision of equal services to the student. Equality in terms of output assumes unequal inputs. Indeed, if outputs are defined as equalization of opportunities to succeed in postschool experiences, then unequal outputs as well as unequal inputs are implied.

Considering first the input side, the search for policy to promote equalization between social groups has turned attention to possible structural changes within the educational system. In Europe, traditionally, dual systems of education separated at the age of ten or eleven those students preparing for higher education from those lower-achieving students destined for terminal education. Since World War II, there has been a distinct movement toward some form of comprehensive schooling. In this trend, European educators have looked to the long-standing experience of the United States with comprehensive schools.

The traditional argument put forth by American educators in favor of comprehensive schools has been in terms of its contribution to social cohesion and to equalization of opportunity for advanced education. The comprehensive school brings under the "same roof" youth from the whole spectrum and provides flexible programs of both college preparatory and terminal nature. While European educational reformers have generally disclaimed any desire to imitate the American pattern, some of the same advantages have been claimed for schooling which allows students from all social classes to extend their participation in a common culture.

Yet as many recent studies have indicated, the American comprehensive school has not obliterated class lines. This is not only because of de facto segregation according to study programs and social activities, but also is the result of the ecological context of American schools.

Thus, one finds even in the United States, where essentially a single public system of preuniversity education exists, that gross variations in the status of schools persist. In a study of urban schools, Herriott and St. John found that schools perceived by citizens to have a low socioeconomic status varied in a large number of ways from those perceived to have high socioeconomic status. For example, the lower the socioeconomic status of the school, the smaller the percentage of parents who attended school events, initiated talks with teachers, or gave their children adequate supervision. Further, the lower the socioeconomic status of the school, the lower the pupils' achievement level (particularly striking were the number of poor readers), the lower the interest in academic subjects and the greater the disciplinary problems.[28]

Herriott and St. John were also concerned in their study with examining hypotheses relating the role of the teacher to the socioeconomic status of the schools. These hypotheses were called (1) the culture-gap hypothesis; (2) the horizontal-mobility hypothesis; and (3) the hypothesis of inequality.

The culture-gap hypothesis refers to the assumption that teachers tend to be middle class in origin, status, and values and, therefore, very different from their lower-class pupils. It

[28] Robert E. Herriott and Nancy St. John, *Social Class and the Urban School* (New York: John Wiley, 1966), p. 204.

was found that indeed teachers were middle class in status, and also varied from pupils in terms of community origin (teachers were more apt to have been raised in a small town). However, "with respect to socio-economic level, it appears that there is as much of a discrepancy between the status of a teacher's own parents and the status of his pupil's parents in schools of highest as in schools of lowest SES." [29]

Those teachers in the schools of highest socioeconomic status tend to have lower status than their pupils, while those teachers in the schools of lowest socioeconomic status tend to have higher status than their pupils. The hypothesis that a greater cultural gap exists between teachers and pupils in schools of low than of high socioeconomic status was thus not supported in this study.

The hypothesis of horizontal mobility refers to the movement of teachers toward schools of higher status. This hypothesis received support from the Herriott-St. John study, which found that schools of lowest socioeconomic status did have proportionally more young and inexperienced teachers than did schools of highest socioeconomic status. Moreover, teachers in the lowest socioeconomic status were least satisfied with their current situation.

But does this situation support the hypothesis of inequality, that is, are schools of lowest socioeconomic status discriminated against with respect to staff? Are younger and less experienced (and less well paid) teachers poorer teachers? What is the effect of low teacher morale on the quality of instruction and on pupil-teacher relationships? Do less contented teachers work harder? In terms of educational qualifications there appears to be little difference between teachers from the schools with lowest socioeconomic status and those from the schools with the highest socioeconomic status. Thus, confirmation or rejection of the hypothesis of inequality depends on answers to the questions raised above—questions unanswerable at the present time.

---

[29] Ibid., p. 25. SES is the symbol for socioeconomic status.

Turning from teachers to the resources for expenditures, the picture again is not very bright as far as the less-advantaged pupils are concerned. Analyses in this direction require an understanding of changes in the tax base and the tax rate between school districts and of the changing patterns of expenditures on education by state and federal governments. It is generally assumed that although the differential wealth among school districts continues to be great, efforts at the state and national levels have gone a long way toward bringing about equalization in expenditures per pupil. Studies of financial inequalities, however, suggest that this view may be unduly optimistic. Federal and state funds do tend to flow in the direction of need, but not in the magnitude necessary.

Thomas, after studying the situation in Michigan, notes: "The inequalities remaining after the allocation of state aid are far from negligible . . . even after state aid had been allocated, the typical pupil in the bottom quintile was receiving an education whose cost—and probably quality—was only 64 percent of that provided to the typical pupil in the top quintile." [30] Danière found the same situation in Massachusetts after studying the effects of the formula for educational equalization in that state:

> Altogether, therefore, and subject to measures of actual performance in applications, it appears that the net result of "opening up" community choice through a "percentage equalization" formula is (1) a loss of opportunity to children of poorer or less responsible communities, (2) a persistent distortion of the original intent to the detriment of poorer communities and to the benefit of the richer ones and (3) a lack of clarity concerning the objectives and performance of the formula.[31]

---

[30] J. Alan Thomas, *School Finance and Educational Opportunity in Michigan* (Michigan Department of Education, 1968), p. 196.

[31] Andre Danière, "Cost-Benefit Analysis of General Purpose State School-Aid Formulas in Massachusetts" (Report to the Massachusetts Advisory Council on Education, 1969), pp. 32–33.

Similar conclusions have been reached regarding the efforts of a number of other states. The failure of higher governmental units to equalize finances, coupled with intradistrict disparities in resource allocation, e.g., qualification and experience of teachers, understandably have led to dissatisfaction among the poorer segments of the population. Dissatisfaction in turn has stimulated the search for alternatives in the control and allocation of educational services. Minority groups are beginning to question whether the best course of action is to fight (through the courts and school boards) for equal financing or to seek direct control of the education of their children.

There are those who argue that needed changes cannot be brought about under the present system of educational control. Portions of the urban black population in particular are advocating local community control of schools. Thus, the inner-city schools would no longer be part of a large, sprawling, urban education system but would be controlled, in terms of program, staff, and so on, by the immediate community. Some blacks have further argued that the appropriate model to adopt once community control is established is a school that would emphasize black values, black identity, and black community.

Another effort at altering educational inputs in such a way as to increase the possibility of school success lies in the area of compensatory education. Only one of the major compensatory programs, Head Start, will be discussed here.

· The research and conceptual base for Head Start was derived largely from the fields of psychology and child development. Experts in these fields generally believe that early childhood training can have highly significant effects on later learning and ability to cope with life's problems. Originally, Head Start was conceived as a small experimental program for a limited number of economically disadvantaged children. Its goals were to improve the life chances of these children in two aspects, directly through additional learning experiences and less directly through health, nutrition, and community development. However, by the mid-1960s, Head

Start had become a key weapon in the U.S. government's new "war on poverty." Nearly overnight, it had grown from a modest experiment to a national policy affecting hundreds of thousands of children. Head Start activities began to include not only summer programs but year long programs as well. Its purposes, in addition to the physical, cognitive and affective development of children, were extended to provide social services and instruction for parents.

Some fragmented research on individual projects and one large-scale evaluation of the overall program have generally indicated that Head Start, at best, has had but limited success in improving school success.[32] The early gains from summer programs in certain learning skills do not persist, and even the longer programs appear to offer few long-term advantages to the recipients. The major conclusions from the only overall study of Head Start to date have been summarized as follows:

1. Summer programs appear to be ineffective in producing any gains in cognitive and affective development that persist into the early elementary grades.
2. Full-year programs appear to be ineffective as measured by the tests of affective development used in the study, but are marginally effective in producing gains in cognitive development that could be detected in grades one, two, and three. Programs appeared to be of greater effectiveness for certain subgroups of centers, notably in mainly Negro centers, in scattered programs in the central cities, and in southeastern centers.
3. Head Start children, whether from summer or from full-year programs, still appear to be considerably below national norms for the standardized tests of language development and scholastic achievement, while performance on school readiness at grade one approaches the national norm.
4. Parents of Head Start enrollees voiced strong approval of the program and its influence on their children.[33]

---

[32] Walter Williams and John W. Evans, "The Politics of Evaluation: The Case of Head Start," *Annals* (September 1969): 118–32.
[33] Ibid., p. 125.

In all fairness, it should be pointed out that Head Start still has a number of strong supporters. It remains popular among parents in many communities where it has been in operation. Some teachers and researchers associated with Head Start feel that only a longitudinal study which examines not only successes but also changes in health and social skills can be considered a proper evaluation. The supporters, in effect, are saying that the data are not all in.

Some of the proponents of Head Start and other compensatory programs argue that poverty may be viewed as a distinctive culture or subculture.[34] The notion of a "culture of poverty" has been useful in concentrating attention on and stimulating study of the more subtle aspects of poverty. Quantitative measures of income, level of education, and type of housing are obviously inadequate for a complete enough understanding of the phenomenon to provide guidelines for the development of ameliorative policy. On the other hand, the concept "culture of poverty" is frequently associated with the idea of "poverty of culture" or cultural deprivation. These last two terms particularly run the danger of taking on ethnocentric characteristics of the dominant middle class and concentrating only on the "negative" aspects of the life of the poor. Moreover, focusing on such facets of the culture of poverty as family and community can lead to ignoring the constraints imposed by the larger society. Reissman has identified two of the features "in the culture and psychology of individuals in low-income groups" that may affect their success:

1. "most disadvantaged children are relatively slow in performing intellectual tasks;"
2. " . . . disadvantaged children are deficit in formal language." [35]

---

[34] See, for example, Oscar Lewis, "The Culture of Poverty," *Scientific American* 215, no. 4 (1966): 19–25; Charles A. Valentine, *Culture and Poverty: Critique and Counter Proposal* (Chicago: University of Chicago Press, 1968); Michael Harrington, *The Other America* (New York: Macmillan, 1962).

[35] Frank Reissman, "The Culturally Deprived Child: A New View," *School Life* 45 (April 1963): 5–7.

But, as Reissman and others have argued, even these traits need not be treated as wholly negative. Slowness is not the same as dullness. And the language handicap in school does not mean that the pupil is inarticulate in speech outside school.

There is probably no single key to improvement of the educational system for poor children. In addition to provision of compensatory education, teachers, materials, and facilities all have to be altered. The teacher's attitude toward the pupil and his potential may be crucial. Reissman reports that a group of poor youngsters commented that "they knew the minute they entered the room that the teacher didn't like them and that she didn't think they were going to do well in school." [36]

And the belief on the part of the teacher that children cannot do well often becomes a self-fulfilling prophecy. Therefore, perhaps the first ingredient for improvement is faith in the child's ability to progress. Accompanying this faith must be understanding. Teachers tend not to live near the schools that serve the poor and for this reason as well as other social barriers, they have little contact with the parents of the children they teach or the community in which the children live.

Apparently two missing ingredients for successful school programs are information and motivation. Parents may not understand the demands of the schools on their children, e.g., homework, available reference works, and so forth. In terms of motivation, poor youngsters may have fewer models of successful people to observe and emulate. The quality and extent of information and motivation may engender more confidence in both parents and children. Confidence in the ability to complete an educational program and in the eventual significance of education increases likelihood of success.

But will these actions be sufficient? The perspective that is taken on the nature of poverty may have profound consequences for courses of action. For example, "The emphasis on

---

[36] Ibid., p. 6.

upgrading those who live in situations of poverty is a little premature if the main ill is with our system of education. It is not feasible to bring individuals out of a condition of poverty into an outmoded educational framework, only to discover that they prefer to return to or maintain a style of life which the middle class cannot comprehend." [37] On the other hand, a focus on educational improvements, occupational opportunities, and the like may have limited effects when encountering constraints exerted by a culture of poverty.

While the confirming evidence is far from overwhelming, we believe that an alteration in the allocation of resources within the schools and compensatory experiences outside the schools can increase the educational performance of the poorer socioeconomic groups. Such policies are likely to be costly and to meet considerable political opposition. Moreover, because efforts in these directions require an extensive period of time before satisfactory results may be attained, commitment among educators and funding groups may wane before such programs can show a high percentage of success. The history of the U.S. government's involvement in new educational projects and in poverty programs in general suggests that a ridiculously quick "return" on the "investment" is expected.

The scope of programs needed to raise inputs to a level that would significantly improve the educational attainment of the poor is large indeed. Our inadequate insight into poverty as well as our ignorance about the capabilities of the schools will undoubtedly result in wasting a certain amount of time combating the symptoms and not the disease. Moreover, we must assume that corrective policies frequently will have a limited or unpredictable effect. We have already indicated some of the changes that might be attempted inside the school. Outside the school the following areas appear to cry out for action:

---

[37] Neil Eddington, "Comment," in *Poverty*, ed. Thomas Weaver and Alvin Magid (San Francisco: Chandler, 1969), p. 177.

1. *Health.* We know that the biological state of a person affects his way of knowing, feeling, and acting. Health services, health education, and family-planning programs need to be made available in greater quantity and improved quality.

2. *Housing.* Dirty, crowded, poorly lighted, and ill-ventilated living quarters are not conducive to physical nor mental health. Several studies have demonstrated a close association between a level of housing and success in school and work.

3. *Income.* The poor need more money. Through a better welfare system, through reduction in unemployment and underemployment, through a minimum salary law, through a negative income tax or other means, the income of poor families must be raised.

4. *Skills.* In order to better compete for the rewards in modern society, the poor must acquire "marketable" skills. It is probably a mistake to rely fully on the formal educational system to develop such skills. Some of them must also be acquired through training arrangements on the job.

But several observers argue that even a massive infusion of resources into the existing school and community structure is doomed to failure. Limiting attention to the schools, Carnoy argues that an alternative to the compensatory education approach is necessary.

> The alternative to this strategy is to reject the concept of a neutral school system implicit in the poor learners–good learners theory, and to assume instead that all groups of children can learn equally well but under different conditions. We may find that children's motivation is affected much more by the structure of the learning environment than by the number of years of teachers' academic preparation. The low probability of success of compensatory programs within the existing framework points to the need for new educational strategies for ethnic and racial minorities if equality is to be achieved.

. . . [We must] create an educational process which does not preconceive social roles or even clearly define what or how a child must learn. This process would require new kinds of tests to measure results and a different kind of teacher to produce them.

. . . The alternative strategy, then, creates equality among groups of children, by believing that all children are equally capable of learning and building an educational structure that allows children to express themselves in various ways, all equally acceptable. This alternative would thus start from the premise that the structure of learning in the schools must be changed to produce something called "equality" rather than accepting the present hierarchical, role reinforcing structure and attempting to overcome its deficiencies with massive infusions of traditional resources."[38]

Summary

A more equitable spread of wealth and an open social structure permitting mobility of the talented typically are among the stated goals of contemporary societies. It is usually assumed that the educational system is of major importance in the achievement of these goals. Through the knowledge, skills, commitments, and motivations they impart, schools increase the potential for occupational success and for social mobility.

There are, however, many uncertainties and qualifications in any interpretation of education as a leveler of society. As we have seen, in the United States educational credentials may not bring similar rewards to different social, ethnic, and racial groups. Further opportunities for acquiring education varies according to family status, place of residence, and so on. We are making strides in learning how to promote more equitable conditions within the educational system but two

---

[38] Martin Carnoy, "Is Compensatory Education Possible?" in *Schooling in a Corporate Society*, ed. Martin Carnoy (New York: David McKay, 197_, chap. 8.

haunting questions remain: Can and should the educational system allow educational programs and standards for evaluation to vary between groups of children? Will the superordinate society then extend the basis for its reward system to respond appropriately? The alternative to movement in these directions may well be a radically different arrangement for offering educational services set in a radically different society.

References

Anderson, C. Arnold. "A Skeptical Note on the Relation of Vertical Mobility to Education." *American Journal of Sociology* 66, no. 6 (May 1967): 560–70.

Bendix, Reinhard, and Lipset, Seymour M., eds. *Class, Status and Power: A Reader in Social Stratification.* 2nd ed. New York: Free Press, 1966.

Carnoy, Martin, ed. *Schooling in a Corporate Society.* New York: David McKay, 1972.

Floud, Jean, et al. *Social Class and Educational Opportunity.* London: Heinemann, 1957.

Fox, Thomas G., and Miller, S. M. "Economic, Political and Social Determinants of Mobility: An International Cross-Sectional Analysis." *Acta Sociologica,* 1966.

Fuchs, Estelle. *Pickets at the Gates.* New York: Free Press, 1966.

Halsey, A. H., Floud, Jean, and Anderson, C. Arnold. *Education, Economy and Society.* New York: Free Press, 1961. See especially part 2.

Miller, S. M. "Comparative Social Mobility." *Current Sociology* 9 (1960): 1–89.

Social Objectives in Educational Planning. Paris: Organization for Economic Cooperation and Development, 1967.

Smelser, Neil, and Lipset, Seymour M., eds. *Social Structure and Social Mobility in Economic Development.* Chicago: Aldine, 1966.

Discussion Questions

1. What is meant by "ascribed status"? What is meant by "achieved status"?

2. Do ascribed characteristics still affect a person's educational opportunities in the United States? Explain.

3. What social and educational changes during the past 25 years seem to make it more likely that a person's life chances will be more influenced by achieved characteristics than were those of people up to that time?

4. What is generally meant when it is asserted that the educational system is biased in favor of the "middle class"?

5. What status differentials would you expect within the American comprehensive high school?

6. Explain how residential location of ethnic and racial groups affects the educational opportunities provided for these groups. Is the problem of residential location becoming greater or less? Explain.

7. Some observers believe that teacher reaction to the minority child is often such that the child is further deprived of educational opportunity. What seem to be the major problems here? What might be done to ameliorate this situation?

8. What are the various approaches to the achievement of more equity within the educational system? Why do some observers argue that equality of educational opportunity can only be achieved under radically new educational arrangements?

choices
in control and planning
in education

4

Much of the content of Part 4 is most directly pertinent to the interests of administrators and policy makers. Teachers, of course, are affected by changing patterns of educational control and changing conceptions of educational planning. Moreover, teachers, through their professional organizations, are increasingly involved in policy formation. Indeed, the demarcation of teachers' prerogatives in decision making from those of the administration may well be a major issue in years to come.

Chapter 7 argues that certain political traditions and the influence of a growing bureaucratization have led to new patterns in the control of education. However, these new patterns are not evolving without conflict, and in certain communities a bitter struggle has emerged, pitting parents against the educational establishment.

In spite of the demands of certain groups for local educational control and the considerable publicity being received by those who argue for "freedom of choice" in matters of schooling, there is a decided trend toward increased attention to educational planning in the United States. The United States is, however, more reluctant than many nations to engage in elaborate forecasting of educational needs. Chapter 8 offers a broad view of the objectives and procedures of educational planning at national and subnational levels.

CHAPTER SEVEN

The Struggle for Educational Authority: The Public and the Professionals *

In earlier chapters we have pointed out that as a society we have come to attach a great deal more importance to formal schooling than was the case in the past. One result of this is that the school has become a threatening institution, both for the students and for parents. Success in formal schooling has become, for most of our young, a virtual prerequisite for success after they leave the schools. Teachers and administrators, although no doubt benefiting in some ways from the new importance of schooling, face greatly increased pressures. Parents and other concerned members of the public, now viewing schools with great concern, have become unwilling to tolerate what they view as inferior or unfair school practices.

Facing demands from the public for reform, educators have responded with a host of "innovations." But the modifications brought about by these innovations have not been sufficient to allay the public's concern and criticism. Inade-

---

* Much of this chapter is a revision of some of the arguments in Gerald M. Reagan and Thomas F. Green, "Polity, Profession and the Urban Public: The Dynamics of School Reform," Educational Policy Research Center, Syracuse University (Syracuse University Research Corporation, September 1967).

quacies abound, as do demands that the inadequacies be overcome. In short, it has been demanded of educators that they make the schools work; that they develop school practices which are effective, efficient, and equitable. And many segments of the public see the educators as not only unsuccessful, but as having failed to bring about even minimal improvement.

The dissatisfaction with the efforts of the educators has given new importance to a very old question. Rather than focusing simply on the question of *what* is to be done to improve our schools, many groups are raising with new force the question of *who* is to decide what is to be done. Most educators and most of the public want our schools improved, even though there are innumerable disagreements as to what should be changed and how the changes might be brought about. But there is further disagreement as to who should have the power and authority to decide. What part are educators to play in making such decisions and what part is to be played by the public? And if we say the public is to decide a certain issue, what constitutes the public? At what level is the decision to be made? When questions such as these are raised, the struggle is not so much one about reforms in schooling practices as it is a struggle for educational authority; a struggle not to establish some program of schooling, but to establish the role of some group in *deciding* educational questions. It is to this struggle for educational authority that we now turn.

The Public and the Control of Public Schools

There is a cherished notion in the history of American education that the public does, or at least ought to, control the public schools.

> The principle of authority most widely accepted by Americans for the administering of schools and colleges is one of public control vested in a board of lay-

men. The lay board is empowered legally to direct the organization and is held responsible for its welfare; it is to have final authority over the work of the employed staff. This principle relates to a wider belief, long a part of the American tradition, that schools and colleges should be directed ultimately by community interests rather than by professional personnel or government departments.[1]

Clark calls this view of educational authority the principle of authority as public trust. But what we *believe* to be the case about the control of schools and the facts of the matter are often not the same. Let us pursue this matter further.

It has been frequently suggested that the American school is an institution close to the people, that schools are "grass roots" institutions in the sense that they reflect community interests and needs. There is little doubt that this has been and is sometimes true. Many communities have controlled and do control their schools. But with some groups and some communities local control is more ritual than fact. And increasingly, when citizens concerned with problems of schooling attempt to influence educational decision making they find it difficult to do so. Indeed, in many cases they find themselves virtually powerless. Schools often prove resistant to change, and educators seem isolated from, and unresponsive to, the pressures brought by the citizenry. Schools, some groups have argued, seem to have become "public-proofed" as the result of an upward drift of educational decision making, the bureaucratization of schools, and the "professionalization" of school personnel.

The upward drift of decision making. Many educational decisions, once made at the local- or community-school level, seem now to be made at higher levels. Many factors have contributed to this "upward drift," which has not been limited to educational decisions.

---

[1] Burton Clark, *Educating the Expert Society* (San Francisco: Chandler, 1962), p. 152.

> An important axiom in political science is that when one level of government is unable or unwilling to meet the desires and needs of people, assistance is sought from the next higher level of government.[2]

Evidence in support of this axiom is great indeed in the case of educational decision making. The authority of state and federal government is used more and more in setting and implementing educational policy. Local political units, including school systems, have been seen as either unable or unwilling to bring about needed changes. As the demand for changes have increased, these units have simply been by-passed. Thus, much educational policy has come to be seen as a problem that is properly, and more effectively and efficiently, dealt with at the state and federal levels. Apparently the traditional demands for "local control" and "local autonomy" of schools have lost much of their persuasiveness for many people.

The increased activity on school matters by state and federal governments has undoubtedly wrought some substantial changes in schools. Yet the changes brought about have not been sufficient to stem the tide of criticism of schools. The reforms initiated have not been accompanied by a decrease in the demand for reform. In some quarters it seems that the demands for change continue to increase rather than decrease. Why should this be? A partial answer may be that some groups and some communities are convinced that even though the changes made thus far may be important, those changes have not been sufficient to improve substantially the educational opportunities available to their youth. Still another part of the answer may be that a growing number of groups within our society seem to have become convinced, rightly or wrongly, that it is within the power of the school to improve the social lot of their children. The increased de-

---

[2] B. J. Chandler, "Forces Influencing Urban Schools," in *Education in Urban Society*, eds. B. J. Chandler, Lindley J. Stiles, and John I. Kitsuse (New York: Dodd, Mead, 1962), p. 6.

mands may also in part be a reflection of a growing ability and willingness of traditionally silent groups to articulate their educational concerns.

There is an additional factor that helps to account for the increasing demands for changes in the schools. For some groups, and particularly those in the inner city, many of the changes made thus far in schools have seemed, like Cinderella's carriage, to turn into a pumpkin. The reforms have promised much and delivered little. Since highly lauded changes from above frequently have had meager results, additional reforms from above have less appeal. When those who control school policies cannot seem to make the schools work, attention is redirected to the question of how those supposedly served by the school can bring about changes within that school. Although our traditional belief indicates that schools are directed by those whom they serve, the facts often contradict that belief.

In our political ritualizations we tell ourselves that in our system of government and of education we allow for diverse interest groups to contend, and that it is in the crucible of public debate and discussion that our political and educational decisions are made. When decisions are made in this way, our ritual continues, the result is majority rule, with a healthy and firm respect for minority rights. But such ritualization or sloganizing may mislead. The claim to decision by majority rule, for example, is misleading unless we specify the government level at which the decision is to be made, the level of the "public" at which the decision is made. When we speak of the advantages of majority rule it may be that we assume automatically that the majority to which we refer is the majority of those most directly affected by the decisions to be made. Certainly we would not claim that every decision, or even most decisions, should be made by a majority of *all* the people in a state or city. For example, if we were to argue that a family should operate on the basis of majority rule, we would presuppose that there is a range of decisions properly made at the family level, and that it is for *that range of decisions* that the majority is to be the majority of family members. And we might also hold that there are ranges of community decisions, city decisions, state decisions, and national decisions. If we make such assumptions about levels of educational decision making, why do we sometimes move a decision from a lower to a higher level? Why do we take a certain range of educational decisions from the level of a neighborhood school and relocate those decisions at a higher level?

When we turn to higher levels of government to bring about changes in schools, we may appeal to either of two assumptions. First, we may assume the problem that the reform is intended to solve has, for some reason, become a more general problem, a problem affecting a wider community. If we turn from individual school systems to a statewide system of policies to help solve the problem of prekindergarten education, we may do so because we hold that the problem is no longer merely local but is one that directly affects all the people of the state. Statewide problems, we might argue, should be dealt with at the level of the state government. The second assumption to which we might appeal when moving decisions to a higher level is that there is a problem, local in nature, which must be dealt with and which is not being attended to by local authorities. That is, we may move a decision to a higher level when the local government—or the local majority—has been either unable or unwilling to act. In cases such as this, the demand that action be taken at a higher level is a kind of appeal to the "wider" majority at the next-higher governmental level.[3]

In demanding that a higher level of government act because a lower level either cannot or will not deal adequately

---

[3] We may be encouraged to accept this second assumption because we have come to understand that tyranny, as well as democracy, can exist at any governmental level. The notion that local government guarantees democracy and that a strong central government insures tyranny has apparently been rejected by many as sheer prejudice. Certainly there is compelling evidence to show that local governments can be as tyrannical as those at any other level. And one safeguard we have against local tyranny is the possibility of having protective or corrective decisions made at a higher governmental level.

with an educational problem, we may still claim that the problem is a local one. Such a demand is a kind of appellate demand—an appeal to a wider majority to help solve a problem or settle a dispute that *is* local. Such an appeal may be appropriate when, for example, the local majority fails to take into account minority rights or when it lacks the resources for a needed reform. It may also be appropriate when the local majority simply cannot agree or cannot act. Furthermore, there may be cases when an appeal is appropriate because the local majority attempts to decide on problems that are not local in nature. In short, the "appellate" strategy is brought into play when it is held that decisions at the local level are being made that should not be made, or when local decisions are not made when they should be made. In contrast, the "new problem level" assumption discussed earlier is used when the problem is perceived as one that is more general in the sense that the problem has direct consequences for the wider public.

We note that neither of these strategies or assumptions that may be used to justify the making of decisions at higher levels suggests that there are no important decisions to be made at the local level. Few persons would make such a claim. We commonly argue that local decisions about education are desirable wherever and whenever it is reasonable to believe that local units can democratically and effectively make those decisions and where the problems are indeed local, i.e., where the decisions do not have great effect on the wider public.

What has happened is that, for many groups and communities, what is called the domain of *local* control is no longer local in any meaningful sense. For example, in any large city, neither the local government nor the local school system is likely to be organized to give the urban poor or the urban minority group (or any other neighborhood group) very much power with respect to the government or schools within their own community. In a sense the failure to recognize a community as a community is a tacit denial that there are governmental or educational decisions to be made by the community. When this happens, most educational decisions that are labeled as local are made by the wider community (of the city or the school system). The neighborhood groups supposedly play their part and exercise their influence by participating at the higher level. For some groups, this presents no great problem. For other groups, who have or perceive themselves as having unique interests and concerns, it often means that those interests and concerns are either ignored or outvoted by the wider majority.

This problem is not, of course, new. The poor, the ignorant, the minorities have never spoken with the full authority that our ritual grants their number. What may be new, however, is that these groups today, in demanding what many apparently regard as special privilege, are in fact demonstrating a readiness to participate more fully in the democratic process described in our ritual. To the concerned groups, it may well appear that seldom is the readiness matched by a willingness to allow community decisions to be made by community members. Thus these urban groups have become, in John Dewey's sense, "concerned publics" and are attempting to function as such. We could see the very existence of such concerned publics as the potential for a more fully democratic society. Instead, we have created a situation in which groups once silent and perhaps apathetic have now donned the dress clothes of democracy only to discover that they have no place to go.

Let us focus on the case of schools. Certainly citizens may and do work together to influence policy of the school *system*, but they are often virtually disenfranchised at the level of the *community* school. In a city with a relatively homogeneous population, this may create no great hardship because there may be substantial sharing of educational interests and purposes. Such harmony of interests does not always exist, and in the larger American cities it may never exist. Interests and needs are diverse, not homogeneous. There will be *some* common needs and interests, but there will also be interests and needs of a neighborhood within a city that are not shared by other groups and communities. And in many cases there is no reason to demand that community interests be sacrificed for the "general welfare." In short, there are problems that concern the local community and that could be solved at that level without damaging effects on the wider public. Even though such problems exist, and even though concerned local communities are addressing themselves to those problems, there is generally no unit, political or educational, through which community groups can work effectively. In short, no matter how local the problem, to influence school-policy decision making through governmental processes, groups generally must work through the larger unit of the school *system*.

Bureaucratization and professionalization. Although typically there is no local political unit corresponding to the neighborhood school, it is sometimes argued that the school systems are generally organized in such a way so as to make up for this. That is, school systems are organized in a way that guarantees that legitimate concerns and demands of a local public are given due consideration at the local school level. In other words, it may be asserted that freedom is granted to school personnel so that those personnel have the authority to respond to the wishes and needs of those served by a particular school. It is indeed possible that school personnel may function in this way. Yet forces are operative in most large school systems that make such responsiveness difficult and perhaps unlikely. These forces are the result, at least in part, of rather rapid bureaucratization of schools and professionalization of school personnel. This bureaucratization and professionalization, although improving schools in some ways, have tended to encourage the educational "Establishment" to allow or even encourage more and more decision making to be taken away from the community and to be given to the managers of the schools. Let us look more closely at this problem.

It has been argued by some that the most significant change in American schools during the last half century has been bureaucratization. Ronald Corwin, a sociologist, speaks of this importance as follows:

The world of the public school teacher is a world of organizations. Indeed the job of teaching as it is known today scarcely exists apart from the organization. It is the perch from which teachers see their students, it is the barrier that teachers erect between themselves and the public, and it is the hierarchy in which they must make their way in order to perform.[4]

Complex organizations are bureaucratized and the school system is no exception.

In speaking of bureaucratization of schools, we should note at the outset that we do not mean *simply* that schools are increasingly marked by inefficiency and red tape, even though that may be the case. But the intent here is not to make bureaucratization evil by definition. Indeed some writers avoid the term "bureaucracy" simply because of such connotations. Etzioni, for example, uses the term *organization* rather than *bureaucracy*.[5] But whatever terminology we use, the process with which we are concerned remains the same:

> In contrast to earlier societies, modern society has placed a high moral value on rationality, effectiveness, and efficiency. Modern civilization depends largely on organizations as the most rational and efficient form of social grouping known. By coordinating a large number of human actions, the organization creates a powerful social tool. It combines its personnel with its resources, weaving together leaders, experts, workers, machines, and raw materials.[6]

Hence rationality, effectiveness, and efficiency are the organizing principles in bureaucratization. Red tape and inefficiency may be the marks of a bad bureaucracy, but they are not definitive characteristics.

[4] Ronald G. Corwin, *A Sociology of Education* (New York: Appleton-Century-Crofts, 1965), p. 3.
[5] Amitai Etzioni, *Modern Organizations* (Englewood Cliffs, N.J.: Prentice-Hall, 1964), pp. 3–4. See also Harold Hodgkinson, *Education, Interaction and Social Change* (Englewood Cliffs, N.J.: Prentice-Hall, 1967), pp. 25–47.
[6] Etzioni, *Modern Organizations*, p. 1.

If schools are becoming bureaucratized, what should we expect to find happening? The major factors to be considered are (1) size, (2) extent of centralization, (3) extent of standardization,[7] (4) extent of specialization, and (5) a hierarchical pattern of authority.[8] To what extent are these factors evident in contemporary schools?

1. *Growth in size.* Clearly the "size" of the total schooling enterprise in the United States has increased dramatically in the past quarter of a century. With the growth of the population there have been more and more students to be educated. And equally important, students are staying in schools longer. Along with these increases in students has come a steady demand for more teachers, more administrators, more schools, and, of course, much more money. This growth has been described in other chapters and need not be further discussed here.

2. *Centralization.* Increased size of the formal schooling enterprise has been accompanied by a rather rapid centralization of schools. During the last two decades, the number of school districts in the United States has been greatly reduced. At the present time more than three-fourths of the students in our public schools are being taught in the schools of fewer than one-fourth of our school *systems.* This centralization of schools has long been encouraged by both professional educators and by some of the critics of American public education.[9] Other indicators of growing centralization include the

[7] Corwin, *Sociology of Education,* pp. 40–43.

[8] Roald F. Campbell, Luvern L. Cunningham, and Roderick F. McPhee, *The Organization and Control of American Schools* (Columbus, Ohio: Charles E. Merrill, 1965), p. 241.

[9] James B. Conant, for example, in his *The American High School* (New York: McGraw-Hill, 1959) strongly recommended that small high schools be eliminated wherever possible. For a good account of the development and changes in school districts, see Campbell, Cunningham, and McPhee, *Organization and Control of American Schools,* pp. 80–109. The decline in the number of school districts is a good indicator of the rate of centralization. In 1947–48 there were 94,926 school districts in the United States. By 1963–64 this number had declined to 31,319.

tendency to have more educational decisions made at higher governmental levels and the growing concern of state and national interest groups over educational matters. The fact of increased centralization seems clear.

3. *Standardization.* Great is the number of educational leaders who have expressed their attachment to the goals of individualized school programs and their concern for individual differences. This concern would seem, on the surface at least, to be the antithesis of standardization. Nonetheless, moving from one classroom to another, or from one school system to another, or from one state to another, one finds that the similarities in schooling are likely to be more striking than are the differences. The infinite variety and the devotion to individualized programs sometimes attributed to the American schools are difficult, if not impossible, to find. Or at least they are not obvious when one begins to examine what actually takes place in the schools. For example, if it is indeed the case that standardized achievement tests are used to measure school achievement the country over, if a relatively small number of textbooks is used in the majority of schools, if procedures of administration and of grading in the curriculum are fairly uniform, if teacher training varies little from state to state, and if class size is about the same wherever one goes, then one may well wonder where that infinite variety is to be found. Indeed, in any society where geographic mobility is as great as in the United States, it is probably desirable that there be a high degree of uniformity from place to place in school administration, teacher training, curriculum, and assessment.[10] Such uniformity is approached by our schools today.

---

[10] Standardization, of course, takes many forms. When many people express their fears of standardization and centralization, they seem to envisage a situation in which at 2:32 P.M. on a certain October 18, every fifth-grade teacher in the country will be reading question 19 from page 68 in the government-prescribed social studies textbook. There may be some grounds for such fear, but such rigidity is not the inexorable result of centralization and standardization. Nor, we must add, is such a condition necessarily avoided with increased decentralization or less prescribed standardization.

4. *Specialization and differentiation.* Specialization of work, or division of labor, a part of the process of bureaucratization, is clearly a characteristic of the modern school. One indicator is departmentalization of high schools and junior high schools, now extended into the so-called middle schools and making sizable inroads into the elementary schools. Another indicator is the proliferation of courses and curricula. Accompanying both these developments is the rapid expansion of "supporting staff" in such fields as guidance counseling, school psychology, reading, physical education, instructional media, and administration. Given the present state of specialization, the modern educational establishment could hardly be seen as following the model of Mark Hopkins on one end of a log and the student on the other. The implementation of such a model today would require a very long log if all the "instructional support personnel" were to have a place on it.

5. *Hierarchical authority.* This bureaucratic characteristic is especially important for those who attempt to influence school policy. At the beginning of this chapter we discussed briefly the traditional and still widespread notion that authority over our schools ought to be in the hands of the public. To borrow the old line about the military: Schools have become too important to be left to the educators.

How in fact are schools controlled? Who does exercise educational authority? In many cases authority is exercised by persons *within* the schools, administrators who are granted considerable authority. Calling this bureaucratic authority, Burton Clark says the following:

> The legal provision that authority rests ultimately with the lay board does not insure that laymen will determine policy. Schools and colleges are organized in an hierarchy of personnel and staffed with full-time, paid officials; operating authority is either delegated to senior officers by the lay board or is assumed in the course of affairs. The board members, part-time and

amateur, are removed from actual operation, while the officials—full-time, expert, informed—are on the spot, making the daily decisions. Even though the board is supposed to make policy and the hired staff to execute it, much policy determination falls into the hands of trained officialdom. The organization assumes, to some degree, the form of a bureaucracy, with a hierarchy of officers assigned to positions that have fixed jurisdictions and duties.[11]

This growth of bureaucratic authority, along with the continued belief in authority as public trust, presents a serious obstacle to those groups that attempt to influence school policy or modify school practices.[12] To whom is any given person within the administrative hierarchy responsible? He is likely to see himself as responsible not to the public he is supposedly serving—at least not directly—but to his bureaucratic superior.[13]

The point here is that it may appear—and people may believe—that educational power and authority are decentralized. The educators themselves are likely to believe this. It may be argued, for example, that the principal of a local school has power delegated to him so that he may respond to legitimate community pressures in such a way that the local school does in fact serve local interests and needs. But the formal delegation of power does not guarantee such responsiveness. In trying to do his job, the principal may view his own author-

---

[11] Clark, *Educating the Expert Society,* p. 153.

[12] A good general discussion of bureaucratic authority can be found in Etzioni, *Modern Organizations,* pp. 75–93. Discussions of bureaucratic authority in schools are found in Campbell, Cunningham, and McPhee, *Organization and Control of American Schools,* pp. 226–55; in Hodgkinson, *Education, Interaction, and Social Change,* pp. 25–47; in Corwin, *Sociology of Education,* pp. 217–300. See also Robert Presthus, *The Organizational Society* (New York: Vintage Books, 1965), pp. 27–58.

[13] See John W. Polley, "Decentralization Within Urban School Systems" in Chandler, Stiles, and Kitsuse, *Education in Urban Society,* pp. 117–28. Polley argues that even with attempted decentralization, the lower bureaucrat tends to make the decisions to please higher bureaucrats, not to please the "public" served by his unit.

ity not so much as being held in "public" trust as in "superior-in-the-system trust." That is, the persons to whom he is directly accountable are likely to be the higher administrators in the system, not the citizens of his school community. Of course there are exceptions. For the most part, however, the administrator is likely to be at least as concerned that his decisions please his superiors as he is that those decisions meet with the approval of and fulfill the needs of the school constituency. For after all, insofar as the power of the principal is concerned, the superintendent giveth and the superintendent taketh away.

Thus the principal may well believe that schools ought to serve the public interests, but it is also likely that he will, in many cases, assume that those interests are best served by "following the rules," by "going through channels," by letting the decisions concerning public interest filter down from those persons in bureaucratic positions where they can see the "big picture." He may listen to those who describe for him the "little picture" of the local community; he may empathize and sympathize; but this does not guarantee that he will view community citizens as those who legitimize his decisions. Given a bureaucratic authority system, the principal is often encouraged to look above him in the bureaucratic hierarchy for legitimization of decisions.

Perhaps one ought not to be too suprised nor treat lower administrators too harshly when their decisions are made not so much to please constituents as to please superiors. But our point here is that the hierarchical structure of authority, rapidly growing in our schools, is likely to frustrate attempts by those on the outside who attempt to modify the workings of the schools. In other words, given a bureaucratic authority structure, lay attempts to influence school policy at the level of the local school are likely to be met by (1) "kicking decisions upstairs"; or (2) making decisions at the local level but with the important reference group being bureaucratic superiors rather than the members of the community.

Teacher Power, the Public, and the Bureaucracy

There are many instances today of bureaucratic authority being challenged by the public, which sees the growth of that authority as a departure from public trust. Bureaucratic authority is also being challenged more and more within the schools by teachers who are asserting that they should have increased power and authority. The teachers' claim to increased authority is often based on the notion of what Clark calls "colleague authority":

> Overall, the long-run trend in American higher education has been for authority to move from external to internal sources, with faculties increasingly contending with the administration about who has authority over what. The faculties march under the banner of self-government and academic freedom, emphasizing equality of relations among colleagues and de-emphasizing administrative hierarchy.[14]

This notion of authority has not in the past been strong in public schools. Public school teachers have traditionally been much more subject to lay control than have most other professionals, and this has discouraged teacher attempts to increase their own authority. Also, the academic freedom of teachers suggested by the notion of colleague authority has not been thought to be necessary for the effective performance by teachers below the college level.[15] But the timidity of teachers is a thing of the past. No longer are teachers as a group referred to as "gutless wonders." Teachers are demanding and getting power.[16] And the trends suggest that teachers

---

[14] Clark, *Educating the Expert Society,* pp. 156–57.

[15] Ibid., pp. 159–60.

[16] In terms of collective action, public school teachers seem to have surpassed their college and university counterparts. For example, it is now common across the country for public school teachers to engage in collective bargaining on matters of salaries and working conditions. This sort of collective action is still a rarity on the college campus.

will continue to demand more and more authority. Clark, for example, says that authority patterns in schools will change as follows:

> Trustee authority will undoubtedly continue to be recognized legally and formally as the dominant type of authority; schools and colleges will continue to have lay boards as their highest formal element. But in actual operation we may expect bureaucratic administrations on the one hand and self-constituted groups of teacher colleagues on the other hand to assert themselves increasingly and contend more actively for decisive influence in school matters. We know that the influence of the expert administrator will increase because the administration will grow in size and will become ever more specialized and expert. Everything we know about bureaucratization and managerial technique points in this direction for the decades immediately ahead. At the same time, the influence of the teaching staff will continue to increase, because the faculty grows in size and also gains influence through its growing expertness. This is most apparent in the case of physical scientists and mathematicians in the universities, but even first-grade teachers are now privy to theories and techniques—Gesell on the "fives" or the "nines" for example—known generally only within the ranks.[17]

Thus Clark expects that there will be growth of both bureaucratic and colleague authority. And if both grow, it is clear that there will also be growing conflict between the two.[18] This struggle for educational authority is complicated further by growing demands for student authority, some of which were discussed in the preceding chapter. Student demands for increased authority have already spread from the college

---

[17] Clark, *Educating the Expert Society,* p. 160.
[18] Corwin, *Sociology of Education,* p. 229; and Campbell, Cunningham, and McPhee, *Organization and Control of American Schools,* p. 253.

campus to the secondary schools. Indeed, even elementary school students have begun to ask for increased student participation in school governance.

As conflict between bureaucratic and colleague authority grows, what happens to the notion that schools should be controlled by the public? Increasing either bureaucratic or colleague authority will produce the potential for increased conflict between school personnel and laymen. The conflict between bureaucratic authority and colleague authority is an intrainstitutional conflict, and an important one. But an increase in *either* of these constitutes a decline of de facto trustee authority, even though a general belief in trustee authority may continue.[19] Thus it may well be that the whole notion of authority as a public trust will become mere ritual, while the bureaucrats and the professionals contend over control of the schools. In the meantime, bureaucrats, teachers, and the public are likely to repeat the ritual of authority as public trust. It is as if both the educator-bureaucrats and the teachers are asking who are the best trustees of education, with neither group seriously considering the possibility that for *some educational questions* perhaps the public is the best holder of the public trust. The failure to consider this possibility may be one of the major reasons that educational professionalism is sometimes viewed by the public as a kind of paternalism.

Many who urge increased professionalization of teachers would disagree with the preceding paragraph. But the point not to be overlooked is that although professionalization *may* lead to a greater concern for the public and for the student-clients, it does not necessarily do so. The growth of professional, or colleague, authority does not guarantee that the professionals will be any more responsive to attempts to change schools than are bureaucrats. Authority may be vested more in teachers and less in administrators without

---

[19] Growth in bureaucratic and colleague authority need not make school personnel unresponsive to the needs and wishes of the public and students. It would, however, make it more likely that school personnel would decide as to what needs should be met in what way.

insuring that decisions are made with the welfare of the students or desires of the parents in mind. Indeed, giving increased power to teachers may in some cases merely replace one bureaucracy with another; i.e., the administrator-bureaucrat may make decisions on what is best for the organization or school system while the teacher-bureaucrat may decide on the basis of what is good for the teachers or the teachers' organization.[20]

Thus it appears that, in some cases at least, to increase teacher authority may represent a drift away from meaningful lay authority. This is perhaps most clear at the level where we would expect the greatest lay control—the neighborhood school. In many cases it seems at this level we accept the paternalistic assumption that educational decisions are best made by those who might be considered outsiders, i.e., the administrators and perhaps the teachers. And if the neighborhood school proves to be difficult for the public to influence, it should not be surprising that many citizens despair of bringing about significant educational change.

We do see citizen despair about our schools. Perhaps the clearest example is found among the urban poor, particularly the black urban poor. They have pointed out again and again that their attempts to modify schools are quickly blocked. And in a sense these citizens, in their objections, are paraphrasing an oft-quoted and oft-criticized statement of John Dewey:

> The man who wears the shoe knows best that it pinches and where it pinches, even if the expert shoemaker is the best judge of how the trouble is to be remedied.[21]

Dewey's analogy is, of course, weak. It is not always the case that the man who wears the shoe knows that it pinches, just

---

[20] This does not mean that the administrator-teacher battle is not important. Colleague authority is different from bureaucratic authority, and changing from one to the other, or placing increased emphasis on one, will make a difference in how a school operates.

[21] John Dewey, *The Public and Its Problems* (New York: Henry Holt, 1927), p. 127.

as it is not always the case that a local community will recognize its educational problems. But we ought not to conclude, as some apparently have, that because Dewey was not *all* right, he was all wrong. There may be all sorts of educational pinches that local communities in our cities do not feel, but there are some pinches they do feel, and these are real pinches.

What is at issue here? Upon what grounds should educational authority be granted? First, it would seem that all three of the groups discussed in this chapter, plus the students, should be participants in holding and using educational authority. Thus the issue is not whether we want authority as public trust or bureaucratic authority or colleague authority or student authority. The questions are rather what part each should play when the decisions to be made are held to be decisions where all groups should participate, and for each group what range of decisions is the special and sole province of that group.

To put this another way, some decisions in the school can and should be made with the participation of more than one group. Other decisions, it seems, are best made by experts, at least if we understand the term "expert" in a particular sense. Teachers, for example, are experts on a variety of questions, partially because of training and experience and partially because of the perspective provided by their position in the school. But there are other questions about which teachers are not experts, but parents and other members of the public are. Administrators, too, face certain decisions that can best be made if left to the administrators. And it seems obvious that there are many decisions to be made that primarily affect students and that students are best equipped to decide.

Summary

We have argued that the upward drift of decision making, the bureaucratization of schools, and the professionalization of school personnel are three changes that are transforming the schools. Although all three have promised reform, in at least some cases they have made the school more distant from the public, more protected from those who seek to modify it. And to the extent that schooling practices are seen by the public as being inadequate in meeting important educational needs of children, professional resistance to the modification of those practices is a crucial and frustrating problem.

Thus professionalization and bureaucratization have been urged as improvements, as means that can be used to minimize the risk of failure that faces every student. For many, these means have not been sufficient to the task. All groups recognize this, and recognize as well that there are educational problems to which no group has answers. But quite apart from the question of what would be the best decision about a particular problem is the question of authority: Who should make that decision? And this latter question, we have argued, needs to be carefully thought out. The position taken here is that authority in schools should not belong to one of the contending groups but should be shared. This sharing would be of two types. First, there are some questions that should be shared by all groups because all are affected and because no one group has sufficient "expertness" to warrant its claim to special authority. Second, for each of the four groups—public, administrators, teachers, and students—there are decisions which can be made best by that group alone and should be the special province of that group.

The situation is a difficult one. There are no easy answers, no easy solutions. Perhaps the problems of schooling in the United States are, as some have claimed, impossible to solve. It is to be hoped that this is not true, but even if it is, the most important truth is that the problems of schooling are too important to be ignored.

References

Campbell, Roald; Cunningham, Luvern L.; and McPhee, Roderick F. *The Organization and Control of American Schools*. Columbus, Ohio: Charles E. Merrill, 1965.

Clark, Burton R. *Educating the Expert Society*. San Francisco: Chandler, 1962.

Corwin, Ronald G. *A Sociology of Education*. New York: Appleton-Century-Crofts, 1965.

Etzioni, Amitai. *Modern Organizations*. Englewood Cliffs, N.J.: Prentice-Hall, 1964.

Hodgkinson, Harold L. *Education, Interaction, and Social Change*. Englewood Cliffs, N.J.: Prentice-Hall, 1967.

Katz, Michael B., ed. *School Reform: Past and Present*. Boston: Little, Brown, 1971.

Presthus, Robert. *The Organizational Society*. New York: Vintage Books, 1965.

Sexton, Patricia Cayo. *The American School: A Sociological Analysis*. Englewood Cliffs, N.J.: Prentice-Hall, 1967.

Discussion Questions

1. In your judgment, what sort of educational decisions, if any, should be made by each of the following? Why?
   a. The public at the level of the local school
   b. Educational professionals at the level of the local school
   c. The teacher at the level of the classroom
   d. The public at the state level
   e. Educational professionals at the state level
   f. The public at the national level
   g. Educational professionals at the national level

2. It has been asserted that what educators take to be professionalism is often viewed by segments of the public as paternalism. Is professionalism in education necessarily paternalistic? Why or why not?

3. In your judgment, what would be the advantages and disadvantages of increasing bureaucratic authority in our schools? Colleague authority? Authority as public trust?

4. To what extent should schools across the nation be centralized? Why? To what extent should educational programs be standardized? Why?

5. Ought the professional preparation of teachers in the United States be more standardized? In your judgment, what would be the likely advantages and/or disadvantages of increased standardization of teacher education?

6. Should parents of school children have a greater voice than other citizens in determining educational programs? Why or why not?

CHAPTER EIGHT

Planning and Policy in Education

The rapidity of technological and social change, the growing faith in the ability to predict the consequences of such change, the increased confidence in man's ability to control his environment, and the rising concern for preservation of human and natural resources have given great stimulus to the respectability and prevalence of planning. The practice of national planning, long a basis for distinguishing between the "socialist" nations and "capitalist" nations, is rapidly becoming common to all nations. Nearly all of the less-developed nations have created planning mechanisms and plans to husband scarce resources and to focus national thrust on goals of development. Nations of Europe have been revitalizing administrative and policy-making bodies by injecting the newer perspectives and techniques of planning. In the United States at the federal, state, and urban levels the notion and the process of planning have been receiving wide attention.

Planning is, then, a concomitant of our age. It may be described simply as an attempt to exercise some control over the future, or it may refer to a specific set of techniques and a rationale for the allocation of resources. Planning is a kind of decision making and, at least in its contemporary meaning, tends to deal with a set of sequential and systematically related decisions. In Waterston's words, it is a scheme of action with certain attributes, which include: "looking ahead, making choices, and where possible, arranging that future action for attaining objectives follow fixed paths, or where this is impossible, setting limits to the consequences which may arise from such action." [1]

Perhaps the range in the conceptions of planning may be viewed on a continuum. At one end would be planning as a strict allocation of resources, establishment of quotas, and the like. At the other end would be planning viewed as information dissemination with no constraints on individual choice.

command or compulsive planning	planning as information dissemination
A	*B*

While it might be agreed that no pure example of either type exists, the socialist nations such as the U.S.S.R., China, and portions of Eastern Europe, tend toward the *A* end of the continuum, and much of Western Europe and the United States tend toward the *B* end of the continuum.

The Nature of National Educational Planning

Many of the concerns and proposals mentioned in the previous chapters, such as the financial squeeze, the demand for efficiency, and the increased reliance on multiple institutional arrangements for instruction, have generated during the last decade an intense interest in educational planning. Changes in authority and control which move educational decision making from local communities to metropolitan and state levels increase reliance on planning. Should the state become increasingly the primary administrative unit in education, as is being predicted by some educators, we may expect the rapid

---

[1] Albert Waterston, *Development Planning: Lessons of Experience* (Baltimore, Md.: Johns Hopkins Press, 1965), p. 9.

development of elaborate mechanisms for planning. There are, however, counter trends represented by demands for increased freedom in educational choice, community control, debureaucratization, and "deschooling" which tend to place less faith in planning and at times are militantly antiplanning.

Given the existing peculiar role of the education system in providing inputs to all other social systems, educational planning can be viewed as fundamental to the achievement of broader planning goals. Like general planning, views of educational planning may be placed along a continuum, at one end of which lies educational planning as the implementation of plans and fulfillment of quotas established by the central government. At the other end of the continuum lies educational planning as a mild guidance system to facilitate the individual's decision making (particularly vocational choice). Most, if not all, nations lie somewhere between the two extremes. Vocational choice, for example, is usually manipulated to some extent through financial or other inducements on the part of the government or firm. Yet no nation has been able to specify in comprehensive detail how each educational institution may function.

The term *educational planning* requires further definition, however, particularly in distinguishing this process from the usual activities in educational administration.

Beeby defines educational planning as:

> the exercising of foresight in determining the policy, priorities, and costs of an educational system, having due regard for economic and political realities, for the system's potential for growth, and for the needs of the country and of the pupils served by the system.[2]

Some would find Beeby's definition too broad and, instead of viewing educational planning as the "exercising of foresight,"

---

[2] C. E. Beeby, *Planning and the Educational Administrator* (Paris: UNESCO, International Institute of Educational Planning, 1967), p. 13.

would prefer to identify it as a technical activity whereby educational targets are established and the derivative adjustments made in the educational systems. In either case the distinction between educational planning and educational administration is largely one of emphasis. As typically used in current literature, educational planning suggests: (1) more comprehensiveness of coverage; (2) a longer time perspective; and (3) more attention to economic and social factors than is typically implied by educational administration.

Viewing the nature of educational planning cross-culturally, it may be argued that countries at different stages of development require different approaches to educational planning and target setting. Alexander King, for example, suggests that three stages of development and their corresponding planning needs are observable:

> Firstly, [in] the really underdeveloped countries where resources are very scarce . . . policies are made essentially on national grounds . . . matters of prestige and local politics dominate . . . once [the] choice has been made, careful detailed planning is extremely important as to rate of implementation and the detailed allocation of resources within the politically predetermined framework.
>
> Countries of the second category, the developing nations, exemplified by the six countries of the Mediterranean Regional Report and many Latin American states, are quite different in their approach, quite different in their needs. . . . The immediate need is for economic development to produce greater resources, which then can make possible a much broader approach to education, thus generating eventually social pressures for more education. The manpower approach is probably the most appropriate approach at the first phase of development.
>
> In the third category, the highly developed countries, social pressure has already developed because of the sufficiency of resources and general prosperity, and it dominates the planning. Here the main requirement is for choice between alternatives. While social pres-

sure planning may be the most important general approach, detailed manpower projections are required especially for higher professional levels and for specific sectors of the economy.[3]

There are three basic questions that require answers before the educational planning process can be carried out: What are the educational objectives? What kinds of data are needed for the planner to relate educational decisions to societal goals? What conceptual framework of society, education, and their various subsystems is most useful in ordering these data? Since we are not so concerned here with the more technical and procedural aspects of educational planning, the emphasis in the following discussion relates to the first two of these questions. The work of the educational planner, as well as that of the general planner, is hindered not only by the inaccuracies in existing national economic, political, educational, etc., data with which he must work, it is further obstructed by the lack of certain *kinds* of data. In the United States these limitations on available data have been recently referred to as the "intelligence gap." As Gross comments:

> Executive officials and members of Congress alike are misled by inadequate interpretations of bad information based on obsolete concepts and inadequate research and collected by underfed and overlobbied statistical agencies.[4]

Objectives of Educational Planning

As described in chapter 1, education performs a great variety of functions and can conceivably serve a number of individual and social ends. Presumably, attempts could be made to

---

[3] Alexander King, "Educational Planning and Development: An International Approach," in *Educational Planning*, ed. Cicely Watson (Toronto: Ontario Institute for Studies in Education, 1967), p. 11.

[4] Bertram M. Gross, Remarks prepared for U.S. Senate Subcommittee on Government Research, as reported in *Summer Orange* 65, no. 2 (June 30, 1967).

plan for any or all of such ends. However, it has been only in such utopias as *Walden Two* and *Brave New World* that schooling and instruction have been designed to develop or reinforce a wide range of individual and social attributes. The stated educational objectives in the real world of planning are of a much more restrictive nature. Indeed, the major elements taken into consideration in educational planning could perhaps be classified under four categories:

1. Adjustment to population change
2. Economic growth
3. Social demand
4. Social welfare and equity.

1. Educational Planning as a Response to Population Change

To many educators and social scientists responses to population changes would not be called planning. However, one of the activities most widely engaged in by educational administrators and planners is the anticipation of the number of classrooms, personnel, and materials needed, judged on the basis of population forecasts. Since this procedure frequently means merely extrapolation of population data, it might not be dignified with the label *planning*. Nevertheless, it is the most fundamental and frequently the only explicit recognition of the structure and size of the future educated population. Since responding to population changes is a part of the educational administration of every national, regional, or local educational system, further discussion is unnecessary.

2. Economic Growth

The ways in which educational systems contribute to the economy of a nation are not precisely known. Indeed, the more studies that are conducted on this problem, the more complex the relationships appear. It is commonly assumed that the higher a person's education the more dependable,

248 · SCHOOLING AND SOCIAL CHANGE IN MODERN AMERICA

flexible (to new job requirements), and productive he is. Yet, the precise relationships, for example, between education and skill and between skill and productivity have not been well explored. Nevertheless, one of the most common approaches to planning for economic development postulates that the economy demands labor with various levels of schooling in fixed proportions. The needed outputs of the educational system at any future date, then, may be determined on the basis of the desired occupational structure (number of professionals, technicians, clerical personnel), and this, in turn, can be determined on the basis of the desired level of goods and services in the economy. This view of the relation of education and the economy is reflected in what is usually called the manpower approach to educational planning. The discussions that follow in this section relate only to the manpower approach.[5]

Probably all nations wish to develop educational policy that will support economic growth targets. The less-developed nations in particular tend to give priority to this goal. One finds, for example, in the First and Second Five Year Plans of India the following statements:

Education is the most important single factor in achieving rapid economic development and techno-

[5] Parnes, one of the foremost exponents of the manpower approach to educational planning, limits approaches to assessing educational needs of any society to two: (1) the manpower approach; and (2) the cultural approach. By culture requirements for education, Parnes refers to "all those requirements, other than for vocational preparation." Parnes recognizes that the difficulty of this approach "lies in specifying the criteria in terms of which educational needs are to be defined and in deciding upon the amount and type of education "appropriate" or "necessary" for the achievement of each.

"The cultural approach . . . stresses education as a social 'investment' to which returns cannot be calculated in money terms—an investment in values that are either indispensable or highly desirable to the society, e.g., an informed citizenry and equality of opportunity."

After this exercise of reason, which appears at least partly designed to demonstrate that economists can be broadminded, Parnes concludes, "I am unable to conceive a set of operations in the cultural approach analogous to those that have been set forth above for the manpower approach." *

* Herbert Parnes, "Assessing the Educational Needs of a Nation," in *Educational Planning*, ed. Don Adams (Syracuse, N.Y.: Syracuse University Press, 1964), pp. 60–61.

logical progress and increasing a social order founded
on the values of freedom, social justice, and equal opportunity. . . . It is one of the major aims of the
Third Plan to expand and intensify the educational
effort and to bring every home within its fold, so that
from now on, in all branches of national life, education becomes the focal point of planned development.
   Education is a determining influence on the rate at
which economic progress is achieved—contribution to
widespread participation of the People in all activities and constructive leadership at various levels.[6]

The same objective is dramatically visible in the educational planning of the Communist nations. Since development of the economy is seen as crucial to the achievement of
all major Communist goals it would follow that one of the
prime concerns of the educational system would be its contribution to economic growth. In discussing the development
of the modern Soviet state, Soviet writers point out that the
first priority was given to the pressing economic problems—
organizing the social economy and controlling production and
management. The emphasis on education for productivity
persists, for in the USSR, as in all nations of the Communist bloc, man the worker is seen as the goal of all socializing
institutions and as an indispensable condition for development in a planned economy.[7]
   In Western Europe and in the United States relatively less
attention is given to education as a driving force for the
nation's economy. Not that education is not viewed as a
national investment. It often is. Returns to the individual and
to society from monies spent on education are anticipated.
Yet, typically, at neither the national nor the local level are
the economic returns the overriding justification for public
expenditures on education. Thus, a government document

   [6] India, Government Planning Commission, *The First Five Year Plan,
The Second Five Year Plan* (New Delhi: Manager of Publications, 1950, 1955).
   [7] *Educational Planning in the USSR* (Paris: UNESCO, International Institute of Educational Planning, 1968).

from Sweden notes that educational policy should contribute to economic development by "producing the right types and amounts of qualified manpower." This goal, however, is seen as subordinate to those of social demand and "the satisfaction of social demand for school places is thus not subject to any restrictions imposed by estimated manpower requirements. . . . " [8]

In a somewhat similar vein, a report from The Netherlands states, "Vocational guidance and manpower forecasts are seen as the instruments to serve the students in making correct decisions." [9]

In the United States where, until recently, planning activities in education were so diverse and decentralized that they may not warrant the label of planning, little explicit effort has been forthcoming at either the federal or state levels to utilize forecasts of manpower needs in the development of educational policy. At the federal level, while there are many agencies and offices that collect and disseminate manpower data, these activities serve as only one of the many inputs into policy decisions at state and local levels. And it has been observed that at the state level "manpower gets less attention than future student demand or problems of finance, organization and educational program development." [10]

The federal government can and does offer financial incentives, draft deferments, and the like in order to make the preparation for certain occupational careers appear more attractive. The availability of scholarships, for example, has probably influenced, particularly at the graduate school level, the career patterns of many young men and women. The chronic oversupply in a number of fields, e.g., secondary school social studies teaching, however, suggests the inadequacy of such arrangements. Indeed, the present teacher sur-

---

[8] *Educational Policy and Planning: Sweden* (Paris: Organization for Economic Cooperation and Development, 1967), p. 47.

[9] *Educational Planning in The Netherlands* (Paris: Organization for Economic Cooperation and Development, 1966), p. 67.

[10] J. K. Folger, "Scientific Manpower Planning in the United States," *World Yearbook of Education* (New York: Harcourt, Brace and World, 1967), p. 203.

plus could have been easily anticipated through the use of the technical tools of planning available.

3. Social Demand

"If the truth were told, nine-tenths of educational planning around the world is of this type [social demand] despite all the lip-service to the more sophisticated varieties of 'education as investment in economic growth.'" [11]

In principle, what is usually termed the social demand or demand-for-places approach to educational planning is the simplest and most straightforward. The objective is merely to provide the schools and personnel to satisfy the numbers of students who demand admission. In practice, this principle is modified to accommodate academic—and possibly other—standards for admission. But at least this objective avoids the controversy over whether education should serve economic or social ends and further avoids many of the sticky technical problems of target setting.

Educational planning in most Western European nations plays down manpower planning and emphasizes the adjustment of educational facilities and programs in response to social pressure. For example, in a national educational plan prepared in Sweden the following educational objectives were specified:

1. All Swedes of school age should enjoy an equal right to public education without regard to income, social origin, sex, or place of residence.
2. The school should aim at safeguarding and strengthening the democratic system.

The so-called *Robbins Report on Higher Education in Great Britain* (Report of the Committee on Higher Education 1961–1963 [London: Her Majesty's Stationery Office, 1964]) is considered a classic example of the social demand

---

[11] *World Yearbook of Education,* 1967, p. 85.

approach to educational planning. The committee preparing the report examined educational planning in a number of other nations (frequently at first hand) and gave consideration to the objective of economic growth, then gaining popularity in much of the world. After a period of study, however, the committee announced that it "reject[ed] the suggestion that they should base any part of their projections on an assessment of economic needs. With the exception of the need for school teachers, they [the committee] harness their recommendations exclusively to projections of demand for places." [12] In another section the report is even more specific: "courses in higher education should be available for all those who are qualified by ability and attainment to pursue them and wish to do so." [13]

The objective of a great deal of the educational planning in the United States is satisfaction of social demand, or at least response to significant social pressure. Beyond the years of compulsory education, all states and local communities have complete high school facilities and many have developed community colleges and state universities. The United States historically has not been particularly concerned with imposing a rigid standard of quality on its institutions of higher education. The wide range in subject matter and in intellectual requirements in American colleges and universities has often dismayed foreign visitors. However, this variety has meant that, subject to financial constraint, nearly every high school graduate can attain admission to an institution of higher education.

4. Social Welfare and Equity

No nation has taken a broad articulated approach to educational planning for the multifaceted objectives of social welfare and equity. Nevertheless, as planning becomes more imperative, as our understanding of the possibilities of ma-

---

[12] Ibid., p. 91.
[13] Ibid., p. 85.

nipulating the educational system increases, and as our social goals become better specified, it is reasonable to anticipate movement in this direction.

We have already seen that the concept of equity or equality of opportunity is somewhat elusive. In chapter 7 we offered several definitions of equality of educational opportunity, each of which suggested a different educational policy.

One definition of equality of opportunity popular in the United States and increasingly prominent in Swedish, English, and, to some extent, other European circles is that of equal educational participation rates among the various social classes. Clearly, adjusting education to manpower needs or merely responding to social demand is unlikely, at least in the short run, to effect equality since (1) skills tend to be most easily acquired by those groups that have already been successful in education; and (2) the level of social demand for education tends not to be equal among various social groupings. Regarding the second point, educational policy in the United States, for example, in favor of compensatory education or in support of different selection criteria for certain disadvantaged groups may reflect egalitarian motives of certain articulate groups in the middle classes as much as it does social pressure from the lower classes. Similarly, in Sweden, the democratic commitments of political leaders bulwarked by the results of pedagogical research may have had more direct influence in bringing about comprehensive schooling than did general parental concern.[14]

Action of the sort that has taken place in educational planning at a national level in most countries to achieve social equity has been limited largely to extension of length of compulsory and common education, legislation prohibiting geo-

---

[14] It should be noted that defining equality of opportunity in terms of standardized selection devices may be considered attractive economically since the numbers of talented by definition are small and therefore the aggregate costs of education are comparatively less. Further, however, this approach to equality may also be politically more attractive, for any lack in educational advantage for the intelligent and privileged (and hence the most articulate and politically sophisticated group) may result in strong pressure for political change.

graphic, ethnic, and other discrimination, and nationalization of examinations. While much educational research has been related to factors impinging on school success and educational participation rates (of various social classes), the results of these efforts have had little direct influence on planning.

Perhaps the most significant response in the United States to the various studies of equality of opportunity is just beginning to be visible at the state and urban levels. For example, the State Committee on Public Education has made a report to the California State Board of Education that states with respect to equality of educational opportunity, "Correction of socio-economic imbalances will be achieved when the average level of educational performance and its dispersion and range do not substantially differ from one school to the other." [15]

Proposals for legislation in this regard suggest: " . . . respective school facilities should be served by administrators and faculties of equal professional proficiency, that the courses of study and the materials therefore shall be of equivalent merit, variety, and range, and that the physical properties shall be comparable. . . .

" . . . the distribution of educational attainments of the pupils shall be similar for each school. . . .

" . . . local districts shall prevent concentration of classes of students and shall seek to mix those of differing race, social and economic backgrounds and academic attainment according to the general mixture of the district." [16]

Clearly these proposals fall far short of what is necessary to equalize educational participation rates among different social groupings.

A somewhat different view may be taken of these objectives. Such bases for educational planning as demography, manpower needs, social demand, and equity concerns may serve as multiple grids in the evaluation of a given educational policy. Thus the creation of new secondary vocational programs, the

[15] "Citizens for the 21st Century: Final Report from the State Committee on Public Education to the California State Board of Education," June 1968, mimeographed.
[16] Ibid.

development of training centers, the transfer of certain school functions to civic agencies, or the initiation of a voucher system might be examined against such grids. From a planning point of view no particular conceptual difficulty is encountered because of, say, an increase in the number of institutions with explicit instructional functions. Practical problems of data gathering (being able to describe the inputs and outputs of the various institutions) and problems of coordinating and implementation may, of course, be greatly complicated. What may be won, then, in terms of flexibility, in quality of instruction, and in savings in cost, may be at least partly negated by increased possibilities of incongruities and maladjustment between the educational output and the needs of society.

Trends in the United States

The emerging issues in the United States regarding educational planning relate to the scope of the planning process and the location of planning responsibility. Is educational planning to consist primarily of making certain quantitative adjustments to educational systems in the light of external pressures and demands? Or will the planning process include certain qualitative aspects of education? And what will be the division of responsibility and initiative between local, state and federal levels?

Chase has summarized the American experience in educational planning as follows:

> In the past, educational planning tended to be sporadic, piecemeal, and confined to the more tangible and more or less urgent aspects of education such as providing facilities for students already enrolled or shortly to be enrolled. It was seldom conceived as a carefully calculated process for reordering the educational system to meet needs for education arising in a given community or society. Planning occasionally, however, represented an attempt to create something in the nature of a grand design, but usually without spelling out in any detail how the design was to be

realized. The resulting plans often consisted of little more than expressions of pious purposes, loose generalizations in regard to the required resources, and extremely hazy delineation of the measures to be taken or even the alternatives open for consideration.[17]

Benson suggests that there are several reasons why the United States has engaged in educational planning less vigorously than many other nations:

1. We are rich and therefore more willing to take chances in the spending of money in relatively unplanned and unmonitored ways.

2. Our educational services are more broadly extended than are those in other countries. Disparities in income distribution are somewhat less distressingly visible.

3. In the United States, both employers and employees hold relatively flexible attitudes toward the necessary and proper fit between a person's education and the job he holds; hence, we have managed—up till now, at least—to avoid serious problems of educated unemployment.

4. We have a blind faith in evaluation as a total substitute for a more complete set of planning activities.[18]

Planning at the School Level

Most planning activities in education, irrespective of objective, have given little attention to the internal dynamics of the educational system. In responding to social demand, planners and administrators have been concerned with the magnitude of input to the educational system and in developing the

[17] Francis S. Chase, "The Status of Educational Planning in the United States," in *Educational Planning in the United States*, ed. Stanley Elam and Gordon S. Swanson (Itasca, Ill.: F. E. Peacock, 1969), p. 40.

[18] Charles Benson, "How the American Education System Looks from the Standpoint of Systematic Planning" (Paper [mimeographed] delivered at the Annual Meeting of American Educational Research Association, New York, 5 February 1971).

personnel and facilities to service the input. In responding to economic and manpower goals, the planners and administrators have been concerned with inputs and outputs but largely in numerical terms. Educational planning for the goals of social welfare and equity, in particular, demands qualitative as well as quantitative educational measures.

In effect, education has been viewed by planners as shown in the following diagram:

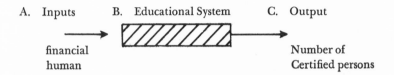

A. Inputs   B. Educational System   C. Output

financial   Number of
human   Certified persons

Such a model is obviously not very satisfying to the teacher or educator who believes that many significant (and interesting) aspects of education lie in what happens inside the system: the nature of curriculum, instructional design, teaching and administrative style, and so on. Indeed, when teachers and educators speak of *quality*, it is these kinds of ingredients to which they refer. The question thus arises as to the possibility of changes in such qualitative aspects of education through the mechanism of educational planning. Before directly considering this question, however, further clarification of the meaning of quality is in order.

R. S. Peters has made a useful distinction by noting that there are "product judgments" and "process judgments" in education. *Product* judgments relate "purely to the degree to which those who had been at a school or a college satisfied the multiple criteria involved in 'being educated.' " [19]

Educational objectives concerned with quality as a product might include: levels or kinds of knowledge and understanding (e.g., theory of skills necessary for economic productivity);

---

[19] R. S. Peters, "The Meaning of Quality in Education" in *Qualitative Aspects of Educational Planning* (Paris: UNESCO, International Institute of Educational Planning, 1969), p. 153.

level of commitment to "what is regarded as value in itself" (or what might be called a noninstrumental attitude); "wholeness" (in distinction to being "trained," an educated person has developed in "all the various forms of awareness").[20]

Any of these objectives or criteria could originate and be imposed from sources external to the educational system or might reflect the predelictions of education.

Process judgments take "careful account of the state of students before they entered such institutions and measured the extent to which they had progressed towards being educated from a different base-line." [21]

Quality as process probably comes close to what most educators mean when they refer to quality of education. There have, of course, been endless pedagogical debates concerning the need to improve the quality of education. Moreover, there is a growing body of empirical research on such topics as the determinants of educational achievement, the structure of a learning environment, and the nature of social interaction in school. However, the results of such experience and research have rarely been systematically utilized in educational planning at the urban, state, or national level. For its part, educational planning, with its concentration on quantitative assessments, has highlighted certain qualitative issues and has suggested areas of research. Yet planning activities have not forced the invention, testing, and application of new learning systems.

Without attempting to analyze the substance of quality education, let us concepualize the task that needs to be done. Again, using a systems model, what is needed is not the very restricted view of education as above, but a fuller characterization of education as a dynamic, many-faceted process. Figure 4 may serve to illustrate our point.

Some behavioral scientists argue that significant advances are being made in understanding of the relationships depicted in figure 4. More sophisticated scientific underpinnings of the teaching and learning process allow the individualization

---

[20] Ibid., pp. 155–56.
[21] Ibid., p. 153.

A. INPUTS

B. SCHOOL PROCESS

C. OUTPUTS

Symbolic

Community Demands
and Supports
Social goals and values
Legal Requirements
Role Expectations

Human

Professionals
Students
Parents (as indirect clients)
Organizational Pattern and
Administrative style

Material

Fiscal Resources
Plant and Physical Setting

Individual educated in:

Affective

Attitudes
Motivation
Personality

Cognitive

Knowledge
Skills

Evaluative

Appreciation
Value Orientation

Physical

Health
Physical Skills

Social

Increased community
involvement
Increased inter-
generational
understanding

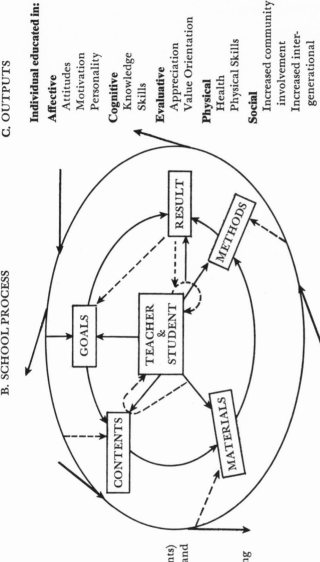

- - - - - - External Feedback - - - - - ->

FIGURE 4

A Systems Model of Education

of instruction, a more systematic development of instructional materials and an improved design of the learning environment. Scientific advance may in time allow a differentiated pattern of instruction where students learn from various methods as suggested by a diagnosis of needs. Most pertinent to educational planning, science increases predictability and if pedagogical and technological innovations represent improvement in the science of education, they are a boon to planning efforts.

A realistic appraisal, however, must conclude that scientific progress in education is at best slow and uneven. The science of behavior is relatively young, nor is it supported by the elaborate research institutes common in physical, biological, or space sciences. It is difficult at the present time to conceive of a process of educational planning that takes into account and measures the several inputs, the dynamic relationships in the school process, and then proceeds to distinguish the subtle outputs. Our level of knowledge and tools of inquiry do not suffice to accomplish this fully even at the local level. Yet for individual research and evaluation projects measures have been employed for all the input and output variables identified in figure 4. A system for gathering such data on a regular and recurring basis then may not be utopian. The contributions of such a procedure are several, for these data would permit planning to come to grips with qualitative factors and allow more sophisticated comparisons with past performance.

The Process of Educational Planning

If educational planning is to become more than manipulation of certain structural features in education, more attention must be given to (1) the social environment of education and (2) the participation of the various "clienteles" of the educational system.

Some space has already been given to describing the inadequate utilization by planners of the range of tentative knowledge that has been accumulated concerning schooling and the linkages between schools and other social institutions. Attention is now turned to the second of these two shortcomings.

The development of an educational plan or a delineation of educational policy, whether conducted at the level of the school district or at the national level, typically involves a small group of educational administrators and other specialists. Limiting involvement in educational planning in this manner is unjustifiable on at least two major counts, however. First, the real authority to implement plans and policies may rest outside this group with some combination of politicians, parents, teachers, or students. Thus, for the sake of efficiency, participation in planning may need to be extended. Second, notions of equity and democracy require that the views of those served by education be given consideration.

A commitment to the importance of nonprofessional involvement clearly complicates the process of educational planning. However, in many American communities, extensive community participation in decision making already exists, particularly with regard to the earliest levels of public schooling. At the preschool level, parents often work closely with teachers and children in planning schedules and programs. But as has been pointed out: "The higher one moves in education or the further one progresses up the planning hierarchy through local and regional to national planning authorities, the more tenuous become the lines of communication between the interested parties." [22]

The problem, then, may be not so much the creation of new structures for the participation of additional groups in planning as the extension of a network already in existence. There is no ready-made answer for the best organizational arrangement to satisfy the conditions being recommended. The depth of democratic traditions in decision making is one condition affecting the level of interaction in the planning process. Another factor is the obstruction to communication resulting from status differences among school personnel and

[22] Susan Balloch, *The Social Environment of Education and Educational Planning* (Paris: Organization for Economic Cooperation and Development, DAS/EID/71. 12, 1971), p. 21.

among citizens. We suggest, however, that extended participation in planning might possibly lessen the harshness of
confrontations between groups involved in education and
most probably can avoid the practice of reacting to conflicts
with hastily conceived ad hoc educational policies.

Dysfunctionality in Educational Planning

Clearly, educational planning whether at the classroom level,
school-district level, or the national level has tended to fall
far short of expectations. National level educational planning
often becomes but a paper exercise—data are gathered and
plans are written, only to gather dust in national offices. At
the local level in the United States we are all familiar with the
written statements of educational objectives (or "philoso-
phies") that never even get translated into plans, much less
become implemented as changes in the schools. Here we
would like to examine briefly some of the reasons for the
failure of planning and consider the dangers of excessive
faith in planning.

Figure 5 may be useful in viewing the educational planning
process at either a micro or macro level. A brief examination
of this model suggests the many points at which the process
can break down. Do the politicians, educational officials, and
school board members clearly identify the educational goals
and objectives? Are the specialists in pedagogy, finance, economics, and statistics able to translate these statements into

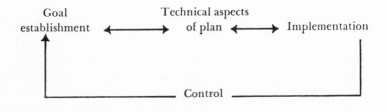

FIGURE 5

The Educational Planning Process

specific quantitative and qualitative targets? Is there the administrative capability to implement the targets? Is there some measurement or judgment of results that provides the direction for adjustments in goals and targets? Successful planning is thus predicated on the coordination of a variety of skills and on the cooperation of a number of persons of different backgrounds and interests. Although space does not permit an examination of the full range of planning problems, one of the most basic planning problems, the formulation of objectives, will be discussed in some detail.

At both national and local levels educational objectives are frequently stated in such terms as helping each student achieve his potential, preserving or improving the democratic way of life, strengthening the moral fabric of society, and creating better citizens. Should statements of objectives phrased in such manner be considered pertinent for planning purposes, or do they represent political statements designed to placate the public?

How can the stating of goals be modified or regularized so that the task of planning is facilitated? We suggest that *to be of maximum utility goal statements should include the following: (1) specification of the time allowed for the policy to produce the desired consequences; (2) specification of the target population and/or institution; and (3) specification of the evidence that is to be taken to count as attainment.*

Specification of time. When talking about goals and goal statements, we frequently use temporal modifiers. For example, we commonly talk of long-range goals or short-range goals or immediate goals. These modifiers give *some* hint about when goal attainment is desired or expected, but the suggestion is far too general and imprecise to be useful to the policy maker. And in many cases we do *not* include any time specification in our goal statements. One can find, for example, goal statements calling for increased teacher salaries or improved physical facilities or higher levels of academic achievement, but making no mention of time.

It may well be that in many contexts in which people discuss goals no consideration of time is important. Nevertheless, specification of time is crucial for planning purposes. *Without a time specification—without an indication of when a goal is to be attained—the planners and administrators must either furnish the time specification or develop a policy without knowing when that policy is to be evaluated.*

Perhaps an example will make the foregoing more clear. Suppose we begin with the following goal statement:

> Goal statement: "It is the goal of the state of New York to reduce illiteracy in the state by ten percent."

Given this as a goal, the policy maker must either specify the time, or design a policy intended to reduce illiteracy but with no claim as to how soon the reduction might occur. Let us assume here that our policy maker chooses to specify time. His goal, as he modifies and restates it, is:

> "It is the goal of the State of New York to reduce illiteracy in the state by ten percent during the next year."

Now, in specifying the time the policy maker may make his own task either easier or more difficult. But the important point here is that in specifying the time, he is in fact setting part of the goal, and not merely designing a policy to achieve an already stated goal.

Target population. The time specification indicates when a goal is to be attained. The specification of the target population is intended to indicate by whom the goal is to be attained. There are a number of ways in which one could categorize target populations. Consider, for example, the following three factors: (1) *target level;* (2) *target group;* and (3) *target comprehensiveness.*

Target level. The level of social organization, e.g., family, school, city, state, nation. Clearly, we do have different educational goals for these different levels, and we sometimes encounter difficulties if we are not quite careful to make clear the level with which we are concerned.

Target group. The particular set of persons or institutions with which we are concerned, e.g., eighteen-year-olds, seventh-graders, families with annual incomes of less than $5,000. Thus, when we combine the target group and the target level we would have sets such as:

Target Group	*Target Level*
(eighteen-year-olds)	in (Syracuse)
(seventh-graders)	in (New York State)
(families with incomes . . .)	in (the United States)

Target comprehensiveness. The degree to which the goal statement demands attainment by the target group, e.g., all, 50 percent, 25 percent, mean, etc. Thus, the target population when specified by level, group and comprehensiveness, would result in population description such as:

Target Comprehensiveness		*Target Group*	*Target Level*
(all)		(eighteen-year-olds)	in (Syracuse)
(fifty percent)	of	(seventh-graders)	in (New York State)
(mean X)	of	(families with incomes . . .)	in (the United States)

The target group may be institutions rather than persons. Thus one could have target populations such as:

All schools in Syracuse
Fifty percent of the secondary schools in New York State
Mean X of all colleges in the United States.

The major point here is that if goal statements are to be of maximum use in planning the target population must be specified.

Evidence of goal attainment. The two preceding sections have been concerned with the specification of when and about whom evidence of goal attainment is to be collected. In addition to this, of course, *the goal statement should make clear what is to be counted as evidence of attainment.*

What should be taken to count as evidence of goal attainment? What should be taken as evidence that a certain policy is ineffective? These are central questions, but they are questions difficult to answer when we look at some goal statements; i.e., some goal statements are such that it would be difficult to get agreement that any particular evidence would be useful in evaluating a policy. What, for example, would be evidence of goal attainment when the goal statement is: "The goal of this school system is to develop good citizens?"

Even a goal statement much less vague may not be specific enough with regard to evidence. Notice the following goal statement: "It is the goal of this school to develop citizens who are law-abiding." Now, the notion of "law-abiding citizens" seems less vague than that of "good citizens," but it remains difficult to say what should be taken as evidence. Will law-abiding behavior of students within the confines of the school do? Or until the age of twenty-one? And must a person obey *every* law to be law-abiding? In short, these goals are stated in such a way that one cannot be sure what is *meant* by the goal, and hence neither can one be sure what should count as evidence of attainment. The claim here is that what is meant by goal attainment must be made clear before evidence of goal attainment can be specified.

The foregoing assumes a distinction between the meaning of goal attainment and evidence of goal attainment. If we hold goal X for student Y, what must be true of Y before we are willing to assert that Y has in fact attained X? To answer this question would require a full explication of what we *mean* when we assert that someone has attained X. We should be clear about this, but we should also recognize that our evidence is often inadequate to support the full-blown assertion that Y has attained X. Thus, we must settle for less. Given the meaning of attainment of X, what sorts of things are we willing to treat as relevant evidence to give some support to the assertion that Y has attained? Suppose our goal is to have Johnny become (or remain) a law-abiding citizen. We observe that Johnny obeys the local law that prohibits jaywalking. Refraining from jaywalking is certainly not what we mean when we say someone is law-abiding, but the fact that Johnny does not jaywalk is relevant evidence. And in many cases, the best we can do is to look at the relevant evidence, even though that evidence is far from conclusive.

What is the point here? Basically, it is that for our own purposes, it is crucial to distinguish between goal attainment and evidence of goal attainment. A goal statement may be clear about neither, and clarifying one may not clarify the other. Goal attainment, for example, might be made quite clear and yet not be directly observable or testable. When this is the case, relevant evidential statements must be provided, even though the evidence described is only supportive rather than conclusive.

Of course, the adequacy of goal statements is only one requisite for successful educational planning. Indeed, conceptually, planning need not be viewed as a process moving from goals to implemented policy. Could not objectives and goals grow out of the process of planning?

Furthermore, in attempting to cover the range of opinions on planning it should be recognized that supporters of "deschooling society" (see chapter 9) might oppose any formal planning on the grounds that it is a form of management which tends to assume the persistence of existing structural arrangements in education. That is, the goal of educational planning typically is to produce a more efficient education for a more efficient society. In addition, any social planning restricts individual freedom and must deny the individual control over aspects of his life. Planners might argue that by restricting some individual rights planning can increase the number of choices open to all persons. Yet, to those who view any organized (bureaucratic) attempt to influence individual and group choices as evil, this argument is unlikely to be satisfactory.

Summary

Educational planning as the process of looking ahead, making adjustments and innovations today as a means for a preferred future, is likely to receive increasing attention in the years ahead. New techniques for data acquisition and processing, the application of economic and fiscal concepts to education, and the development of more elaborate managerial techniques have contributed to a rapid improvement in the technology of target setting and resource allocation. But the demands of public and government for accountability in educational policies have added to the necessity of planning.

Moreover, irrespective of our level of insight into the functioning of the educational system, teachers and students, as well as administrators, have a role to play in planning. This is so because a plan at the local or national level that does not reflect to some degree the views of teachers and students is not likely to be implemented. But more fundamentally, when planning becomes more than an attempt to improve the system of pupil and financial accounting it ceases to be the exclusive activity of technicians. Planning viewed as a tool for creating a quantitatively and qualitatively different educational system should as a matter of principle involve groups central to the educational process. Teachers and students may not be versed in the techniques for handling demographic and economic data but they are in a position to judge the effect at the classroom level of new pupil-teacher ratios, additional training requirements for teachers, and variations in curricula or evaluation procedures.

As the possibilities increase for making judgmental and qualitative data available, the potential of educational planning grows. Breaking open the black box of education allows us to tinker with some of the more subtle aspects of education, thus permitting planning to become a more powerful tool for efficiency, innovations, or rigidity. However, it is well to remember that educational planning thrives on quantification, and at present statistics can satisfactorily describe but a few of the elements of a learning environment.

References

Adams, Don, and Miner, Jerry. *Educational Planning*. Syracuse, N.Y.: Educational Policy Research Center, Syracuse University, 1970. Mimeographed.

Bereday, George Z. F., and Lauwerys, Joseph A., eds. *Educational Planning: The World Yearbook of Education, 1967*. London: Evans Brothers, 1967.

Organization for Economic Cooperation and Development. *Social Objectives in Educational Planning*. Paris: OECD, 1967.

Morphet, Edgar L., and Ryan, Charles O., eds. *Planning and Effecting Needed Changes in Education*. Denver: Designing Education for the Future, June 1967. Idem, *Implications for Education of Prospective Changes in Society and Prospective Changes in Society by 1980*.

Sizer, Theodore R. "Educational Planning and Individual Freedom," *Comparative Education Review* 10, no. 3 (October 1966): 381–89.

Discussion Questions

1. Why is educational planning receiving increased attention today in many nations?

2. What are the more common societal and community goals for which education is planned?

3. Who are the educational planners? What are their skills? What are their motives?

4. What weaknesses do you find in the manpower, social demand, and equity approaches to target setting in education?

5. What are some of the ways in which educational planning might be used as a tool for conservation or innovation?

6. Is there a moral issue involved in educational planning? Who decides: Should we plan?

options
in designing
educational change

5

Part 5 concentrates on the emergence of a number of major choices in educational reform. In so doing many ideas and problems mentioned in earlier chapters are brought into focus through consideration of possible educational innovations and alternatives. Here as elsewhere in the book the emphasis tends to be on schooling at the system level. Relatively little attention, for example, is given to the many new programs and techniques being considered in the classroom.

In the context of educational changes in the past many of today's proposals must be viewed as radical. Who would have predicted a few years ago that some American public schools would temporarily close their doors for lack of funds? Who would have predicted that some school boards would enter into contracts with private enterprises to teach children reading and other skills? Who would have anticipated that advocates of the elimination of schools would receive serious attention?

CHAPTER NINE

Alternatives in Education

The decade between 1960 and 1970 must be viewed as a very romantic period in education. Schools became the focus for planners who sought vast social and economic changes, for politicians who sought to build more national cohesion, for citizens who wanted more of the good life their society had to offer. The early 1960s saw considerable agreement about the power of schools to generate new levels of modernization and to respond to the needs of industrialized social orders. Educational systems were seen as the producers of skilled manpower and the new knowledge requisite for technological advancement and economic growth. Schools also inculcated pupils with the discipline, attitudes, and motivations requisite to the demands of industrialization. Human capital became viewed as more valuable than physical capital, and intrepid economists identified the differential value in percentage points. Educated people were said to produce more on the job, adjust more quickly to the demands for new skills, and demonstrate more commitment to their work.

Proponents of education found other contributions as well. Schooling purportedly curbed population growth because the better-educated were more rational and saw the folly of large families. Most important of all in the minds of many was the faith that the educational system promoted social mobility for the poor—and few appeared to question the legitimacy of mobility as an overriding ambition.

By the late 1960s and early 1970s skepticism and even disillusionment had set in. If educational systems generated economic growth, they did so in an indirect and exasperatingly slow manner. Undoubtedly schools imparted and strengthened attitudes and disciplines useful in an industrial social order. But precisely how and at what expense they did this often appeared unfathomable. Most damaging of all was the realization that more and more schooling did not necessarily result in an equalization of opportunity for the available goods and services of society. Clearly schools were imperfect instruments as social levelers. And an obstreperous few even questioned whether the good life should be defined in terms of more of the same.

The view of the teacher was likewise changing. The teacher was less frequently viewed as the impartial broker between innocent childhood and adult fulfillment. Indeed, to the harshest critics, the teacher was the witting or unwitting pawn in a system that was more than slightly fraudulent. The teacher was telling the students that if they acceped his wares the world would open before them equally; but time proved his promise false.

Bulwarking these various dissatisfactions was the realization that the costs of schooling were reaching alarming proportions. Some nations were spending one-third of their annual national budgets on education. School costs around the world were rising faster than enrollments and faster than national incomes. In the United States heavy reliance on the local property tax for the support of schools meant not only that a sharp limit was placed on available resources but also that the wealthier areas could support better schools. (The wealthier could also partake of available, expensive private schooling while, with a kind of perverse consistency, supporting the rights of the poor to control their own schools.) By the early 1970s the situation had reached such a crisis stage that several American communities temporarily closed their schools for lack of funds.

Since the voices of dissatisfaction were heard from many quarters, the nature of the discontent was understandably varied. Any easy classification of the depth or kinds of criticism is sure to be an oversimplification, for education was merely one of the institutions to come under fire in a period of turmoil. As has been reiterated throughout this book, however, for those concerned about schools and their social environment a few problems stood out. First, the demand for increased educational services and the competition for scarce financial resources everywhere gave rise to calls for efficiency within the educational system and in terms of its fit with other institutions. Second, societies had placed tremendous burdens on their schools to equalize opportunities among various groups of citizens. Clearly, educational systems were not up to this task. Third, and least clearly articulated, was the hope (or, occasionally, the demand) that there could be a new level of freedom for the individual expressed in terms of all social choices, including the choice of an education.

The outgrowth of the mounting dissatisfaction and criticism of existing educational policies was a growing willingness on the part of citizens and professionals to consider innovations within and, more radically, alternatives to, existing patterns of education. Brief note of some of the proposed educational reforms has been made in previous chapters, but for purposes of review and further analysis the various available options are examined in more detail here. Attention particularly is given to the implications of a number of different policies under consideration by educators and citizen groups. These alternatives are not necessarily mutually exclusive but have been identified separately for purposes of clarification.

The Pedagogical and Technological Option

Advances in an understanding of the teaching process and the development of educational technology have provided a growing array of choices in the instructional process. Innovations resulting from pedagogical and technological progress are fully described in textbooks on curriculum and teaching methods, and no attempt is made here at a comprehensive review. Our concern is only in understanding the general direction of such change and in assessing its magnitude.

Many of the innovations have as their purpose the increased efficiency of schooling. Efficiency may be defined as either "achieving the greatest amount of output from any given set of inputs" or "achieving a specified amount of output utilizing a minimum quantity of inputs." [1]

Improved efficiency in education could come from one or more of the following actions:

1. Reducing the time required to achieve the educational objectives
2. Reducing the unit cost of inputs necessary to achieve the objectives and
3. Reducing the inputs per student.

Improvement in the efficiency of the educational system is expected to come from efforts toward all three of these directions with an emphasis perhaps on points 1 and 3. In education as in industry the approach to reduction of time required to fulfill a task and to raise the quality of the effort has been through a commitment to role differentiation and specialization. Educators apparently associate increased role differentiation and specialization with increased professionalization. Departmentalization as commonly practiced at the secondary school level is one example, of course, of specialization of roles —in this case based on academic disciplines. Further specialization is frequently predicated, however, along the following lines: (1) new roles within instruction to include TV teachers, master teachers. teacher interns. teacher aides. instructional materials specialists, learning diagnosticians, learning therapists, and so on; (2) new roles within educational administra-

---

[1] Daniel Rogers, "Productivity and Efficiency Within Education," in *Education in National Development*, ed. Don Adams (New York: David McKay, 1971), p. 47.

tion including budget specialists, planners, and operations analysts.

Specialization presumably raises the quality and perhaps reduces the time required to accomplish instructional and managerial tasks. Instructional specialization and technology may also allow economy of size, that is, a decrease in the average cost of accomplishing some educational objective. For example, educational television may permit more students to receive instruction without an accompanying increase in numbers of teachers or in administrative costs. In a similar manner managerial specialization and technology may allow larger school systems, a smaller ratio of administrative and clerical staff to students, and the efficiency of centralized resources, e.g., science and media equipment centers.

Curiously, literature in professional education has given remarkably little attention to the social and individual problems accompanying specialization. Even if one cannot agree with the somewhat hysterical pronouncements that specialization necessarily means dehumanization, there is no denying the frustration and emptiness associated with many occupational roles today, including many of those in education. Not only humanists, but certain persons within the managerial profession as well are worried about alienation from the job even though such alienation may be viewed only as an obstruction to greater productivity.

Some difference of opinion persists regarding whether pedagogical and technological advance in specialization and use of technology is to "teacher-proof schools" or to "school-proof teachers." At times, technologists when discussing media, programmed texts, computer assisted instruction, and other prepackaged learning materials appear to wish to structure learning in such a way that teachers have few choices to make. The implied assumption is that materials and experiences designed by experts lessen the possibilities of being utilized successfully when tampered with by the average teacher. The classroom teacher may, as in the case of programmed materials, administer the learning medium or may, as the case of television teaching, offer supplementary instruction. For those who would "teacher-proof schools," however, the classroom teacher plays at most a minor role in the professional task of selection and design of learning experiences.

Those who would "school-proof teachers" make the teacher the central professional figure as far as instruction and evaluation are concerned. The goal is to treat the teacher as an applied scientist competent enough to transcend any administrative, organizational, or financial limitations that might be obstructive. Many teacher preparation programs apparently have as an objective the creation of such a teacher, although research and evaluative skills are rarely well developed among teachers.

Some behavioral scientists argue that a science of pedagogy is beginning to emerge which will permit a different, more truly professional relationship between teacher and student. Advancements in the science of pedagogy will, for example: (1) generate much more reliable information to be used as the basis for differentiating among students and (2) ultimately allow a differentiated pattern of instruction where students learn from various methods as suggested by a diagnosis of needs undertaken by teachers and various specialized school personnel.

At times, in terms of programs being recommended, those who would "teacher-proof schools" and those who would "school-proof teachers" appear remarkably in agreement. Note, for example, the following definition of what is involved in any instructional process:

1. Setting up new forms of response . . . a very evident characteristic of learning is the increasing precision of the student's response . . .
2. Setting up new kinds of stimulus control . . . teaching the student to use previously learned skills in response to new subject material is the pertinent instructional task, and this involves transferring stimulus control to new subject matter . . .
3. The maintaining of behavior . . . not only is the ex-

pert's behavior (the behavior of an individual who has fully mastered a certain subject matter) guided or controlled by the subject matter, but with increasing competence it can be characterized as self-generating and highly independent of environmental supports . . .[2]

These three stages in instruction can be and have been incorporated in the programmed materials prepared by media and technology specialists. The link between behavioral scientists and technologists is obvious. Both groups appear capable of making an easy analogy between learning and, say, the production of rolled steel where progress is monitored, prescription is automatic, and evaluation is rigidly standardized. Yet, most proponents of a more specific pedagogy would probably reject such an oversimplified analogy. The teacher has limited power to control the learning environment; moreover, given the changing needs, desires, and motivations of individuals there is a question of how much the teacher *should* attempt to control. Certainly there is a strong argument that the best education is not only adapted to the individual but to a large extent determined by him. On any hand, anything resembling a science of pedagogy, or even a technology of instruction, appears only on a distant horizon.

The Organizational and Political Option

A number of wide-reaching changes in the structure and control of educational activities have arrived on the scene in the last several years. Many changes, such as those referred to in the last section, involve only minor adjustments in administrative and teaching styles. Consolidation of smaller schools into a single larger school and other efforts to foster economies of scale, lengthening the school day or year, and an increased sharing of specialized facilities with community

---

[2] Robert Glaser, "The Design and Programming of Instruction," in *The Schools and The Challenge of Innovation* (New York: Committee for Economic Development, 1969), pp. 184–85.

organizations are examples of policies that might reduce the cost of schooling but are unlikely to affect radically its structure or control.

However, there have been more fundamental alterations in the delivery of educational services. One group of such changes could be placed under the label of nonformal education. Revolutionary societies such as China and Cuba have initiated literacy and vocational training programs outside the formal educational structure utilizing a wide range of social, political, and occupational groups as contexts for such efforts. Factories and farms as well as schools are seen as having explicit educational functions. Many other developing nations, while not necessarily emulating China and Cuba, are seeking routes outside their school systems to disseminate information and knowledge. Industry and governmental agencies, for example, are increasingly called upon to carry more of the burden of skill training. In Western Europe and the United States a variety of ad hoc extraschool training programs can be found. Table 19 offers one attempt at comparison of formal and nonformal educational programs.

The move toward efforts in nonformal education was stimulated by a variety of conditions.[3] First, increasingly there has been a realization that school systems typically are poor places for the training of many occupational skills. They tend to be inefficient in time, frequently produce a low level of compe-

---

[3] The term nonformal education typically refers to those instructional programs and learning experiences not provided by the regular school system. A more detailed description is offered by Coombs:

"Non-formal education refers to the wide assortment of organized systematic educational and training programs *outside* the formal system, designed to generate skills and knowledge relevant and useful to particular sub-groups in the population and labor force—e.g., farmers, training centers, extension services, rural youth programs, work-oriented literacy projects and in-service training for rural administration, small industry, and farm cooperative management. The sponsorship, control, and financing of non-formal education is widely scattered among different government agencies and private organizations." *

* Philip Coombs, *Non-Formal Education for Rural and Agricultural Development*, International Council for Educational Development, 1 January 1971, mimeograph.

tence, and therefore, are expensive per unit output. More-over, school systems adapt only slowly to the need for new skills generated by technological change. Second, a group of semi-literate youth exists, particularly visible in the less-developed nations, but also present in advanced industrial societies, who have dropped out of the early stages of the regular school system. These rejects from the regular educa-tional structure can, with training, become more productive members of the labor force and better citizens. Third, there has been a growing criticism that schools are taking on more functions than they can perform in a satisfactory manner. Fourth, school systems as large-scale bureaucracies have often become unresponsive to community interests. A relocaliza-tion of control appears in order.

Reimer, long an advocate of devising alternatives to the present school systems, has arrived at certain generalizations regarding the availability of services typically provided by

TABLE 19

Some Characteristics of Nonformal and Formal Educational Programs

Nonformal, Nonschool Programs	Formal School Programs	Variable
On a continuum from high to low degree of structure, but usually the latter. Little inter-relatedness of com-ponents.	Relatively highly struc-tured. Functionally in-terrelated set of units hierarchically ordered, i.e., a graded sequential system.	Structure
Usually task- or skill-centered; dictated by functional needs of par-ticipants. May reflect values conflicting with status quo and elites.	Generally academic, abstract, and often "ethnocentric." Highly verbal, reflects status quo values of elites.	Content

TABLE 19 (*continued*)

Nonformal, Nonschool Programs	Formal School Programs	Variable
Short-term, present-time orientation. Often part-time, evening study. Flexible timing of activities.	Future-time oriented. Full-time attendance stressed. Lock-step inflexible sequence of activities.	Time
Uncoordinated, fragmented, diffuse. Voluntary organizations predominate. Greater degree of local control. Decisions often made at program level.	Coordinated control, national, regional, or religious bureaucracies predominate. Elites influential in higher control positions.	Control
Low visibility, may be on the job or at home. Participants bear fairly low costs. High efficiency of locale utilization, i.e., functionally related to learning.	Highly visible, expensive, fixed in place. Often state-supported. Urban preference. Low efficiency of plant utilization. Learning physically isolated from application.	Locale
Great variation but stress is on resocialization, acculturation, and the learning of practical skills and knowledge to be used in work or community situations. Terminal. Seeks to supplement or complement formal schooling.	Stress on socialization, enculturation, and perpetuation of educational bureaucracies. Legitimization of existing elites, their values and behaviors. Conferring status, selection for more schooling, and possible elite recruitment. Seeks to bring youth into conformity with the values of adult institutions.	Functions
Payoffs tend to be tangible, immediate, and related to work or	Payoffs tend to be deferred promise of long-term gains in sociocul-	Rewards

TABLE 19 (*continued*)

Nonformal, Nonschool Programs	Formal School Programs	Variable
daily life: i.e., increased material well-being, productivity, self-awareness, and power to control environment.	tural and economic status.	
Teacher helps student interact with, and master, the material to be learned and applied. Content centered. Methods are relatively flexible and related to application and performance-standard needs.	Knowledge is standardized, transmitted from teacher to pupil in the classroom. Teacher-centered. Teaching methods dictated by policy and are relatively inflexible and noninnovative.	Method
Learners are from all age groups, i.e., not age- or place-defined. Job mobility concerns predominate. Great variety of teacher qualifications and motivations.	Students are age-defined, predictable, often urban in outlook and frequently seek social mobility. Teachers are formally certified and their statuses correlated with location in the school hierarchy.	Participants
Great variation in costs per program and per student vis-à-vis costs for comparable educational programs in the formal system. Economies of size not often possible.	Costs are standardized by level and increase moving up the structural hierarchy. Economies of size possible.	Costs

SOURCE: Adapted from Rolland G. Paulston, *Planning Non-Formal Educational Alternatives* (Pittsburgh: University of Pittsburgh, International and Development Education Program, October 1971), mimeographed, pp. 3–5. As suggested in the title of the table, Professor Paulston has attempted to sharply contrast formal school programs from nonformal programs. While the drawing of rigid distinctions is useful in gaining a general perspective on possible similarities and differences, the areas of overlap tend to be ignored.

school systems.[4] Drawing on his experience and the perceptions of several teachers and educators from a number of nations, Reimer concludes:

1. Similar educational experiences are available to upper class children of pre-school age, to middle class elementary school children and to lower class high school children, i.e., there appears to be a lag of about six years from one class level to another in the availability of such educational experiences as trips, music, books, or theatre of a given kind.

2. Such selection and certification services as tests, advanced placement and provisional admission are little utilized by the upper class, are seldom at the option of the lower class, and thus serve almost exclusively the upwardly mobile middle class.

3. Individualized services, i.e., tailor-made education, indoctrination and custodial care, are the prerogative of the upper class, the use of mass-produced services characterizes the middle class, while the lower class, which has only marginal access to mass-produced services, has a range of informal educational opportunities which the other classes do not fully share.

4. All of the functions performed by schools are also available independently, and in almost any combination, either commercially or as functions of non-educational institutions, somewhere in the world if not in any one country.[5]

While the validity of Reimer's conclusions would seem to at least vary from society to society, his observations are nonetheless stimulating. His two basic points relate to (1) the pervasive inequity of the present system of schooling and (2) the wide availability from alternative sources of many of

---

[4] Reimer defines the school system as the institutional union of four social functions: custodial care, selection for social roles and social status, value formation, and cognitive education. See Everett Reimer, "Alternatives in Education" in *Education in National Development*, ed. Don Adams (New York: David McKay, 1971), p. 86.

[5] Ibid.

the functions now performed by schools. Many of the current functions of schools, such as custodial care, selection, certification, and even instruction, could be performed by commercial enterprises. Or many of such functions could be redistributed to the home, church, firm, and labor union.

The availability of learning opportunities outside the regular school system of a nation has rarely if ever been investigated in depth. Marien, however, offers some crude estimates on the magnitude of the total "educational complex" in the United States. Under his classification there are formal and informal educational institutions. The formal category, in addition to the core institutions of primary, secondary, and higher education, includes a peripheral group composed of corporations, military, proprietary, correspondence, vocational training, antipoverty programs, educational television, other adult education, and other child education. The informal educational institutions include national media (television, radio, print, films, recordings), local cultural facilities (theaters, museums, zoos, planetariums, fair grounds, historical sites, libraries), social organizations (family, church, political process, clubs and associations, and peer groups), and personal media (telephone, mail, personal tape recordings).[6]

Marien estimates the periphery to have had an enrollment of 44.2 million students in 1965 (only 9.4 million less than the enrollment of the core). He makes no attempt to quantify involvement in informal education. The 44.2 million students include 14.5 million in organization training (business, government, and military; on-the-job training and formal classes sponsored by the organization itself or another institution); 7.8 million in proprietary or trade schools; 2.8 million in antipoverty programs (including programs formerly in the Office of Economic Opportunity and programs under the Manpower Development Training Act); 5.0 million in correspondence schools; 5.0 million taking formal courses via

---

[6] M. Marien, "Notes on the Education Complex as an Emerging Macro-System," in *Global Systems Dynamics*, ed. E. O. Attinger (New York: Varges, 1970), pp. 225–44.

television, and 9.1 million in other adult education (including programs conducted by core institutions, libraries, churches, Red Cross, Great Books, community centers, etc.). Because of obvious problems of duplication, estimates of "other child education" are not included in the above totals, although Scouts, Little Leagues, dancing classes, summer camps, and the like serve to supplement the educational services in the core schools.

The above classification differs from that of many writers who tend to include under the label of nonformal education much of what Marien classifies as periphery. The imprecision in conceptualizing extraformal education clearly inhibits attemps at describing its boundaries, analyzing its functions or measuring its output.

Clark describes three nonformal educational *systems* in the United States. One is run by private business, the second by the military establishment, and the third by private voluntary organizations.[7] In describing the scope of nonformal education Clark noted, for example: (1) that some of the largest industrial firms were spending as much money on training as the instructional budgets of many U.S. universities; (2) the amount of Sunday school space in the churches of some communities was equal to the classroom space of the local schools; and (3) over 35,000 "specialty" schools exist outside the regular system to teach a wide variety of skills ranging from advertising to ventriloquism.

Let us look more closely at the notions of commercialization and redistribution of educational functions. This option, in effect, argues for a widening or broadening of what might be termed educational space. That is, more people and more objects become viewed as sources for learning. Examples of

---

[7] H. F. Clark and H. S. Sloan, *Classrooms in the Factories* (Rutherford, N.J.: Institute of Research, Farleigh Dickinson University, 1958); idem, *Classrooms in the Military* (New York: Bureau of Publications, Teachers College, Columbia University, 1964); idem, *Classrooms on Main Street* (New York: Teachers College Press, Columbia University, 1966); H. F. Clark, H. S. Sloan, C. A. Herbert, *Classrooms in the Stores* (Sweet Springs, Mo.: Roxbury Press, 1962).

learning resources, in addition to the teacher-in-school, might be: books, games, art products, nature products, and people. The question becomes not so much one of identification of an extended list of possible resources as (1) a decision as to which educational arrangement is best suited to perform any given task; (2) determination of the action necessary to make available such potential learning experiences; and (3) the allocation of resources for learning.

Recommendations for new arrangements for the financing of education are linked to a broadening of educational space, and have included the establishment for each child of an educational account, the provision of educational credit cards and utilization of various new tax sources. Receiving most attention in the United States has been the idea of education vouchers (briefly referred to in chapter 2). Under a voucher system parents would use public money to purchase education for their children in public or private schools.[8] Under one proposal the student would submit the voucher at the school of his choice and the school, in turn, would forward the voucher to a government agency for repayment.

The assumptions underlying the notion of education vouchers appears to be:

1. The existing public schools are not providing an adequate education. This is particularly true with respect to urban and minority children.
2. A voucher system, by giving students a choice, stimulates educational competition through which the good schools emerge and the bad are driven out of business.

Proponents believe that a voucher system would overcome the racial limitations inherent in many neighborhood schools, for if the schools that cater primarily to minority groups did not improve they would lose their customers. The Office of

---

[8] One of the most comprehensive analyses of voucher systems suggests seven different models. See Christopher Jencks, *Education Vouchers: A Preliminary Report on Financing Education by Payments to Parents* (Cambridge, Mass.: Center for the Study of Public Policy, Harvard University Press, 1970).

Economic Opportunity (OEO) has declared its intent to experiment with voucher systems in a number of urban areas. Spokesmen for the OEO apparently have concluded that working through the regular school systems, regardless of the size of financial input, will produce little significant change in the opportunities or "life chances" of the poor.

Probably the best reason for experimenting with educational vouchers lies in the increase in educational choices they might generate. Presumably parents could seek out traditional teacher-oriented approaches, Montessori schools, "free" schools, or a variety of other programs that appeared to satisfy their children's needs. Because of the need to tailor instruction to satisfy particular sets of clients, innovations and reforms might be expected to increase. Moreover, placing finances and, therefore, control to a large extent in the hands of parents circumvents the public school bureaucracies which generally have not been noted for their flexibility and innovativeness.[9]

Clearly a voucher system may represent a threat to the existing public school systems. The National Education Association and the American Federation of Teachers have taken positions in opposition to voucher plans and apparently will not even support modest experimentation in such direction. Some groups, such as the American Jewish Congress, have expressed fear that education vouchers because of potential competitive position of parochial schools would lead to a breakdown in the traditional separation of church and state. Moreover, the reaction of the minority communities, which, according to designers, would profit greatly from education vouchers, has not been completely favorable. The NAACP, for example, has cautioned that vouchers may lead to segre-

---

[9] The history of the idea of a voucher system for financing public education is often traced to the eighteenth-century statements of Adam Smith. More recently, since the 1950s, American economist Milton Friedman has been arguing for vouchers and the competitive school economy they would stimulate. One of the persons who has most popularized the idea and helped organize operational experiments with vouchers is Christopher Jencks. See Jencks, *Education Vouchers*.

gated schools and points to the support of the idea by southern and northern racists.

Indeed, the lack of organized support, the absence of a clear constituency, is one of the most significant shortcomings of the voucher proposal. The idea of education vouchers has been generated and promoted by a limited group of intellectuals financially supported by the U.S. government and a few private foundations. Dissatisfaction and frustration with the public schools has not led to a ready acceptance of vouchers. Activists in urban areas seek more control than provided through the role of passive consumers. Then, too, there are those social scientists, educators, and citizens who despair, in the case of the poor, of any form of schooling that will be able to close the opportunity gap between advantaged and disadvantaged.

Even if competition in the educational marketplace produces better instruction, the success of education vouchers must rest on the wisdom of the parents. Do parents have the information and insight to choose the best available education? Or would they succumb to the slick sales approach and the gimmicks of the educational enterprises? But do marketplace conditions always produce the best commodity—are Detroit automobiles and supermarket foods the epitome in the application of this approach? And wouldn't the better-educated and better-informed groups (the middle and upper social classes) learn to take the most advantage of this system as they have with the regular school system?

Frequently associated with the idea of education vouchers is the concept of accountability. Proponents of voucher systems claim that parents, at least indirectly, through their purchasing power can hold educational institutions accountable for the amount and kind of learning they promise. More directly, however, accountability may be applied through performance contracting in either existing schools or in any devised alternative. For example, there is experimentation in some communities to hold regular teachers accountable under contract (performance contracting) for certain measurable increases in the children's learning. Performance and accountability contracting with commercial organizations for the accomplishment of certain specified tasks is also being attempted in a few school districts throughout the United States and is under consideration in a number of others. In an experiment receiving widespread attention the city school board in Gary, Indiana, contracted with a private corporation to administer the entire program of one school. The corporation, Behavioral Research Laboratories of Palo Alto, California, guaranteed to raise the achievement level of the students or to return its fee for any child who fails.[10]

Accountability in this and other less comprehensive experiments in performance contracting appears to be solely in terms of test scores. This obviously places a high credibility on standardized achievement tests—a credibility not fully deserved in their somewhat checkered history. Much of the criticism by the National Education Association and other professional education groups on schemes of accountability and performance contracting lies precisely in this direction. The NEA, for example, has identified the necessary conditions for teacher involvement with performance contracts: [11]

1. Teachers must be involved through their local associations as a basic condition of the contract. This involvement must extend from the planning of the contract objectives through the evaluation of the performance of the contract.
2. Other measurements in addition to the so-called standardized achievement tests must be used as measures of student learning.
3. Learning objectives must be developed with community and professional involvement and must be the basis for the requests for bids on the contract.
4. All contracts must include the provision—the so-called "turnkey approach"—that will make it possible

[10] James A. Mecklenburger and John A. Wilson, "The Performance Contract in Gary," Phi Delta Kappan 3, no. 7 (March 1971): 406–10.
[11] Education Digest 36, no. 8 (April 1971): 4.

for all innovative aspects of the contract to revert to the regular staff and program of the school.

5. The contract must provide for the maximum use of school personnel who must be given adequate preparation in the processes related to the contractual objectives.

6. All pupils must be under the close supervision of professionally trained and certificated personnel.

7. Contracts must be limited to genuinely innovative approaches that are neither likely nor possible within the school's program.

8. Contracts must not be in conflict with negotiated agreements between school boards and local associations and must not violate the established legal rights of teachers.

The Revolutionary and Anarchistic Option

The most radical option in considering possible educational changes is the elimination of school altogether, indeed, the elimination of the school tradition. This is the proposal of Ivan Illich and his followers who suggest:

All over the world schools are organized enterprises designed to reproduce the established order, whether this order is called revolutionary, conservative or evolutionary. . . . Everywhere the loss of pedagogical credibility and the resistance to schools provides a fundamental option: Shall this crisis be dealt with as a problem which can and must be solved by substituting new devices for schools and readjusting the existing power structure to fit these devices? Or shall this crisis force a society to face the structured contradictions inherent in the politics and economics of any society which reproduces itself through the industrial process? [12]

---

[12] Ivan Illich, "The Breakdown of Schools: A Problem or a Symptom" (Cuernavaca, Mexico: Draft Paper, CIDOC, 1971), p. 2.

Illich assumes that schools are "breaking down," therefore attention should be focused on the nature of learning in a deschooled society. In this regard two questions must be raised: "Will people continue to treat learning as a commodity—a commodity which could be more efficiently produced and consumed by greater numbers of people if new institutional arrangements were established? Or shall we set up only those institutional arrangements which protect the autonomy of the learner—his private initiative to decide what he will learn and his inalienable right to learn what he likes rather than what is useful to somebody else?" [13]

Needed, then, is an arrangement whereby the learner has much more freedom of choice than under any formal educational arrangement which exists today. Such freedom may only be expected under special societal conditions. As Illich admits, education could only cease being the task of some special agency in a new social order.

Two other statements by Illich may help in understanding the nature of the argument and the scope of his proposal.

Many students, especially those who are poor, intuitively know what the schools do for them. They school them to confuse process and substance. Once these become blurred, a new logic is assumed: the more treatment there is the better are the results; or, escalation leads to success. The pupil is thereby "schooled" to confuse teaching with learning, grade achievement with education, a diploma with competence, and fluency with the ability to say something new. His imagination is "schooled" to accept service in place of value. Medical treatment is mistaken for health care, social work for the improvement of community life, police protection for safety, military poise for national security, the rat race for productive work. Health, learning, dignity, independence are defined as little more than the performance of the institutions which claim to serve these ends, and their improvement is

_____
[13] Ibid., p. 1.

made to depend on allocating more resources to the management of hospitals, schools, and other agencies in question. Not only education, but social reality itself has become "schooled." [14]

Equal educational opportunity is indeed, both a desirable and a feasible goal, but to equate this with obligatory schooling is to confuse salvation with the Church. School has become the world religion of a modernized proletariat and makes futile promises of salvation to the poor of the technological age. The nation-state has adopted it, drafting all citizens into a graded curriculum leading to sequential diplomas not unlike the initiation rituals and hierarchic promotions of former times. The modern state has assumed this duty to enforce the judgment of its educators through well-meant truant officers and job requirements, much as did the Spanish Kings who enforced the judgments of their theologians through the conquistadors and inquisitions.

Two centuries ago the U.S. led the world in a movement to disestablish the monopoly of a single church. Now we need the constitutional disestablishment of the monopoly of the school and hereby of a system which legally combines prejudice with discrimination. The first article of a bill of rights for a modern, humanist society would correspond to the first amendment to the U.S. Constitution: The State shall make no law with respect to the establishment of education. There shall be no ritual obligatory for all.[15]

Further elaboration is necessary to grasp the full measure of the "deschooling" thesis. The other options identified have not called into question the institutionalization of education. Changes in curriculum and in the uses of technology do not alter the fundamental relationship between teacher and learner, nor do alternatives in the patterns of control.

[14] Ivan Illich, "Why We Must Abolish Schooling," *New York Review of Books*, 2 July 1970, p. 9.
[15] Ibid., p. 11.

294 · SCHOOLING AND SOCIAL CHANGE IN MODERN AMERICA

These innovations, for example, still require professional teachers, an explicit curriculum, and a hierarchy of certification (and hence the assumption that official knowledge is the most important knowledge).

We noted in earlier chapters that a major difference between modern industrial nations and traditional societies is that in the former power and status are less frequently inherited. In contemporary societies, particularly the technologically advanced ones, knowledge is power. But schools, through a certification system, control that knowledge which opens doors to occupational and social advancement.

Proponents of "deschooling" argue for a "secularization of teaching and learning." Removing control over what is taught from teachers, schools, or other set of prescribed institutions is viewed as the only policy that can fully free the learner to seek, retain, or discard knowledge at his pleasure. A teacher becomes defined as a knowledgeable person who wishes to teach. A student is viewed as any person who wishes to learn.

To some extent such secularization merely gives recognition to the fact that (1) much is learned in informal relationships anyway and (2) informal learning because it is more fun increases motivation to continue learning. Second, there is the assumption that a system of teachers and institutionalized learning, in effect, renders knowledge a commodity treated as private property. Access to knowledge and its uses must then be a cornerstone of the deschooled society.

A deschooled society implies a social structure that cannot be found in any society today. Contemporary revolutionary societies such as Cuba and China have attempted certain radical reforms in their educational systems, such as promotion of part-time and ad hoc training programs and in general extending the opportunity to teach and to learn among wider segments of the population. Yet, even in these nations, the most significant part of education (in terms of rewards to the individual or in terms of support by the government) remains institutionalized as part of a giant governmental bureaucracy.

What is being called for, then, by the proponents of deschooling apparently is nothing less than the end of bureaucracy. But more precisely, what sort of society is envisioned and what organizational arrangements in education will be tolerated remain unclear. For example, are voluntary associations for the purpose of acquisition or dissemination of knowledge necessarily in conflict with deschooling? How about museums and public lectures? In a situation of complete "freedom to teach and freedom to learn" is there to be no protection of the young, weak, and stupid from the strong and clever? Why should the influence of peers, parents, and friends be more salutary in the design of a good education than that of teachers?

The central concerns of Illich and his followers relate to authority and autonomy. They advocate nonauthoritarian education and the enhancement of individual autonomy. As Spring has pointed out, these concerns are in the tradition of the social and political philosophy of anarchism:

> . . . anarchists oppose the existence of the state in any form because it destroys individual autonomy by legislating laws which determine individual action. Anarchists in the nineteenth and twentieth century have argued that the state and its laws exist for the protection of the political and economic elite. This rejection of the state includes democratic societies where the individual is required to sacrifice his autonomy either to the majority or a representative. The state has also been viewed as a mechanism which protects economic systems which allow for the exploitation of one man by another man. Working from this perspective, anarchists have found themselves in the interesting position in the twentieth century of being equally opposed to the political and economic system of both the United States and the Union of Soviet Socialist Republics. Secondly, anarchists have believed that individual autonomy means an individual who is able to make a

choice free from all imposed dogma. This means that to freely determine one's actions one has to establish his own values and goals. This has meant the rejection of all institutions which attempt to make the individual into something. Of particular importance in this respect has been the objection to the school and the church as institutions which limit autonomy by molding character.[16]

Perhaps it is here in the literature of the anarchists that the most fundamental insights regarding deschooling are to be obtained. Authority in the hands of the state is not merely dangerous but fundamentally corrupt in that it represents dogma and values to be imposed on the individual. In this light the notion popular in American tradition that public schools educate free citizens would thus be seen as a contradiction. Free citizens evolve only where autonomy exists for the learner to choose the style and substance of his learning.

Summary

There are two highly visible trends today in the structure of educational systems. One is characterized by such terms as planning, efficiency, and accountability. The other is described by such terms as equity, equality of opportunity, and equal "life chances." It is to support the objectives implied in these two trends that most basic structural changes and major innovations have been recommended. Increased use of technology, cost/benefit analyses, manpower forecasts, new budget systems, voucher arrangements, and promotion of competition between public and private educational enterprises are but a few recommendations that purportedly promote a more efficient and effective educational system. Promotion of racial balance, compensatory education, and elimination of socially discriminatory evaluation instruments are a few of the efforts at promoting more equitable schools.

---

[16] Joel H. Spring, *Anarchism and Education: The Dissenting Tradition* (Cuernavaca, Mexico, CIDOC, 1971), pp. 1–2.

A possible third force in educational change also has emerged. Not well operationalized into experimental programs, this alternative is nevertheless subject to considerable discussion and conjecture in educational circles. There are those who argue that changes of the order mentioned in the above paragraph are not sufficient to produce efficient and equitable education. Needed, they say, is a fundamentally new approach to education supported by a new society. Bureaucratic arrangements of structured schooling must be replaced by guaranteeing more responsibility and freedom for the learner. The deschooled society envisioned presumably allows more meaningful learning to take place and generates new levels of creativity.

While it is difficult to envision that the near future will bring deschooled societies, experimentation with all facets of education appears likely to continue. New instructional arrangements outside the regular school system and new attempts to extend the linkages between schools and other institutions are likely to proliferate. Flexibility in both patterns of control and use of technology may well give new responsibility to the learner, at least within prescribed limits. The limits, of course, are influenced by professional associations and unions and by an increasingly powerful educational bureaucracy. Ultimately, however, direction and extent of educational reform and change will be controlled by the social and political climate and the harshness of fiscal reality.

References

Education Vouchers: A Preliminary Report on Financing Education by Payments to Parents. Cambridge, Mass. Center for the Study of Public Policy, Harvard University Press, 1970.

Illich, Ivan. *Deschooling Society.* New York: Harper and Row, 1970.

Reimer, Everett. "Alternatives in Education" in *Education in National Development,* ed. Don Adams. New York: David McKay, 1971. Pp. 85–97.

Discussion Questions

1. What social pressures have given rise to the demand for fundamental changes in instructional, administrative, and control patterns of educational institutions?

2. What conflicts arise due to the different objectives of those who would reform or transform education?

3. Why does the traditional pattern of education persist, i.e., teachers, teaching relatively homogeneously grouped students with a multilayered organization? Why are teachers viewed as the major direct source of instruction?

4. What would living in a debureaucratized society be like? How might the functions of government, welfare, and education be performed?

5. How do you think most teachers (or administrators or parents) view the certification of teachers?

6. How do teachers' unions and professional groups react to the notions of accountability and performance contracts?

index

Index

Acculturation, 83
Achievement motivation, 15
Adelman, Irma, 18
Alienation, 44–50, 102
American Federation of
    Teachers, 164, 288
American Jewish Congress, 288
Anderson, C. Arnold, 187, 188
Anomie, 45

Becker, Gary, 143
Beeby, C. E., 244
Bell, Daniel, 42, 43
Benson, Charles S., 67–68, 256
Berg, Ivar, 155
Biological technology, 41
Blair, Philip M., 191
Blau, Peter M., 182
Bowles, Frank, 196
Bowles, Samuel, 179, 189
Brookover, Wilbur B., 86, 134
Bureaucratization, 218, 221,
    227, 228–33, 239
Bush School, 27

California State Committee on
    Public Education, 254
Carnoy, Martin, 211
Chase, Francis S., 255
Child-rearing patterns, 93
Clark, Burton, 221, 231, 234,
    235
Clark, H. F., 286
Clausen, John, 84
Coleman, James S., 200, 201
Community school, 226
Comprehensive schools, 202–03
Conant, James Bryant, 66
Continuing education, 158
Corwin, Ronald, 227
Credentialism, 120
Crockett, Harry J., Jr., 182
Culture-gap hypothesis, 203–
    04

Danière, Andre, 205
Debureaucratization, 244
Demographic change, 58–62
Deschooling, 294, 296

Development decade, 9
Dewey, John, 226, 237, 238
Differentiation, 231
  educational, 24–30
  societal, 20–23
Diploma elite, 121
Domhoff, G. William, 33
Dreeben, Robert, 94, 96
Drucker, Peter F., 158, 164
Duncan, Otis Dudley, 182, 187

Economics of education
  correlation studies, 142
  residual approach, 144
  social and individual returns,
    143
Economies of scale, 72
Educational complex, 285
Educational efficiency, 70–71
Educational expenditures, 63
Educational planning process,
  262
Educational technology, 54–57
Efficiency, 11, 65, 168
Empathic capability, 15
Enculturation, 83
Equality of educational
    opportunity, 172–213
  definitions, 201
  discrimination in acquisition
    of schooling, 188–92
  planning for equity, 199–212
  school culture, 194
  school selection procedures,
    195
  tracking, 197–98
Equality of opportunity, 127
Equity in education, 65
Erickson, Edsel L., 86
Ethnocentricity, 31

Etzioni, Amitai, 228
Experimental schools, 74–75

Family planning, 60–61
Feldman, Arnold S., 187
Fertility control, 60
Friedman, Milton, 74

Generation gap, 102, 109
Gottlieb, David, 47
Gross, Bertram M., 246

Hagen, Everett E., 16, 17
Head Start, 206–08
Henry, Jules, 103
Herriott, Robert E., 203
Hodgkinson, Harold L., 173,
  180
Horizontal-mobility hypoth-
    esis, 203–04
Human capital, 142
Hypothesis of inequality, 203–
  04

Illich, Ivan, 68–69, 291, 293,
  295
Industrial revolution, 131
Innovational personality, 16
Instructional technology, 54–57
Intellectual technology, 43
International Project for the
    Evaluation of Educa-
    tional Achievement, 73

Jackson, Elton F., 182
Jaffe, A. J., 147, 155

Kahl, Joseph A., 180
Keppel, Francis, 66

King, Alexander, 245

Labor force structure, 51–52
Liberal education, 160

Manpower, 134, 135, 145
Manpower system, 136
Marien, M., 285
Marsh, Robert M., 22
Marx, Karl, 48, 176
McClelland, David C., 15, 16
Mead, Margaret, 104
Mills, C. Wright, 49
Modernization, 9
    measurement of, 20–23
    modern man, 19
    modern society, 19–20
    norms and values, 94
    process of, 13–16
Morris, Cynthia Taft, 18

National Education Association, 164, 288, 290
Nonformal education, 281–85
Normlessness, 45
Nyerere, Julius, 90

Occupational structure, 130–42
    educational attainment, 148–54
    international, 140
    technological change, 133
    United States, 139
Occupations
    education, 161–63
    level of schooling, 155–57
Office of Economic Opportunity, 285, 288

Parsons, Talcott, 94

Paul VI (pope), 49
Peters, R. S., 257
Planning
    command planning, 243
    communist nation, 249
    educational, 242–68
    human resource planning, 134
    information dissemination, 243
    local school level, 256–57
    manpower planning, 134, 147
    technological change, 44
    United States, 249–53
    Western Europe, 249–53
Political development, 17–18
Postindustrial, 13, 92
Postindustrial society, 11, 42, 63
Potvin, Raymond H., 61
Productivity, 70

Reich, Michael, 189
Reimer, Everett, 68, 281, 284
Reissman, Frank, 208, 209
Robbins report, 251
Rogers, Will, 109
Rogoff, Natalie, 182

School enrollments, 64
School-proof teachers, 277, 278
Schultz, Theodore W., 144
Silberman, Charles, 165
Social learning. See Socialization
Social mobility, 91
Social stratification
    comparison of equality of opportunity, 183

Social stratification (*continued*)
    education and social mo-
        bility, 186–88
    scales of reward, 177
    social class, 174–84
    social mobility, 174–86
Socialization, 81, 83–106
Socialization agents, 92
Sorokin, Pitirim A., 175
Specialization, 20–21, 28, 231,
    276, 277
St. John, Nancy, 203
Student-clients, 236
Student revolt, 102
Systems model of education,
    259

Teacher-bureaucrat, 237
Teacher-proof schools, 277, 278
Teachers, 2
    demand, 166–67
    morale, 204
    nonspecialized, 27
    roles, 54, 69–70
    specialized, 29

teacher competence, 2–5
Technocracy, 11
Teen-age revolution, 108–16
Thomas, J. Alan, 205
Traditional society
    norms and values, 24–26
Tumin, Melvin, 187

United Nations, 9
Urbanization, 38–40, 120, 130
USSR, 197

Van Dyke, Jon, 49, 50
Vocational education, 159
Voucher system, 74, 287

Warner, W. Lloyd, 179, 180
Waterston, Albert, 243
Weber, Max, 176
Weiner, Myron, 14
Westoff, Charles F., 61
Whiting, John W. M., 83

Youth culture, 100, 102, 105